AF531631

MANAGEMENT IN GOVERNMENT

MANAGEMENT IN GOVERNMENT

Edited by

M.K. Singh

&

A. Bhattacharya

DISCOVERY PUBLISHING HOUSE PVT. LTD.

NEW DELHI-110 002

Edition-2011

ISBN 978-81-8356-907-1

Published by

DISCOVERY PUBLISHING HOUSE PVT. LTD.
4831/24, Ansari Road, Prahlad Street,
Darya Ganj, New Delhi-110002 (India)
Phone: 23279245, 43764432 • Fax: 91-11-23253475
E-mail: discoverypublishinghouse@gmail.com
dphbooks@rediffmail.com

Printed at:
Mehra Offset Press
Delhi

Preface

The phenomenal growth of commercial enterprises in the past decade or so has been the outcome of an equally remarkable spurt in surplus purchasing power, wage increase, liquidity of holdings and the advent of consumerism impelled by the remarkable technological development during the period. Enterprises and industrial conglomerates, trading services and hire-purchase firms alike have had to move fast to be equal to the opportunities provided by a growing national as well as international market. Industry and enterprises have had to change gears in a big way.

These new parameters apply as much to government and its manifestations, especially since all key resources in terms of raw material and administration of their prices are in the hands of government and its agencies. Management in government is not limited merely to the efficient functioning of public sector enterprises; beyond this it goes to efficacious use of the vast resources in men and expertise which it deploys through its numerous agencies and departments. Working for the public goods implies enormous responsibility for government and therefore what is of significance is not the quantity of men and materials deployed, but *how efficaciously* these are deployed and utilised. This collection of articles, papers, extracts and contributions draws its theme from the various interfaces of management in government and the benefits it seeks to provide in the larger interest of the country's people. The numerous programmes of poverty alleviation and rural development, of industrial expansion and planned growth require concerted and precise use of the available resources in men and materials for government to acquire credibility and achieve success. The present compilation needs to be viewed in this perspective.

In our efforts we have been assisted in generous measure by our many colleagues and friends, professional managers and experts consultants. They would be too numerous to list—suffice it to say that without their guidance these papers and articles would not have been brought together into a cohesive whole. Nonetheless, we feel it our bounden duty to acknowledge the fruitful discussions we have had with Prof. P. Sarveshwar and Dr. Arun Nimbalkar of the Institute of Corporate and Industrial Management, Bombay; Dr. S. Ganesan of the Textile Managers Association, Aurangabad; Shri K. R. Wadhawan of the Centre for Research in Management Sciences, Manila, and Smt. Urvashi Palekar, Documentation Officer, Institute of Corporate Management, Faculty of Economics, University of Lagos, Nigeria.

Excellent computer and secretarial support services were provided by S/Shri Sameer Kak, Arvind Goswami and Raghuraj T. We are grateful to them.

We have attempted to minimise all printing errors, but hasten to add that we alone are responsible for those that still remain.

M. K. Singh
Akash Bhattacharya

Introduction

Management may be defined as the process of efficient functioning based on correct choices and actions. However, in the moderu world which is increasingly dependant on large organisations, the most significant situations are those which require organisational management. This implies decision and action in a context which is characterised by organised group or collective activity and the goals or objectives towards which the group effort is directed.

These objectives are pursued by managers, who make decisions pertaining to the desired objectives and concerning relationships among resources—the people, money and machines, materials and methods which can be effectively deployed to attain those objectives. Managers then see that their decisions are carried out and that they have the desired effect. When necessary, they use *control actions* to redirect their resources toward the desired objectives. Since managers of large organisations cannot literally to each and every thing that is required as a result of the decisions that are made, organisational management is a process of *working through others* to achieve broad organisational objectives, such as profit or social welfare, or specific objectives such as the development of a new product with success potential of the efficient and time-bound construction of a power plant.

Management may thus be thought of as involving two major elements, *planning* and *control*. These two aspects of management apply to all areas of organised activity, such as the modern large firm represents. Planning involves decisions and actions concerning the future of the organisation. What type of business should be taken up? What kinds of manpower mix will be needed for effective functioning in the 1990s? What impact will increased leisure time have on the utilisation of the contemplated products?

Control involves decisions and actions related to the present organisations. How should production be scheduled to optimise machine-utilisation time? What should be the efficient allocation of workload among various levels of manpower? What mix of newspaper-radio-TV advertising would be best suited to the products?

Every manager is involved to some degree in both planning and control, but the jobs of many managers emphasise the control component. This is, in fact, true of many jobs which have the word 'planning' in their designation. The job of a production planning manager, for instance, is largely control oriented as it stresses the present and the immediate future rather than the long-term future—which is an intrinsic aspect of correct planning.

Every manager is involved to some extent in both control and planning, but the job specifications of most managers emphasise the control component. This is, in fact, true of most jobs which have the word planning in their designation. However, it appears that where planning, control, management and implementation in government are concerned, the bureaucratic monolith suffers from several inherent limitations. The District Magistrate (DM), for instance, is also a manager of a special kind at the grassroots level, in addition to being expected to perform as an able administrator of the government's various welfare and development programme. At another point in the spectrum is the head of the public sector enterprise who is required to be management expert as well as financial controller. At yet another slot in the vast bureaucratic spectrum is the policeman—whether beat constable or commissioner or inspector-general—who cannot shelter behind any pretext in the law and order scenario; he patrols and protects both common citizens and the important persons of the country. The spectrum is indeed vast and the interfaces between management in government and the countrys peoples are countless.

In conventional terms, it is the public sector enterprise, with the "commanding heights" it aspires to, that has been seen as typical or representative of the mechanics and dynamics of government in action. It is the public sector which draws maximum flak, primarily because huge sums of money are involved in setting up, nurturing and developing these dinosauric high-tech creature—and yet they don't seem to be paying their way into the public confidence. The public sector phenomenon—or non-phenomenon—in India also has come to typify management in government. The question that arises is: what would be valid in a welfare state—management by principle or management by reason? To illustrate, when the 'Gold Control Order' was enforced in the 1960s in India, a number of petty goldsmiths committed suicide; similarly, hundreds of poor alcohol addicts died as a result of the policy of prohibition as they drank whatever poisonous brew was available within their limit means his needless of life was in addition to the huge losses to the exchequer. These are instances of 'management by principle.'

In this context it may be mentioned that the whipping post is the Bureau of Public Enterprises (BPE), which has been subject to much misplaced criticism. The BPE has the unenviable balancing act between the devil and the deep sea; the trade unions perceive the role of the BPE as that of "a fifth wheel" to the coach or a backseat driver. Several trade unions in the late seventies went to the extent of moving a High Court to issue an injunction for restraining the BPE from interfering in the process of collective bargaining (by issuing guidelines for wage increase, for example). Most Boards of Directors of public enterprises have been resentful of what they prefer to describe as the Bureau's "interference." (The oft-quoted example of the BPE's "interference" in a non-eventual way is its directive to public enterprises that all their staff cars should be of the same colour.) The problem seems to be of defining the parameters of coordination of the activities of the numerous units in the public sector.

An interesting description of 'non-management' has been provided in the following words: "The most important determinant of the future performance and pace of development of public sector in India is the issue of autonomy. . . But this generous mood of continuing the autonomy as a more important factor of motivating the management by public enterprises to step up their physical and financial performance, however, proved to be a short happy summer. The pleasant walk and talk in the corridors of secretariats of government and in the rooms of ministers by the high public sector managers, more particularly by the Chief Executives and between them and the ministers and secretaries is a vanished summer glory. Today the top public sector managers, according to sources close to them, have to face awkward queries, rebuffs and embarrassing postures from junior secretariat officers with senior officers and ministers becoming unavailable to them to let them speak on the problems of their enterprises." The use of the imeprial fiddlestick has become the order of the day.

Then there are several other aspects which require immediate attention. The burgeoning crisis of the IAS-IPS latent confrontation aggravated by the existence, and even encouragement, of lobbies in the corridors of power, the deteriorating standards of public services with accountability going overboard, the growing mood of cynicism among the general masses where the public dealings of the bureaucracy are concerned, the well-acknowledged fact that funds earmarked for programmes such as the RLEGP and IRDP do not reach the intended beneficiaries, the indifference of the banking sector to the genuine neends of the ordinary, small enterpreneur despite declared policies and other factors are in their collective effect striking persistently at the very roots of sound and purposive management of the country's affairs.

There is much that is good in our system where management by and in government is concerned. The bureaucratic structure may be monolithic but therein lies its strength too. The bureaucrat has met his necessary and stimulating match in the technocrat. More than once it has been demonstrated by a wilful, discerning—and just—minister that by and large what works is the good old principle "Perform or perish." Bureaucracy and technocracy together can combine into a powerful engine of growth and development. That is the need of the day.

There are no easy solutions as evolution sans problems would be suspect in growing world and for striving mankind. The constants would appear to be good administration and the will to excel. There is enormous cynicism in the words of Cicero, the great Roman orator, statesment and philosopher who said over two thousand years ago: "Every people deserve the government they get." The maxim today ought to be: "Every people elect the government they want."

The papers in this present compilation would not have pretensions to definitiveness and emulation. They merely provide a framework, hopefully a working framework, within which the stupendous task of taking a giant like India into the next century has to be performed. As such, they will, it is hoped, prove useful not only to bureaucrats and administrators but also students and researchers in the area.

Contents

Contents

1

Value Management in Government

R.V. GOPALAKRISHNAN

Governments periodically reiterate their good intentions of their imbibing thrift. History, nevertheless, tells us that they get invariably caught in the vicious circle of increasing government expenditure and for meeting the same, 'digging up' fresh channels for their revenue. This cycle goes on, leaving the nations less-cost-effective and more deficit in financing.

Government of India is no exception! Their revenue has escalated from about Rs. 32,000 crores in 1970-71 to about Rs. 13,100 crores in 1980-81, Rs. 15,800 crores in 1981-82; and about Rs. 18,100 crores in 1982-83.

Revenue disbursements were slated to go up by over Rs. 2,200 crores (14 per cent)—from the previous year in 1982-83, the year declared by the Government of India as Productivity Year, which in other words meant that it would make more conscious and intense efforts to become more cost-effective and better-performing.

US Experience

What have other Governments done to become more cost-effective and better performing? A look at the USA, a federal democracy, should throw some light on the magnitude of efforts involved.

Methods Improvement

Being burdened with excessive paperwork and less effective methods of operations, the Government of USA embarked on a 'Work Simplification Programme' as far back as in 1949. The President and the Congress directed that each department of the Government should systematically review the effectiveness of its programmes and the economy of its operations and reward supervisors and employees for outstanding performance. Their Army Work Simplification Programme, for example, effected in 1955 alone as many as 11,156 improvements, saving $ 13.36 millions—an impressive return of about 18.1!

By the end of the 50s, military budgets were soaring high. In order to keep a check on it, several wings of US military, such as US Navy Bureau of Ships, and Army Ordnance Crops adapted Value Management (VM)—the systematic functionally-oriented team-approach, relating functional-worth to the cost of producing goods—for unearthing ,unnecessary' costs.

McNamara Revolution

In the early '60s' Robert McNamara, the then US Secretary of Defence, while grappling with the esculating cost over-runs in defence projects, introduced into the Department of Defence (DoD) the mandatory use of Network Planning and Control and Planning-Programming-Budgetting-System. O.her departments were quick to follow suit.

McNamara recognised Value Engineering (VE) as *key* element 'in the drive to reduce costs' and issued a directive in 1962 for its inclusion as a *mandatory* requirement by the Armed Services Procurement Regulations. The VE Programme was incorporated in 1964 as a part of a Cost Reduction Programme already on in DoD aiming at a cost reduction goal of $ 6,000 million, progressively by 1970!

DoD defined VE as 'a systematic effort directed at analysing the functional requirement of the DoD systems, equipments, facilities and supplies for the purpose of achieving essential functions at the lowest total cost, consistent with the needed performance, reliability, quality and maintainability'. This organised methodology is also known by several other names, such as Value Administration, Value Analysis. Value Assurance, Value Improvement and Value Management.

DoD's use of VE consisted of two elements: an in-house VE effort, performed by Defence personnel and a VE programme for contractors to stimulate them to develop and submit VE Change proposals for changing those contract specifications, purchase descriptions or statements of work, which they felt would impose costly non-essential requirements. The incentive was provided by giving the contractor pre-determined share of the audited gains resulting from the proposal he submitted. Innumerable seminars and workshops were held for Defence personnel and contractors for this purpose.

Direct responsibility for VE programme in DoD was assigned to the Secretaries of Army, Navy and Air Force. The US Comptroller General (the counterpart of India's Comptroller and Auditor General) had been evencing a keen and vigorous *longstanding* interest in the use of VE as a means to help reduce government acquisition and ownership costs, as "our purpose is not primarily to expose but to purpose." Encouraged by the impressive gains from the VE Programme of DoD, (maximum returns as high as 82:1), other Government Departments, such a National Aeronautics and Space Administration. Transportation, Health, Education and Welfare, effectively introduced suitable VE-incentive clauses in their contracts.

The US Post Office Department earnestly embraced Value Management in 1967. It was heatening for them to save as much as $ 700,000 per year, by analysing the value of their largest-selling stamp alone—13 cent denomination selling 3.6 million pieces a year—andrationalising its size from 0.84″×0.39″ to 0.66″×0.78″.

In the '70s, the Public Building Service of the General Service Administration (the counterpart of our Central Public Works Department) adopted Value Management for better cost-effectiveness in construction. In 1973 alone, they saved $ 2.5 million—a return of $ 13.7 for every dollar invested in their Value Programme.

Zero-Base Budget

Jimmy Carter sought the Governorship of Georgia State in the early '70s on the promise that he would not levy an extra cent from the tax-payer during his tenure. The only other 'gutty' person who made a similar promise was Henry Ford I. In 1910's he claimed "I'll make a car, which will cost less every year!" Both could make genuine efforts and keep their promises !

Carter, on his getting elected, adopted Zero-Base Budgeting, an extension of Value Engineering, for Georgia in 1973. This methodology "forced" each departmental head to examine and evaluate different ways of performing the functions required of the department, while estimating its annual budget grants. This process of evaluating functional worth with the service-cost helped the departments establish their priorities *right* and locate unnecessary costs. The result was that the administrative costs were not only contained but reduced, while the quality of service improved considerably.

Many departments in the US Governments, in the late '70s, adopted one or more integrative approaches—such as Zero-Base Budgetting and Management by Objectives—in order to become more cost-effective and better-performing.

Continuous Pressure

The 1973 oil embargo as well as the threat of competition from foreign cars prompted the federal Government to impose better efficiency standards on American automakers. The Energy Policy and Conservation Act, passed by Congress in

1975 in the face of vigorous opposition from the automobile industry, demanded *yearly* improvements in the efficiency of new cars.

The Act stipulated that by 1985, the average car sold in the US must be able to travel at least 27.5 miles per US gallon of petrol or diesel—double the mileage achieved by 1973 models. Later on, the Department of Transportation established new standards of fuel consumption for light trucks and other vehicles as well.

The US Automobile industry, although 'caught with pants down', steared effectively and quickly through radical re-designs of their cars to satisfy the 1975 Act. VE accelerated their adoption of technological innovations, such as the transverse-mounted engine, the front-wheel-drive and the use of new light-weight materials. With double the fuel-economy, the General Motor cars, for example, weighed on an average only 3600 lbs in 1980, in contrast to 4600 lbs in 1970. The next target is to bring down the weight to 3100 lbs by 1985! The Government's initiative is thus 'paying dividends.'

UNIQUENESS OF VM

VM has proven its uniqueness in cutting *quickly* across departments and achieving better results in shorter time and, most often, at lower costs. Though hailed as a 'simple' methodology, the VM approach is organised, and it progresses through different phases of work, demanding a lot of efforts from the VM team-members.

The swift selectivity of VM is astonishing! A VM team can quickly unearth a few functions, for the performance of which excessive costs are mostly incurred. This is done by comparing the worth of the function performed by each component with the cost of the component. Many methods are there for such evaluation of functions.

Take the Annual Revenue disbursements on a macro-level, for example. The cost-functional worth comparison, evolved by a VM team of Senior Administrators, may look like Table 1.1:

TABLE 1.1

VM Project: Annual Revenue Disbursements Cost-Functional Worth Comparison

Head of Account	*Revenue Expenditure %*	*Basic Function*	*FW %*	*C-FW %*
1. Defence Services	27	Defend Nation	21	6
2. Interest Payment	20	Service Debt	15	5
3. Grants-in-aid and Contributions	19	Aid States and Institutions	16	3
4. Agricultural and Allied Service	9	Ensure Produce	18	
5. Administrative and Fiscal Services	8	Maintain Administration	6	2
6. Social and Community Services	7	Facilitate Welfare	10	
7. Economic Services and others	10	Maintain Production etc.	14	
8. Total	100	Maintain Services	100	16

On the face of it, the functions, 'Defend Nation', 'Service Debt', 'Aid States and Institutions' and 'Maintain Administration' are, in the wisdom of the team, incurring excessive costs to perform them. The team can similarly go into the micro-level of each service and identify 10-20 per cent functions which cost of 10-30 per cent more than their functional worths.

Two VM Examples

Two projects may be cited to illustrate the swift selectivity of the VM approach. The first project was a Power Distribution System for which the team came up with the following cost-functional worth comparison (Table 1.2.)

TABLE 1.2

VM Project: Power Distribution System Cost-Functional Worth Comparison

Component	*Cost* %	*Basic Function*	*FW* %	*C-FW* %
1. Transformers	26	Change Voltage	22	4
2. Conduits	24	Provide Protection	16	8
3. Conductors	13	Transmit Power	20	
4. Emergency generators	11	Provide Emergency-power	15	
5. Switchgears and Panels	16	Switch Power	17	
6. All others	10	Several functions	10	
7. Total	100	Distribute Power	100	12

It was evident that functions 'Provide Protection' and 'Change Voltage' incurred costs more disproportionate to their functional worths. These functions were then taken to the next phase, *viz*., the Creative Phase, for alternate ways of performing them. Final evaluation of alternatives led to the installation of lower-cost plastic conduits suitably encased and a different type of distribution system eliminating some transformers.

The second VM project was a metropolitan slum improvement programme brought to a recent VM Workshop by the officers of the concerned Metropolitan Development Authority. Developmental projects of this nature envisaged to cost over Rs. 40 lakhs per urban slum are undertaken on loans from World Bank. Organised VM team-efforts, if made at their design stage itself, can help to conserve *at least* 10 per cent of their costs.

The VM team's cost-functional worth comparison is shown in Table 1.3.

TABLE 1.3

VM Project

A Metropolitan Slum Improvement Programme
Cost-Functional Worth Comparison

Component		*Cost* *Rs. lakhs*	*%*	*Basic Function*	*FW* *%*	*C-FW* *%*
1	*2*	*3*	*4*	*5*	*6*	*7*
1.	Water Supply	6.07	14.3	Supply Water	32	
2.	Sewerage System	6.13	14.5	Dispose Waste	21	
3.	Street Lighting	9.60	22.7	Remove Darkness	10	10.7 (II)
4.	Schooling	10.50	24.8	Impart Education	12	12.8 (I)
5.	Cottage Industries	1.50	3.8	Train People	6	
6.	Road Development	6.95	16.4	Provide Access	17	
7.	Miscellaneous	1.50	3.5	Improve Environment	2	1.5 (III)
8,	Slum Improvement	42.35	100.0	Improve Slum	100	27.0

Needless to say that the two functions, 'Impart Education' and 'Remove Darkness' were selectively taken further to develop alternate ways of performing them, Brainstorming on alternate ways of performing these two functions generated as many as 45 and 43 ideas respectively. The team finally short-listed two ideas for each of the two functions for more detailed evaluation. For the function 'Impart Education', the two most attractive alternatives were found to be :

A dormitory type of building; and

A building for the 'combined' operation of Primary and High School on shift-basis.

The envisaged cost-savings on either of these alternatives were put at 25-30 per cent of the present cost or about Rs. 2.5-3 lakhs.

The two short-listed alternatives for the second function 'Remove Darkness' were:

Flood-light illumination, increasing the distance between lamp-posts; and

Lighting from Bio-gas plant, suitably developed in conjunction with the public-conveniences sceptic-tank units.

The former was envisaged to save about 15 per cent or Rs. 1.4 lakhs, while the latter could be much more attractive in saving nearly 30 per cent or Rs. 2.8 lakhs of investment.

Because of the intense involvement of the concerned people in the final decision-making, resistnace to change is significantly diluted. Quite often, the organisation gets more ready for the impending changes!

A review of VM gains show that two or more of the following factors have been responsible for the gains achieved by the VM team-approach.

Recognition of advances in technology.

Questioning specifications for value.

Application of additional designs, skills, ideas and information available, but not previously utilised.

Recognition of changes in user's needs.

Design turned to value.

Feedback from field test or use.

Removal of deficiencies in design.

What Can Be Done Now?

A VM team of 5-10 Senior Administrators from different departments *most* concerned with the project can effect a 10-30 per cent improvement in cost-effectiveness, if it works either on a full-time basis for 3-4 months or on part-time, *viz.* meeting 2 hours a week or 4 hours a fortnight, over 8-12 months. A full-time VM Co-ordinator can facilitate many VM teams in parallel.

If the Government is committed to contain costs and improve services, the Secretaries to the Government should prepare an *agreed* shortlist of about 100 VM projects which, in their combined wisdom, have to scope for cost-effectiveness to the tune of 20 per cent of the total cost. It should result in the initiation of appropriate VM teams of senior Administrators for those VM Projects.

All developmental projects and programmes exceeding Rs. 50 crores each and all contracts exceeding Rs. 10 crores each should *mandetorily* have the VM approach before their final approval for their execution.

Suitable incentive clauses should be incorporated in all contracts over Rs. 10 lakhs encouraging contractors to challenge specifications and propose changes for value improvement. A pre-determined share of audited gains may be given to the contractors in recognition for their efforts.

Value-consciousness has to be created among government personnel. This demands a massive effort on the part of government and will require collaboration with several institutions.

The Government must make sure that the large number of productive enterprises both in Government and Public Sector, should systematically and intensively practise the VM approach, dovetailing it to their annual planning process and their budgetting and auditing procedures.

Last but not the least, employee-involvement is a critical factor in implementing Value Management changes quickly. A realistic Suggestion Award Scheme, combined with many other ingenious ways of involving employees such as employees' participation in Management, will dilute their resistance to change and accelerate VM gains.

It is heartening to find that our Army, Navy and Air Force and some public sector enterprises, such as SAIL and BEL have been organising themselves systematically for Value Management efforts.

Much more intensive efforts are, however, needed from our public enterprises for exploiting the VM team-approach fully. Besides, it is all the more important that the sick public enterprises should adopt Value Management in order to find ways and means for their survival.

The Committee on Public Undertakings emphasised, as far back as in 1967, that Value Management offered considerable scope for cost reduction and that all public enterprises should undertake it systematically. The Bureau of Public Enterprises found in 1975 that this technique had not been adopted by most of the units in a systematic manner and 'felt' that it ought to be adopted by all public enterprises. 'For this purpose an inter-departmental Committee may be formed, who may draw upon an action plan and lay down priorities for organised Value Management,' the Bureau recommended.

Institutions of Management Education, such as Indian Institute of Management, Bangalore, have been introducing the VM methodology to hundreds of practising Managers and Administrators participating in their programmes every year. Indian Value Engineering Society (INVEST), formed in New Delhi an 1971 has been disseminating this concept through their Seminars, publications and National Conferences.

The scope for VM gains in India is tremendous. The organised VM team-approach, well supported by the Government and well dovetailed into contractors' incentive clauses and employees' suggestion schemes can conserve our annual costs in India to the tune of Rs. 10,000 crores and more and thus accelerate the revitalisation of our economy. It should finally reflect in better products and services at lower costs for the consumers and the taxpayers.

In the '80s, when the costs are escalating even within the same year, it is not only appropriate but is absolutely essential for the Government to weave the VM team approach into the fabric of its structure *suitably* in order to get the best value out of every rupee spent.

2

Management by Trust—An Experiment

R. S. DWIVEDI

There have been several approaches to Management which include Scientific Management approach, Human Relations approach and Behavioural Science approach. Scientific Management approach put stress on efficiency and ignored interpersonal relationships at work. It was assumed that if "one best possible way" was devised, people were selected and trained to fit it and accordingly paid the highest level of remuneration, management would be able to achieve maximum possible efficiency in the organisation. However, this assumption proved to be invalid because of its short-sightedness. Several dysfunctions developed jeopardising the working life and efficiency at work. Because of these dysfunctions of the Scientific Management, Human Relations movement emerged in organisational settings. Hawthorne experimenters were the founders of this approach to management. In this approach emphasis was on human factors, such as attitudes, informal groups, recognition, participation and interpersonal relationships. The main focus was on the satisfaction of human needs.

Several researchers attempted to show the relevance of human factors in work settings. Studies conducted on these lines related to autocratic, democratic and *laissez faire*styles and their impact on human behaviour, reduction of resistance to change through participation, and initiating structure versus consideration, close versus general and task-centred versus people-centred styles of supervision. The major objective of these researches was to show the dysfunctions of traditional approach and the significance of human relations approach in managing human resources. These contrasting approaches to management are designed as theory "X" and theory "Y" respectively.

An analysis of the above approaches reveals that in the classical approach, distrust is the dominating force, while in the human relations approach, trust is the major consideration. Several behavioural scientists have substituted human relations approach by behavioural science approach in recent years and started working on this basic theme.

These behavioural scientists lay stress on trust and confidence in different dimensions of management. However, hitherto, there has not been any concerted effort to evolve a global trust-based approach. This article deals with "Management by trust" as an integrated behavioural science approach to management.

What is Management by Trust?

Management by trust has been defined as a dynamic system, based on definable measurable and developable units of trusting behaviour, involving the attainment of effective performance through optimisation of organisational structures and processes, assimilation of conflicts and integration of goals. It is a powerful managerial system and can be viewed as a process of management. It is a continuous activity in the organisation based on precise units of trusting behaviour of both managers and workers. Trusting behaviour can be defined, measured and developed. It is supportive in character and involves lack of hostility and indifference. It increases in an individual a sense of trust in self and in others in such a way that others can do the same. In fact, the individual has to trust himself and others and become trustworthy in the eyes of others. Trust can be at individual, group and organisational levels. It helps the individual to be himself, to exercise self-control and make the best possible contribution to effective performance. Effective performance means maximum possible attainment of organisational goals: quality and quantity of goods and services produced, reduction of turnover, absenteeism, indiscipline, grievances and unrest and attainment of maximum possible satisfaction of individual needs. Moreover, trust optimises different types of organisational structures and decision making, communication, control, leadership and motivation processes. It means that trust facilitates the attainment of more output than the sum of inputs. Furthermore, trust facilitates assimilation of conflicts which means that conflicts are resolved in a manner that leads to constructive rather than destructive consequences. Finally, trust helps in the integration of individual, group and organisational goals, which means that there is an understanding that individual needs and group and organisational goals can be achieved simultaneously. Accordingly, management by trust is a dynamic system involving six inter-related, inter-dependent and interacting factors. These factors include trusting behaviour, effective performance, optimisation of organisational structures, optimisation of organisational processes, assimilation of conflicts and integration of goals. Each factor in itself embodies several interacting and interdependent sub-factors. The major feature of these factors and sub-factors is that they are mutually re-inforcing and supportive.

In the light of the author's research and experiments of the MIT programme in two leading organisations in India, some guidelines have been evolved which are outlined below:

Measurement of Trust and Distrust

At the very outset of the programme, attempts are made to measure trust and distrust at individual, group and organisational levels. At the individual level, trust involves assured reliance of the individual on others and his perception that others (*i.e.*, follow-workers) have also assured reliance on him. In addition, interpersonal trust involves trust of the superior in the subordinate and that of subordinate in the superior as visualised by each of them. The symptions if superior's trust in the subordinate include perception of the subordinate that his superior allows him to work with confidence and renders support. It involves consistency in word and action of the superior as viewed by the subordinate. The symptoms of trust of subordinate in superior are loyalty, predictability, accessibility and availability. It means that the superior perceives that the subordinate its personally loyal to him, that his behaviour can be predicted in different situations, that he is flexible in his approach, and that the available to him even if not asked for to do so. In general, the individual level trust involves firm belief that the individual can put himself, his status, his career and even his life in others's hand whom he trusts with full confidence and knows that he will not be exploited deliberately or accidently, consciously or unconsciously. This confident expectation at the interpersonal level is a two-way process. It is not possible to maintain individual level trust if both the individuals are not extending their trust towards each other. Group level trust involves measures related to consensus of opinion and ideas and absence of destructive competition. It means that members can sacrifice their personal opinions and ideas for the sake of group working. Finally, organisational level trust involves opportunity in the organisation to take risk and to make experiment. It means that members in the organisation believe that there is full freedom to make innovations regarding the job even at the cost of financial or other types of loss. As soon as trust and distrust at individual, group and organisational levels are measured with the help of a scale, attempts are made to demonstrate significance of improving trust and decreasing distrust in the organisation.

Determining Relationships of Trust and Distrust with Performance

The researcher collects performance data from the organisational settings. Data relate to production, morale, absenteeism, turnover, tardiness, grievances, indiscipline, unrest, accident and merit ratings. Correlational analysis between trust and distrust measures and different performance factors is conducted and interactive effects of other variables are eliminated by patial correlations. In the organisations studied so far, trust has positive relationships with productior, morale and merit ratings and negative relationships with absenteeism, turnover and tardiness. On the other hand, distrust reveals negative relationships with production, morale and merit ratings and positive relationships with absenteeism turnover and tardiness. Although several relationships are not statistically significant because of the small size of samples, the relevance of increasing trust and decreasing distrust has been recognised by both researchers and the managements of the two organisation. This is followed by several MPT interventions to achieve effective results.

Optimisation of Organisational Structures

In the two organisations, there prevailed traditional structures before study. These structures encouraged distrust in many ways. The basic conviction of these structures was that people could not be trusted and if they could not be trusted, they must be carefully watched. Accordingly, measures such as close supervision, managerial controls, guarding, security, sign-out, etc., pervaded the organisation climate. The formal leader is responsible for problem solving. Attempts were made to keep interaction on an impersonal basis because of the fear that "familiarity breeds contempt." Formal rules and procedures rather than informality and spontaneous self-directed behaviour were the characteristic modes of action in the organisation. It was assumed that people could not be trusted to make decision for themselves and, therefore, they should be directed and controlled. Distrust generated distrust and the entire climate was perverted.

To improve the organisational climate in the two organisations, several measures were taken. In general, individuals were encouraged to define their new responsibilities and attempts were made to encourage more and more amount of delegation and decentralisation. In particular, major lines of action taken include formation of groupings based on divisionalisation, establishment of a 6-tier uniform hierarchies of complements, development of cohesive and versatile work-teams, dignified designations, multiple management, installation of a system of built-in motivation, formal statement of responsibility and implementation of different new personnel policies. Several group meetings and discussions were conducted to formulate detailed programme for the implementation of the above measures in the organisation. Specifically, the entire organisation was divided into several divisions based on product, area, functions and inter mix. A hierarchy of 6-tier complements, including deputy manager, assistant manager, senior supervisor, supervisor, senior chargehand and chargehand, was established throughout the organisation to provide clear-cut line of advancement. Attempts were made to develop work-teams based on mutual choices and optimal work loads. Individuals were given dignified designations so that they could enjoy self-esteem in the society. Several committees such as Executive Committee, Trust Development Committee, Review Committee. Works Committee and Functional Committees were established. These committees, provided several advantages of group dynamics. Decisions made by these committees are likely to be effective both at formulation and implementation levels. This multiple management system is to be very crucial from the standpoint of development of junior managers. Several measures have been taken to introduce different types of financial and non-financial incentives in the organisation to provide built-in motivation. Responsibilities of individuals, both technical and non-technical-are to be defined with their collaboration and embodied in their job profiles. Personnel policies relating to promotion, increment, job-rotation, job enrichment and enlargement, trust development, etc., have been formulated with the involvement of people and embodied in a manual of the company. Several difficulties were encountered in the organisational design because of misconceptions of the old timers and doubts of the top management. Largely, it was feared that with the implementation of the proposed structure, seniors would lose their power and authority. It was further held that the proposed structure was justified in view of the quality of the people (of course, this indicated distrust) in the organisation. However, through constant effort by the researcher, the management in the first organisation was convinced of the need for redesigning the structure, largely. However, in the second organisation, progress was not very satisfactory initially in the redesigning of the organisational structure because of certain situational factors; of course, it picked up in course of time.

Optimisation of Organisational Processes

In the two organisations under study, organisational processes were initially distrust-based. Decision making, communication control, leadership and motivation processes were largely limited in many ways. In general, there were attempts to deliberately distort information and engage in destructive conflicts to acquire competitive advantage. Because of these tactics, quality of decision suffered heavily. Communication was marked by malicious motives as well as suppression of true feelings for fear of punishment. Individuals communicated merely to protect themselves rather than accomplishing organisational goals. Excessive amount of control was exercised. In view of distrust, management by crisis or drive was the major approach to management. This was the symptom of breakdown of manage-leading to confusion and incompetence. Leadership was marked by either exploitative or benevolem autocratic styles based on distrust. Formal leaders feared that subordinates would make mistakes as they were not capable of doing things. Accordingly, they put stress on close supervision and hovered around watching and checking. This resulted in self-conscious behaviour. People were motivated from 'outside' by using "carrot and stick" approach. To improve the above processes, several measures were formulated after individual and group discussions. These measures include:

—Brain-storming, workers' participation, scientific tools and techniques to optimise decision making process;

—Innovations in downward, horizontal and upward systems of communication;

—Encouragement of human factors in the establishment of standards and objectives, evaluation of performance and taking corrective actions to optimise control;

—Evolving behavioural styles suitable for and unique to the culture of the organisation to optimise leadership; and

—Introduction of a number of monetary and non-monetary techniques to optimise motivation process.

Specifically, brain-storming technique has been introduced in problem solving process. Workers are now frequently involved in decision making in so far as it affects them. Several operatons research techniques such as, waiting line, linear programming etc., have been introduced to optimise disicion making process. Attempts have also been made to assure that downward communication does not simply provide the work-related instructions and procedures, but it also provides feedback, indoctrinates goals, and gives a rationale for doing the job. Horizonal communication is strengthened to accomplish effective co-operation and manage conflicts. Upward communica tion system is optimised by trust to get constant feedback from employees using techniques, such as attitudinal surveys, exit interview, and suggestion system Control process is optimised by trust at different stages In brief, individuals are involved while setting goals, evaluating performance and taking corrective measures. Leadership process is optimised by giving utmost stress on consultative and participative approaches and other techniques based on managerial grid, etc. Finally several monetary incentives and non-monetary incentives, such as recognition, challenge, advancement, a sense of achievement, etc., are used to optimise motivation process. All the above measures have been implemented, especially in one organisation because of high level of enthusiasm of young executives and by the effectiveness of the organisational structure optimised by trust in preceding step.

Assimination of Conflicts

Conflicts occur at individual, group and organisational levels. At individual level, there are intra-personal and inter-personal conflicts. Individual is exposed to several types of conflicting situations in the form of frustration, goal conflict and role conflict. This causes adverse effect on his health, if not managed adequately, causing nervous break-down, heart attack and ulcer, etc. Interpersonal conflict is frequently accompanied by personality conflict in organisational settings. Interpersonal conflict start from the top and may influence the working of the individuals from top to floor level. In addition to individual level conflict, there is conflict at group level which many include conflict between formal and informal, line and staff, functional groups and finally, between labour and management groups. Conflict can also ouccur within these groups because of lack of trust. Finally we may have conflict at organisational levels which may include intra-organisational and inter-organisational conflicts. Union-management conflict is an organisational conflict.

There are also conflicts within the union and management organisations. If conficts occur in a trusting climate at different levels, it has positive consequences; it provides innovations and creativity. However, if it occurs in a distrusting climate, it is highly damaging to the individual, group and the organisation. Therefore, at this step, attempts are made to assimilate conflicts in the system to obtain "dither effect". At the very outset, organisational behaviour is analysed to diagnose causes of conflicts. This follows modification of intervening varibles, such as communication, influence, responsibility, motivation, co-ordination and decision making processes. Although some of these processes are already optimised by trust in the preceding steps, further efforts are taken to modify them with a view to facilitating the management of conflicts at different levels. Other approaches to assimilate conflits include use of peer leaderships, development of interaction-influence network, principle of supportive relationships, integrative goals and consensus, and deemphasised status and depersonalised problem solving process. Specifically, every individual is indoctrinated to exercise leadership on his fellow-workers to mobilise his behaviour in the appropriate direction. This follows use of supportive relationship as guiding force in day-to-day behaviour. This principle asserts that the individual has to give respect to other individuals, especially those with whom he differs. The feeling of integration of goals at different levels is injected and consensus of opinion is generated through concerted efforts in group meetings and discussions. Status symbols are disguised so that individual is not disgusted by them. Finally, in problem solving process, attempts are made to consider contributions as emerging not from the individuals, but from the group to avoid any unpleasant feelings on the part of participants. This procedure facilitated assimilation of conflicts in the first organisation to a substantial extent. In another organisation, attempts are being made to experiment with these measures. Results accomplished are that management is attempting to develop union, while union is attempting to facilitate attainment of management goals. Likewise, different groups and individuals are able to manage their conflicts more effectively and make their constructive applications for effetive results. This follows the last element in MBT system.

Integration of Goals by Trust

At this stage, measures are taken to integrate goals of the individual, group and organisation in a trusting climate. The preceding steps taken in the organisation provide a framework to implement this step. Usually, efforts are made to review, consolidate and reinforce several measures introduced earlier. This follows efforts to evolve a procedure in line with the culture of the organisation in several group discussions to accomplish integration of goals. The procedure embodies several techniques including innovations in organisational design and leadership, optimal staffing and job design, control and compensation systems, appraisal and orientation system, staff-line integration and improvement in supervisor-subordinate relationships. In organisational structures, further modification is made by introducing linking pin system to bring different groups together. By linking pin is meant an individual who occupies membership in two groups; in one he may be a member and in other a leader. This individual facilitates integration of two groups in several ways. Morever, authority and power are assigned to the individuals not in terms of their positions in the structure but in terms of their functional contribution to the attainment of goals and responsibilities in the organisation. Innovation in leadership is achieved by encouraging the leadership style for which subordinates have preference. The leader and subordinate have power to control the reward and penalty system as well as to determine membership in the group and its structure. Staffing patterns are diagnosed to ensure that they are optimal for the attainment of goals. Jobs are redesigned to ensure commitment. Managerial control is given to the individual being controlled rather than to the superior. It means that subordinates have to maintain their own performance data. The superior has to approach the subordinate to obtain the data. Individuals are compensated not only in terms of their contribution to attain tangible results, but also intangible results, such as morale, trust development, improvement of climate, etc. Performance appraisal is done not by the superior but the individual ltimself. As soon as individuals join the organisation an orientation programme is designed to familiarise them with organisational culture and goals. Besides, several measures are taken to integrate staff and line groups by providing increasing participation to the line. Finally, superior and subordinate relationships are improved by encouraging them to practise trusting relationship and giving increasing amount of exposure and feedback to each other. Most of the above measures are being practised by supervisory personnel in the first organisation. These measures are being tried in the second company. The results accomplished through these measures are highly significant. Individuals have started perceiving that they can attain their own goals in the best possible way by ficilitating attainment of goals of the groups and the organisation.

Development of Trust

In addition to the above steps, several measures are taken to develop trust and minimse distrust in the organisation. These methods concern individual and group. Among individual methods, organisational behaviour modification technique and meditation are worth mentioning. In OB Mod technique, trusting behaviour of the individual is reinforced by giving some suitable reward while distrusting behaviour is ignored by discouraging it. In meditation, the individual devotes at least 10 minutes in morning in analysing the magnitudes of trust and distrust in his day-to-day behaviour with a view to enriching it with trust and confidence. These techniques are found to be highly useful. Group techniques include sensitivity training and transactional analysis. People are exposed to these techniques in training programmes being launched as part of longterm development. However, no scientific measures have been taken so far to assess the impact of these techniques on trust development. In one of the organisations, subordinates have given feedback that these techniques have helped them to improve their trust in different walks of their lives, besides the organisational settings. In addition to these individual and group techniques, several other methods were used in the long-term MBT training programme. These method included business games in decision making, simulution, communication experiment, case studies embodying different levels of trusting and distrusting climates, Johari awareness window, confrontation meetings between actual and simulated labour-management groups, a series of lectures in human relations, motivation and morale managerial effectiveness, communication and management by trust. During training programmes attempts have been made to measure leadership effectiveness as well as managerial orientations of the participants and provide feedback during discussions in seminar Although specific measures have not been taken to evaluate the training programme, several participants have reported that their behaviour and performance has improved markedly and they are better equipped to deal with their environment effectively. One of the senior executives said that as a result of exposure to MBO measures his adjustment had improved substantially not only within the organisation, but also in family settings.

Effective Performance

Finally, in one of the organisations, follow-up study reveals the levels of trust have increased while those of distrust decreased it different levels. Three per cent increase in trust and three per cent decrease in distrust as a result of MBT programme during a 21 monthperiod, have led to one per cent increase in employee morale an over 50 per cent (35 per cent in real terms) rise in production of the plant. Specfically, during a six month peirod of follow up there has been a significant rise in the production in different departments. In addition, there have been substantial reductions in the rate of turnover absenteeism, tardiness and accidents. The relationship between union and management is marked by cooperative attitudes. Financial position of the company has improved substantially and it is embarking upon a remarkable technological innovation very soon. Perhaps, the self-reinforcing, spiralling circle of management by trust has started working in the company.

3

Building an Effective Modelling Capability: A Practical Guide for Managers

PHIL CHARKO AND DAN HARVEY

The use of models or computer modelling systems as an integral part of managements' organisational planning and decision-making processes is growing rapidly in both the public and private sectors. Questions of effectively developing a modelling capability, relevant to particular management needs, must be dealt with if this trend is to be successful.

In this article the authors address the major challenges managers face in building an effective modelling capability in their organisation. Using forecasting and simulation modelling in financial and operational activities as examples, they outline the fundamentals of modeling and develop general guidelines and principles for use in modelling systems development. Also described are the technical considerations managers must take into account: how to assess genuine requirements; selecting

Reprinted from Optimum, Volume 13-4, 1983, Minister of Supply and Services, Canada, Bureau of Management Consulting Ottawa, Canada.

optimal hardware/software combinations; managing modelling activities; and strategic consideration concerning model use.

Recently, governments have begun to emphasise the use of coordinated planning process in both financial and operational areas. This emphasis, combined with greater availability and access to data, resulting from increased use of computer technologies, has created widespread management interest in the potential and use of models to support planning and decision-making activities. The issues and questions connected with this developing trend toward the use of computer-based modelling in management, and with how in effective modelling capability can be developed and used by managers for their organisations, provide the essential focus of this article.

By Way of Backgrouud

Defining the Model

Simply stated, models are nothing more than representations of reality. Their purpose—as perform experiments to find answers to particular questions. What may be surprising to some is that wherever decisions are made, modelling inevitably is involved—even if only at the intuitive level. How formal or structured a model becomes varies greatly. Formality depends on the explicitness of relationships among the model's elements and its basic assumptions.

At the least formal level models are intuitive—such as a mental map of city. At the second level of formality, relationships among elements remain non-explicit. However, relationships are based on well-understood theory. The operating statements or balance sheet of an agency are examples of such models. At the third level are models having clear statements of specific relationships and assumptions. In econometric model of the Canadian economy fits into this category. It is also at this third level that computer models are found. Here basic relationships are translated into computer language. For our purposes, the approach to model building advocated in this guide is based on developing these formal computerised modes from the less formal or structured models that currently existen the organisation at intuitive levels.

Management Decision-making and Modelling

The notion that the purpose of modelling is to support management decision-making is not unfamiliar. However, model developers have demonstrated a tendency to forget this purpose and the major implications it has on the type of model managers need. For example, organisations often attempt to design one model to support all types of decision making—from long-term strategic planning decisions to detailed resource allocation. Models must be designed to support specific types of decisions if the major benefits of modelling are to be gained.

To take this point further, models can be used to support several types and levels of decision making by management, including (but not at all limited to):

long-term strategic planning;

the preparation of Multi-Year Operational Plans;

responsibility centre budgeting; and

resource management processes such as cash forecastings and inventory control.

Management decision making for each area involves different variables. The net result is that the nature of formal models supporting each decision area has to be different. Models for strategic planning decisions, for example, should consist of variables such as socio-economic trends, product demand, aggregate costs, volumes and output measures. Budgetary process models, on the other hand need elements which reflect individual responsibility centre expenses or detailed work-load measures. Too often, this specific design purpose relationship is ignored, limiting the effectiveness of models and of the decisions made using model outputs.

There is another dimension to modelling/decision-making interactor which has to be recognised by managers. This dimension encompasses the organisational impacts of using models in formalised decision-making activities. Model building requires an explicit identification of all relevant assumptions and relationships inherent in making management decisions. For example, a model could identify a definite relationship between work load and person-year resources. Obviously, this type of identification is essential for effective decision making. The difficulty lies in the fact that such explicit statements can cause tension and discord within an organisation unless there is a consensus at senior management levels about such assumptions. On the 'up' side, however, where there is consus models can serve as a common focus for decision making thereby ensuring that all types of planning are closely and effectively linked. This last point suggests some of the benefits an organisation and its managers can expect from development of a formal computerised model.

Benefits of Computerised Modelling

Computerised modelling tends to result in two basic type of benefits. First, there are efficiency gains. Computer models make calculations feasible which would be impractical and costly to perform manually. As well, modes allow for the efficient use of various types of statistical and econometric techniques and interative calculations thereby permitting more efficient testing of assumptions and more precise analysis of a wider range of variables. Stated more generally, managers can deal with a wider range of questions and issues because of the efficiencies of modelling using computer technology.

The second type of benefit—the increase in management's knowledge and understanding of the organisation and its internal processes—is even more important than simple efficiency gains. Formal models test a manager's intuitive understanding of the organisation and its environment. Using models helps pinpoint areas where information and data are laking and where knowledge of organisational processes is weak. Ultimately, this promotes better planning and decision making because of better knowledge and insight into the needs of the organisation, This benefit can also be extended. Where different groups participate in the development of a model, as should be the case, the increase in understanding is shared, allowing for the integration of efforts of diverse groups such as programme, financial and planning staff.

It must be cleary stated, however, that formal model building in and of itself does not result in better decision, making. Modelling may result in more accurate forecasting or the efficient generation of countless scenarios, but it does not automatically lead to better organisational decisions. There must be an increased understanding of the organisation, combined with integration of effort, for better decisions to be the result of model building and use. Managers must view models as learning tools for their organisations and focus on this during the process of developing a modelling capability.

Development Modelling Systems—Some General Guidelines

Recent data processing literature about modelling and forecasting is filled with articles advocating a variety wide of approaches and hardware/software combinations. "Financial Modelling on Main-frames"; "Desk-top Financial Forecasting," "Crystal Balling on Micros"; to name a few examples.[1] Other articles warn of the dangers inherent in the model development process itself; "Effective Use of Strategic Planning, Forecasting and Modelling in the Executive Suite;" "Corporate Planning Models that Failed;" and "An Over-view of a Decade of Corporate Modelling in the UK."[2] illustrate these types. For managers seeking to gain the benefits of compulerised modelling, the technical issues and options they face seem formidable. Take heart—the development of an effective modelling capability need not be particularly difficult, lengthy or expensive.

There are a number of useful general guidelines and well-tested principles available to managers wanting to follow a practical approach to the development of an effective modelling system. Using financial modelling as an example, the following are particularly useful (as well as being applicable in other fields):

Develop small systems to meet a genuine (need the model can be expanded later if necessary);

take an evolutionary user-driven design approach which begins with prototypes and permits end-user control over model operation;

avoid the so-called 'professional vices of the accountant and management scientist in the design of the system;

utilise system designs and software which minimise the programming task; and

maximise use of current staff for the development and maintenance of the model.

Many modelling attempts in the public sector failed during the early '70s, because model designers focused on generating numbers rather than pursuing a specific management purpose. Models developed to respond to a genuine problem will be examined critically by management because the results of modelling exercises will be relevant to the organisation. Equally, results will be used in decision making if and when they are relevant, credible and comprehensive to managers.

Closely related to focusing on specific problems is the need to emphasise results. Obtaining useful results quickly, rather than canvasing all possible requirements for all potential users before developing modellings programmes, is important if models are to be successfully utilised by management. This approach is called user-driven computer design, as opposed to pre-specified design methodologies previously used.[3] With user-driven design, systems, are developed on a prototype or pilot basis. They use high capability software, thereby minimising the need for professional programmers on staff in the organisations. The main impact of this approach is that an evolutionary process involving continuous interaction with system users is developed. There is no freezing of designs as in conventional project life-cycle design processes. Changes to designs occur from initial development activities up to, and even after implementation of the modelling system.

The third guideline is meant to serve as a warning about prevalent practices in the design of many simulation models. Models designed to be used as an aid to executive decision making should not allempt to perform excessively detailed or overly sophisticated routines. Detailed costing or excessive optimisation routines are examples of the biases of accountants and management scientists which can reduce model utility for management. While extra detail can add accuracy, it also increases complexity. Complexity involves high costs, particularly when modelers utilise complex software. Complexity adds to development, testing, and decumentation times. Overly sophisticated routines can limit model credibility since decision makers must put their faith in techniques they may not fully understand. Better decisions will emerge only where managerial insight and understanding increase, a process inhabited by the use of excessive detail and complicated techniques. The purpose of financial and other planning models is to enhance decision making, not to produce forecasts which are accurate to the tenth decimal place. Elegance and fine detail are not always virtues.

The fourth principle noted is to design systems and select software that minimise the programming task. The technical considerations segement of this paper outline the ranges of software and hardware options available for managers. It should be noted here, however, that programming should promote the best fit between a manager's needs and understanding of the organisation and the computer model being designed. The necessary nerative, evolutionary approach to ensure this fit is inhibited where unnecessarily complicated programming is used.

With respect to the last principle, a variety of staff at all levels in the organisation must have a good understanding of both how the mod.l works and its basic assumptions. The benefits of increased understanding and integrated decision making will be lost where current staff are not involved fully in the development and operation of the modelling system.

The basic steps in the development of a modelling system consistent with this approach can be summarised as follows:

establish model objectives;

develop conceptual design;

choose software and processing approach;

programme and test the prototype;

examine the prototype (users);

add user-driven features;

undertake needed documentation, implementation and user-testing activities; and

monitor, evaluate and refine the model.

With small model systems, managers can proceed through these steps informally; for larger systems, a more structured approach is desirable.

Adoption of these guidelines and principles and the eight-step development programme will result in practical models. These will serve genuine management needs while minimising the risks of failure or of under-utilisation.

Some Technical Issues

The previous section focused on general practices designed to ensure that models are effectively integrated with management and organisational needs. In this section, a number of more technical issues are addressed—from this same perspective. These include design principles, software selection, processing approach, project management and implementation.

Before discussing these areas, however, it is important to differentiate between two general types of computer models; those used for forecasting and those performing simulations.

Forecasting models are those where the primary technical problem is the development of accurate forecasts. Simulation models are used where the emphasis is on accurate replication of relationships or statements needed to conduct a variety of 'what-if' analyses. Size and complexity of the model, and the related software and hardware alternatives, are quite different for the two types of models. In practice, models usually, combine elements of both forecasting and simulation. Nevertheless, the distinction between types is useful. The relative emphasis of forecasting or simulation in the needed model helps determine the optimal approaches and configurations of hardware and software.

Design Principles

To produce the conceptual design of the modelling system. 1 number of basic questions must be answered;

Why is this modelling exercise being performed?

What data are available?

What is the availability and skill level of staff to produce and run the model?

There are at least three plausible reasons for producing a model. First, the need to have very accurate forecasts, such as those for a budgetary forecast; which must be rigidly adhered to. In this case, a detailed forecasting model is appropriate. Second, the need for rough forecast figures (such as in preliminary planning work). Simple , easily produced models fill such requirements well. Finally there is the need to gain an understanding of what is actually happening within a system or area under evaluation. Often it is this last need which ends up as most important, even when not initially the main objective of model development. The very act of producing a model stimulates discussion, thereby creating a better understanding of needs which can lead, eventually, to integrated decision making. In any event, a good knowledge of why the model is being built is essential.

It is important to know what types of data are available for the modelling exercise and how reliable the data are. Early examination of the data available can keep the model designer from wasting time and money. For example, if good historical data series are at hand, detailed time-series models can be built; with only limited historical data, sophisticated time-series modelling is impractical.

The availability and skill level of staff may also limit design options. Obviously, staff with appropriate skills are necessary in the model creation stage. However, this seldom presents insurmountable problems. Where such design/development skills are not available in-house, outside consultants usually can be found. The real issue is whether can not the internal staff are capable of running and understanding the modelling system when it is finished. It is imperative that in house staff know how a model runs and (on a general level) what is does. If the model too complex for the staff to run and interpret, it won't be used. The whole exercise will have been wasted.

Computer Software Considerations

After those general issues are dealt with, managers step into more technical considerations, namely. the particular software and hardware with which the prototype model will be develop. Originally, for many computer applications, choice of hardware determined which software or application language would be used. Later, this rule of thumb was reversed and selection of software became the determining factor, a situation arising from the fact that many applications were available on only a limited number of computers. Now even this situation is changing. New versions of the most popular software packages are available for all sizes of machines, and for different manufacturers.

For the purposes of this guide, four software options are considered. These are listed below in the order of increased programming complexity.

electronic worksheets, (*e.g.*, Visicalc, Supercalc);

modelling packages, (*e.g.*, Suffix, Flares, Empire);

'simple' programming languages such as APL and BASIC;

standard high level languages such as FORTRAN and COBOL.

As a general principle, software should be chosen so as to minimise programming costs without sacrificing the required level of complexity. Table 3.1 summarises major software types and their characteristics. Within each class of software there are curly wide variations in characteristics and flexibility. For example, programming requirements vary somewhat in each type of 'simple' language, exemplified by APL and BASIC. These variation have to be considered to determine which is best for any particular application.

TABLE 3.1

Comparison of Software Types

	Electronic worksheets	*Timesharing modelling packages*	*Simple langanges*	*Standard pro-gramm-ing lan-guages*
1	*2*	*3*	*4*	*5*
Technical training required to produce model	Little	Moderate	Maderate	High

(*Contd.*)

1	*2*	*3*	*4*	*5*
Size of model accommodated	Moderate	Large	Large	Large
Potential for technical sophistication	Moderate	High	High	High
Potential for large using data bases	Little	Good	Good	Very good
Effort required to produce model	Little	Moderate	Moderate	High
Cost to run model	Very low	Moderate	Moderate	Moderate
User control over model	High level of control	High-Moderate level of control	Varibale level of control	Low level of control
Flexibility of model to accommodate changes (*i e.*, maintenance)	Very accommodating	Accommodating	Somewhat resistent	Resistent
Ease of testing model	Easy	Easy	Somewhat difficult	Difficult
Extensiveness of documentation required	Minimal	Minimal	Moderate	High

Software—Some Descriptions and Considerations

Electronic worksheets: The major advantage of electronic worksheet software is that there are no programming requirements at all. The relationships between data and desired output figures are simply specified in quasi-arithmetic formal on the basic worksheet itself. For example, the summation of a column of figures, B, with 10 rows, would be expressed as SUM (B1: B10) placed in the worksheet location where you expect to find the answer. Electronic worksheets are recommended for simulation models of a fairly small size (relatively small amounts of data), where there is a limited need for statistical functions, and limited report formating requirements.* For example, electronic worksheet software is ideal for 'what-if' simulations of an agency's basic operating statement.

Modelling packages: The major advantages of modelling packages over electronic worksheets are their capability to handle larger amounts of data, their greater interfacing capabilities, and their potential for a wide variety of statistical manipulations. There are disadantages to such packages, including higher costs and more complexity in programming. As well, with a system using modelling packages, it is a virtual necessity to have a tramed staff member dedicated to the task of running the system a substantial portion of his/her time.

'Simple' programming languages: Simple programming languages, such as BASIC and APL, offer excellent flexibility and reasonably quick results. Models involving detailed, non-standard data manipulations can ae effectively programmed in either of these languages. The primary disadvantage of even such simple languages is the need for a specialised programmer for initial model development, model maintenance and any model upgrading. This increases both development time and costs.

*There are a number of electronic worksheet products that do offer compatibility with data base, and statistical software, and which permit large volumes of data.

Standard programming languages: A decade ago, most corporate models were programmed in standard languages such as FORTRAN or COBOL. Today, there are few systems which can optimally be developed in either one. Considerations which might require their use in system development include existing policy dictates or the fact that programmers are readily and continuously available. Standard languages do have many disadvantages. Most in-house data processing organisations with the language expertise have large backlogs and are unable to deliver modelling system prototypes or designs within reasonable timeframes. Users also must consider the evolutionary aspect of modelling systems and the need to have assured future support, neither of which is readily accessible given present standard programming languages situations.

Computer Processing Considerations

In addition to software concerns or considerations, managers must also be aware of hardware or processing systems and their relative attributes. Major differences exist among the major processing options available: single-user microcomputer systems; commercial time-sharing systems; and in-house data processing systems. Since each major processing approach has disadvantages, no single approach can be recommended for all situations.

To begin, there is a fundamental disanction between single-user micro-computer based systems and either commercial time-sharing systems or inhouse data processing. Micro-computer systems seem to encourage greater experimentation, are less intimidating and are very compatible with the evolutionary approach. From a psychological point of view, models built on microcomputers appear to be an extension of the manager's own office and seem to integrate with the organisation more easily. In contrast, time-sharing systems, either commercial or in-house, are generally much more task-specific and can be quite intimidating.

Most modelling systems require, at the very least, a terminal and printer facility. Basic rental, storage and operating costs for a moderately complex model using a timesharing system amount to between $ 2,000 and $ 4,000 annually. A good microcomputer system, including the software, can be purchase for about $ 3,000 to $ 10,000. This could be more cost effective than time-sharing or central facilities. With the microcomputer systems, however, there is less support to users. With time-sharing systems, a wider range of expertise is available. On the other hand, costs can mount quite rapidly and unexpectedly with time-sharing systems. Costs of running in-house with the central data-processing department will vary, depending on the system, although as suggested earlier, the crucial consideration is level of service. There is often a backlog of applications to be programmed with resulting reduced service capability. Table 3.2 summarises some of the advantages and disadvantages of these three processing options.

There are two major returns to be realised from the development of a formal modelling system capability within an organisation. The first is the precision and ease with which the immediate forecasting or simulation problem can be solved. The second is the development of a much better conception of the environment of the organisation and specific relationships within it and the impacts these have on the organisation's activities. This latter return is an evolving benefit. The model provides the impetus for rethinking long-standing assumptions about organisational processes. Management of the project team and implementation of the system must be undertaken with these benefits firmly in mind.

As often is the case, however, there are trade-offs involved. Sometimes the only way to get a system operational is to hire someone to develop the model outside the organisation, either because of time contraints or because resource people with the requisite technical, software, and hardware knowledge are not available in-house. This approach often results in a loss of benefits to the organisation. It is often the outside technical

TABLE 3.2

Comparison of Processing Options (User's Perspective)

	Micro-computer based system	*Commercial time-sharing systems*	*In-house data-processing*
Basic costs	Basic single user system \$ 3,000-\$ 10,000 (one-time cost)	Storage operating terminal rental annually (small system) \$ 2,000-\$ 4,000	Variable
Administrative costs	Moderate	Low	Low
Availability	110%	95%-98%	Variable
Flexibility for accommodation of system or design changes	Software & hardware dependent but within these limitations excellent	Software hardware dependent but within these limitations good	Software/ hardware dependent, variable
Risk of hardware problems	Moderate	Low	Variable

analyst/consultant who gains the best knowledge of the system. In-house development obviously provides a better chance that the benefit of increased insight will be realised and that the model will be integrated into the organisation's decision making.

There are other disadvantages to working with resources from outside. Using a service bureau exclusively can mean that certain software and hardware options are automatically excluded. Moreover, service bureau and contract programmers can only respond to well-defined requirements. They cannot determine exactly what it is a manager needs in the same way someone experienced with the organisation can.

Model analysts play an absolutely vital role. They must be familiar with the organisation, the basic data the required calculating techniques and the programming language. If the analyst must be from outside the organisation then managers should ensure that by the end of the project the analyst's role has been effectively taken over by a staff member. Managers developing modelling systems must conduct the project in a way that ensures the expertise gained in developing the model remains with the organisation and evolves to meet future needs.

In the area of implementation, efforts should be created toward ensuring adequate model development, documentation model testing, and user training.

Testing for even small applications has to be thorough. Simple test data or hand calculations can be employed to ensure that the model functions as intended. Where models are developed outside the organisation, a second phase of testing called end-user testing, is required to ensure that the end user can operate, maintain, and if necessary, develop the model further.

The more complex the model and calculations, the more necessary it is that documentation respecting data sources and assumptions be developed. This is particularly true for models with an extensive forecasting component. In these cases, the documentation required is not the programming documentation often called for in systems development methodologies. Rather, it is the detailed description of forecasting assumptions, techniques and algorithms that is required: in other words, a detailed description of what the model does and why is absolutely essential. A modelling system will produce a new, formal concept of the environment of the organisation and existing input/output relationships. To realise these insights to the fullest, relationships should be explained and understood by as many members of the organisation as possible. The more traditional programme documentation—such as flow charts, file descriptions, variable names and so forth—is required in detail only for systems using standard languages. It is required in summar, from only, where more user-friendly programming languages have been used in model design and development.

The amount of training that is needed will depend on the nature of the model itself and the starting point abilities of in-house staff. As a general rule, models should be developed to be run interactively. In this case user-friendly features such as menus, HELP and BACKUP routines should be integral to the model processing system to provide on-the-spot assistance. With more complex models, a user manual explaining options and maintenance requirements is essential. Staff need to be familiar with the assumptions of the model, its operation and with the programming language if second-level benefits are to be maximised. The implementation effort itself can be used to phase it training over the necessary period of time. The success of training efforts is often simply a question of encouraging and developing the original enthusiasm for the system generated during its initial development.

More generally, managers need to be sensitive to the interdependence among end-user testing, training, and functional documentation, and the possibility for synergistic returns if all three factors are dealt with effectively. The first year following the development of the model is the period used for these activities.

Some Final Words

We are in the midst of a technological revolution —a revolution in both hardware and software. The computer is, more and more, a tool with the potential for being used by everyone in their dairy activities. The ideas of user-driven design and user-friendly equipment would have been unthinkable even a few years ago. Now there is software and the needed equipment to undertake tasks which until recently were the remain of the computer expert. With more and better technology, which is increasingly user friendly, a fundamental change in roles can take place. The creation and use of relatively sophisticated management support tools, such as the types of models mentioned in this guide, need no longer be a 'back-room' activity dependent on highly trained experts. Model creation can increasingly be an activity performed by the staff and the manager who will use the model and in results. The implications for management and for decision making are significant to say the least, as are the benefits to be gained if the potential offered by the modelling revolution is exploited.

In part, realising the potential offered by modelling systems will require a major shift in the general approach which has been used up to now for the development and use of models. Technical issues, which in the past have been paramount, have to be replaced with a new emphasis on managerial and organisational concerns. The high degree of centralisation of modelling activity can be replaced by decentralised user-generated models. The dependence on technical expertise, while not eliminated, can be reduced by effective use of that expertise and conscious development of skills in user organisations directing development activities. Dependence on information generated elsewhere, and subject to error because of incomplete understanding can be replaced by user-directed generation and control of information essential to effective decision making.

The tools are available. The technology is suitable. The potential exists. Will it be realised?

REFERENCES

1. P. Cliff "Financial Modeling off Main Frames" *Computer Decisions*, August 1981, p. 63; D. Brown, "Desk top Financial Forecasting", *Financial Executive*, July 1981, p. 16; R. Perry, "Crystal Balling on Micros", *Computer Decision*, September 1981, p. 60·

2. T. Naylor, "Effective Use of Strategic Planning, Forecasting, Modeling in the Executive Suite", *Managerial Planning*, January/February 1982; Ang, of Criva, "Computer Planning Model that Failed", *Managerial Planning*, September/October 1980; P. Gringer, J. Woolter, "An overview of a Decade of Corporate Modeling in the Executive Suite", *Accounting and Business Reserach* Winter, 1980, p. 4.

3. James Martin, *Application Development, without Progrommers*, Prentice-Hall Inc, 1982, pp. 51-68.

4

Toward the Development of Administrative and Management Capability in Developing Countries

KEMPE R. HOPE
AUBREY ARMSTRONG

Introduction

In recent years it has become increasingly obvious that administrative reforms and the development of management capability are necessary in developing countries for the carrying out of social and economic policies and the achievement of socio-economic goals of development. Furthermore, it has been recognised that the administrative and management capability which are necessary must be different from the conventional organisational reforms. Thus, western concepts applied in the

Reprinted with the permission of the authors from 'International Review of Administrative Sciences', Vol. XLVI, No. 4, 1980.

Dr. Kempe R. Hope is Professor of Economics and Finance and Chairman of the Business Administration Department. Daemen College. Amherst, New York. Mr. Aubrey Armstrong is Management Consultant with the United Nations, New York.

interest of development of administrative and management capability in the less developed countries (LDC's) would tend, of necessity, to be ineffective.

This paper examines some of the measures necessary for the creation and development of administrative and management capability in the LDC's for the further promotion of their growth and development.

One way of fostering administrative and management capability is to organise major administrative and management reform programmes. Major administrative and management reform programmes are defined as specially designed efforts to induce fundamental changes in public administration and management through system-wide transformation, or at least through measures for improvement of one or more of its key elements, such as administrative and management structure, territorial organisation, budget management, planning process, personnel practices and other administrative and management processes, in response to significant changes, actual or anticipated, in the environment and role of public administration.

A large number of developing countries organised programmes of major administrative and management reform in the past, but did not always clearly stipulate the specific objectives to be achieved through such programmes or spell out the time frames for various actions. Consequently, in such cases, the reform programmes had only a limited effect on public administration for development. For this reason, the objectives of any administrative and management reform programme should be properly enunciated to provide at least the basis for evaluation of results.

To ensure effectiveness of major administrative and management reform programmes, it is also necessary to pay special attention to their preparation and implementation phases. As far as possible, it is desirable to involve all concerned in the reform process, and to minimise uncertainties, tensions, and resistance among affected organisations and functionaries, which are frequently found to accompany major changes. The implementation of reforms should also include training and briefing in new measures, provisions for feedback and corrective action, and assistance in installing new systems and methods.

A related approach to reforming public administration for development in LDC's, is to directly relate pertinent measures to national plan objectives, strategies, sectors, and programmes in the plan itself. Described as "administrative and management planning", it calls for spelling out and providing for specific administrative and management requirements for implementing development plans concurrently with preparation of their economic, social and technical analyses and components. Administrative and management planning to develop implementing organisations and systems is indispensable to any comprehensive development effort. Attention should therefore be drawn to the importance of measures to increase administrative and management capability for economic and social development, the desirability of making such measures an integral part of development plans at all levels, as appropriate, and the need for such measures to be adequate to enable governments to achieve their goals. Now, let us focus our attention on some more specific measures for creating administrative capability and improving the management of development in LDC's.

Manpower Planning and Training

First, there exists an absolute necessity for training in LDC's. Apart from the removal of the continued existence of the colonial mentality, education and training are necessary to create a stock of trained managers and administrators. This therefore means an attempt at proper manpower planning and assessment. Manpower planning and assessment go far beyond tabulation of supply and demand indices of the labour force. It must take into consideration the broad spectrum of problems of human resources development. Planning and assessment of manpower should be a part of the development plan of any developing country, and should be coordinated with education planning and training. In the LDC's, manpower planning is of vital necessity, but has always been a shortcoming of post-independence development planning in these economies. This shortcoming manifests itself in the negligence or unconcern of the governments and to a lesser degree, in the lack of qualitative and quantitative techniques necessary for such planning. Manpower planning is needed in LDC's to ensure the adequate supply of manpower for public organisations which would meet quantitative, qualitative and time requirements of national development plans and programmes. It is therefore necessary to anticipate changes in manpower and skill requirements likely to occur as a result of national development plans, and to initiate timely actions to meet them. Manpower planning, as part of the broader planning process, is a useful tool in this respect to deal with the problem in a systematic rather than haphazard manner. It will also provide the basis for planning educational and training activities at various levels. In the LDC's, manpower planning could at least be started for the public sector and be eventually extended to include other sectors of the socio-economic system.

All developing countries which are facing the challenge of accelerating economic and social development, with the consequent responsibility for providing the necessary human and material infrastructure, depend critically in this respect on the capability, motivation, and performance of the personnel in the public services. It is therefore important to recognise the government work force as an indispensable element in national development and irrespective of the system of recruitment of these public servants, there is a need to improve their capability through training. By training, we mean the act or process of making a person fit to perform certain tasks. Training is necessary because no matter how well qualified a person may be at the time of recruitment, he or she still has certain inadequacies, and therefore much to learn before becoming a really effective civil servant. This is the reason why in some countries a person who is newly recruited into the Civil Service must first go through a period of training before being assigned to specific duties. In France, and in countries governed in the French tradition, public administrators for example, must go through a period of training in a national School of Administration before joining the various services of the Central Government. This type of pre-entry training can be easily undertaken in the LDC's.

Equally important is in-service training. In many countries, national institutes of public administration have been established for the most part to provide in-service training at the lower management and middle management levels. This may entail a short orientation course of a few days to acquaint a new recruit with his organisation, its environment, and the general nature and conditions of work; it may entail some induction training to each specific tasks and may last a few weeks; or it may involve a more general training programme to enhance the administrative capability of a new recruit and may last for any length of time.

However, in view of the urgency of the work of national development, the traditional method of on the job training is often too slow. Sometimes learning by doing or by trial and error is not only slow but also costly. A formal training programme often speeds up the learning process and thus brings the civil servants, including new recruits, to a better standard of performance. The economy of this matter is one of the reasons why formal training has become important in development administration and management and should be one of its key features. It should be recognised, though, that some form of tutelage and on-the-job training is indispensable in the Civil Service and that self-development and learning from experience and mistakes have their place. But a formal training programme can be used to shorten the time required for a person to learn, to help avoid some of the costly errors of the trial and error method, and at the same time, to maintain a degree of uniformity in the substance of training.

Another critical factor in the effectiveness of in-service training programmes pertains to their substantive content[1]. In-service training, by its very nature, tends to be very general and invariably not geared to any specialised career development, which results in a Civil Service plagued with dilettantism, immobility, and anti-intellectualism. To make in-service training productive, measures must be undertaken that would meaningfully relate training to career development of an individual civil servant, to the processes of recruitment, posting, promotion and other terms and conditions of service such as probationary period and examinations. In-service training is not carried out in vacuum. It functions in an environment of policies, procedures, standards, and institutional objectives and has intimate relationships with other strategies of management. It is important to make a sharp distinction between the mere availability of training programmes and their effectiveness in promoting development objectives. Formal training programmes, both pre-entry and post-entry, in many countries are excessively theoretical and frequently of little operational value. Some are traditional and not development oriented. Some are only for system maintenance and are not change oriented. Some are borrowed without modification from highly developed countries and are irrelevant to the national environment. There is a stong tendency to duplicate university courses in North America or Western Europe rather than to shape courses to meet carefully defined training requirement of the governments concerned. Such mistakes must be avoided.

A development administrator today must be a person of inteligence and character, a child of his national culture, a person with good intuitive judgement, and at the same time, a person with a rational approach, a person with an open mind and broad vision, one who shows concern for society as a whole, has a good sense of justice and is well informed and aware of the political implications and social consequences of his actions and judgements. Such a person must also indentify his or her objectives with the overall development objectives of the nation. In other words, he or she must be development oriented.

Training of civil servants or development administrators must be conceived in very broad terms. It is important to bear in mind that education and training in public administration are long-term processes. No single programme of education or training is able to cover all areas. Some must learn in educational institutions, some in formal training programmes, some through apprenticeship and self-people's understanding and support of social and economic development activities and, as a result, gain the benefit of their own contributions to these activities, and of personal and group adjustments to necessary changes.

Decentralisation should extend both to the lower units in the central hierarchy and to units at the lower levels of government, especially local governments. The latter is especially important because many development efforts must be made at the local government level. Also, the people must be so organised at the local level that they accept the national objectives determined at the centre and actively work towards their achievement. In other words, successful development in these fields depends on public cooperation, especially at the local level where development policies are mainly implemented. Such cooperation may take many forms, including provision for popular participation in the development process, especially in the making and execution of policies, and involvement of local governments in national development, as well as the establishment of national agenicies responsible for assining in the improvement of local government.

Political Organisation and Leadership

The improvement of a nation's administrative and management capability is highly dependent on support from the political leadership. The role of the political leadership is indeed the most crucial factor to be ascertained in the process of national development[5] and hence in the improvement in the administration and management of development. Political leadeship is the arbiter of, rather than one participant of factor among many, in the process of national development. In most LDC's the lack of the political leadership's role in support of major administrative and management change can be traced to have resulted from their own concern for maintaining their elite status and authority. This elite status and authority is so crisply controlled that it is difficult for society to penetrate.

Leading support to administrative change and refrom requires, therefore, commitment on the part of the political leadership. Commitment here involves an overriding desire to promote rationality, rise of productivity, social and economic equalisation, improved institutions and attitudes. All of these aspects of national development combind will hopefully produce the administrative and management machinery needed, while at the same time generating further change. The promotion of these ideals points toward modernisation and is directly opposed to the desire for the maintenance of the *status quo*. Not only should the political leadership be committed to these ideals in the interest of a just society and better development administration, but it should also be resolute enough to recognise such actions as helpful in resolving any problems pertaining to any identity crises.

If a country's leadership takes little interest in management and administration, downgrades administration and management in national priorities, and is ambivalent about reform, then reform agencies find themselves conducting technical exercises with little impact on administrative and management performance. This is less true of *ad hoc* task forces which depend less on elite support than professional acceptance.[6]

Economic and social development is dependent on effective statesmanship within a favourable political environment. Stagnant societies tend to reflect the lack of dynamic political organisation. Since development consists of social action and change, it requires both enlightened political leadership and the support of influential elements in the population. The two are significantly interrelated. Develpment cannot be successful without a substaining philosophy of doctrine, political action on a dramatic order, and effective organisation for the mobilisation of popular support.

Political leadership refers to that body of topmost decision markers those legal and/or actual responsibility is to make final authorities decisions on each of the issues and problems it is concerned with. In this sense political leadership as a concept and category of analysis, is constant, while its actual membership or personnel composition is variable. Therefore, the structure of a government should be of a character that encourages responsible political action and facilitates the involvement of a wide cross-section of the citizens in the development process. The character of the constitutional system and the relationships between political officials, on the one hand, and administrators on the other is thus an important element.

The political universe is the context of actions of political leadership; the political system is the major, yet manipulable, instrument that broadly structures and defines the behaviour of political leadership; and politics is the method by which political leadership performs its role. It is thus that political leadership determines goals, selects methods, and gives direction. Society develops or fails to develop according to the extent to which its political leadership is intelligent, creative, skillful, and committed. Without this requisite function of political leadership, there will be no increase in administrative and management capability, no progress, no direction, no development.

The qualities necessary to exert administrative and management leadership are as numerous as they are difficult to define. It is all very well to mention such traits as initiative, resourcefulness, ability, understanding, and commitment, as being necessary constituents of leadership, but it is impossible to construct a workable model made up of all the virtues deemed basic to the ideal political leader, since certain patterns of leadership apply to certain, but not all, situations. A political leader may be successful in one situation, a failure in another.

However, it can be said that a political leader is successful if he can guide others toward a goal. This may involve administrative and management reform, getting essential work done on time, carrying out legislative mandates and so on But in addition, it can mean also the look into the future, the understanding of ultimate possibilities, the improvement of practices and the enlargement of the boundaries of action. The true political leader has some vision into the future as well as an eye for present reality.

Economic Development

Apart from the obvious need and advantages of economic growth, it influences the level of the administrative and management machinery. Government machinery and its operations are of the greatest consequences in developing countries, and the success or failure of the machinery hinges on the effectiveness of the development effort. Increasing levels of economic development would indicate the need for increasing level of development administration, which in turn influences the impact of development planning—since the secret of successful development planning lies not only in sensible politics but also in good public administration.[7]

Moreover, higher levels of economic development do result in more revenue being available for the implementation of development projects, and it also tends to increase the absorptive capacity of the country. With more readily available financial resources, government budgets can be properly augmented and the necessary inputs required for administering and managing the development effort can be acquired.

Budgets play crucial roles in the development administration process because they entail a compulsory and direct transfer of resources. Hence, it is very important that the budget reflects the relative levels of resource allocation and capital formation to be achieved in the economy with respect to the existing revenue available.

The success of economic development planning depends, to a significant degree, upon the effectiveness of management and administration. K. William Kapp was not exaggerating when he indicated that a quantitatively inadequate or qualitatively defective system of public administration will not merely retard the development process, but may defeat the entire development effort in an even more decisive manner than any temporary shortage of capital or an unfavourable monsoon.[8] Thus the strategic significance of public administration in economic development is to be found in the fact that it implements the plan, that it releases popular energy and initiative as well as community effort, and that it channels latent propensities for cooperation and self-improvement into productive activities.

To call public management and administration a strategic factor in economic development is not equivalent to considering it as the only factor, or for that matter the primary cause. The process of growth and development is neither set nor kept in motion by one factor alone. Public management and administration is at best only one of several factors in economic growth. It is strategic in the sense that it influences and determines the success of the entire development plan, and that it is susceptible to deliberate social control and change.[9]

The role and significance of administration and management are greatly enhanced if economic growth becomes the objective of a deliberate economic plan. A national development plan is essentially a blueprint of public policies designed to bring about certain results which would not be forthcoming without it. Indeed such a development plan may be said to be a decision determining the strategy of government action embodied in rules, regulations controls, directives and impulses, all of which are designed to increase output and productivity. To be practical and effective, the plan must not only be a general scheme, but one which is adequately worked out in detailed directives by careful planning of the different sectors, and it must give instructions for the specific inducements and controls by which the realisation of those directives is effected.[10] It is clear why, under these circumstances, public administration and management assume a key role in the development effort. Directives and controls must be applied, inducements have to be implemented, and the progress and development process must be recorded and supervised so that the necessary adjustments can be enacted and effected as they become necessary. If government assumes these responsibilities of initiating directing and promoting economic development through various policies and reforms designed to channel investments and to overcome structural obstacles and social rigidities, the establishment of an effective system of administration and management, and an efficient Civil Service, are bound to assume an unparalleled importance.

Coordination of administrative and management decisions concerning the allocation and investment of national resources must be an essential element of development effort if it is to achieve its goal and objectives. The objective of the development effort should, therefore, be redefined to include the creation and expansion of administrative and management capability for resource mobilisation and plan implementation. Expansion of local government administrative capacity to identify and execute investments promoting growth with equity must also be given higher priority in national development policy.

Conclusions

The administration and management of development in the LDC's is still a legacy of their colonial past. The colonial political system was a mere bureaucratic system. It was centralised and no separate institution for political and administrative functions existed. This created a blurred distinction between the "administrative" and the "political", and the result was obviously a highly politicised bureaucracy. Policy was largely formulated and implemented by the colonial overlords. The bureaucratic colonial administration has now been replaced by native politicians who also exercise centralised authority and control. Politics is now the order of the day and the development administration machinery is inept.

It is therefore evident that the creation of a suitable machinery for the administration of development is of vital necessity and should be made a priority endeavour. The success of such an endeavour depends on a number of factors as outlined above. The expanded role of government into social and economic areas has increasingly demanded new and improved conceptual and operational frameworks so that national development is manageable and practicable. However, while the need for rapid development has been vividly felt, and national programmes for the satisfaction of these growth needs constructed and articulated, less attention has been devoted to the requirements of programme implementation including the operational characteristics and the organisation systems through which these end goals are attainable.

Effective administration needs autonomous, yet interdependent, centres of activity that can provide resources for, and exact performances from each other. A healthy economic system, a strong political organisation and leadership, proper manpower planning and training, and effective decentralisation and communication are necessary for improving administration. Otherwise, bureaucracy takes over at the expense of society.

Public administration and management has a great part to play in the development effort. It can supply the facts, apply the methods, and evaluate the record. It need not assume responsibility for making overall plans for a better society, but it can and should be in a position to stimulate, support, and carry out plans that are politically accepted. It is the instrument of accoplishment.

REFERENCES

1. For more on this see Faqir Muhammad, "A Change of Orientation in Public Administration Training" in Irving Swerdlow and Marcus Ingle (eds.) *Public Administration for the Less Developed Countries*, Syracuse: Maxwell School, Syrause University, 1974, pp. 90-100.

2. Moshe Wess, "Some Suggestions for Improving Development Administration". *International Review of Administrative Sciences*, vol. 32—1966, No. 3, p. 194.

3. C A.P. St. Hill, "Towards Reform of the Public Services: Some Problems of Transitional Bureaucracies in Commonwealth Caribbean States", *Social and Economic Studies*, vol. 19, March 1970, p. 139.

4. Harold F. Alderfer, *Public Administration in Newer Nations*, New, York, Praeger, 1967, pp. 54-55.

5. T. Tsurutani, *The Politics of National Development*, New York: Chandler, 1973, p. 25.

6. Gerald E. Caiden. "Development, Administrative Capacity and Administrative Reform", *International Review of Administrative Sciences*, vol. 39—1973, No. 4, p. 340.

7. W. Arthur Lewis, *Development Planning*, London: Allen and Unwin, 1966, Preface.

8. K. William Kapp, "Economic Development, National Planning and Public Administration", *Kyklos*, No. 13, 2/1960, p. 198.

9. A factor may be said to have strategic importance if it has real power to control other factors and to determine the general character of the results; and it has peculiar strategic importance if, in addition, we have power to control it. See I.M. Clark, *Strategic Factors in Business Cycles*, New York; National Bureau of Economic Research, 1934, pp. 6-7.

10. Gunnar Myrdal, *Economic Theory and Underdeveloped Regions*, New York: Harper and Row, 1957, pp. 83-84, and C. Russu and E. Radulescu, "The Strategy of Development and the Management Training Requirements", *Management Training Review*, No. 2, 1977.

5

Management of Rural Development Some Aspects

K.K. CHAUDHURI & M.S. MISHRA

Introduction

An attempt has been made here to highlight some of the methodological as well as management aspects of rural development which often do not receive sufficient emphasis on promotion of rural development. The following aspects have been discussed in this paper: (i) understanding rural reality and local needs; (ii) mobilization and utilization of resources; (iii) planning and coordination; (iv) appropriate organizational and institutional structure; and (v) issues in monitoring and evaluation.

In India, rural development began through community development programmes followed by the programmes for increased agricultural production and rural employment. In early areas rural development was considered synonymous with the growth of agriculture and allied sectors. The objectives were approved productivity in rural areas, increased income levels and provision of minimum levels of food, shelter, education and health. The programmcs launched by the Government of India upto the Fifth Five Year Plan Agency and large sectoral as well as sectionable nature. For example, Intensive Agricultural District Programme (IADP), Small Factors Development Agency (SFDA), Tribal Area Development (TAD), Hill Area Development (HAD), Draught Prone Area Programme (DPAP), Command Area Development (CAD) etc., were initiated in different parts of the country keeping in view the development of certain sectors and sections of rural India. But these programmes could not achieve uniform success and often failed to fulfil the objectives due to a number of 'internal' and 'external' factors. Therefore, it would be worthwhile to evolve an appropriate integrated rural development approach and its management based on the experiences of previous programmes, strategies, achievements and failures.

The objectives of rural development of a country should be the optimum utilization of human and natural resources of the rural area for the enrichment of the quality of life of the rural masses *i.e.*, by raising their standard of living above poverty line and making them self-sufficient. The meaning of rural development is not to just provide some physical infra-structure like a school, or better drinking the water and health services, or seeds of a high-yielding variety together with fertilizers and pesticides. The approach should be comprehensive, *i.e.*, apart from the items mentioned above other inputs must come in together. Integration of integrated rural development means not only comprehensiveness and coordination of inputs but also compatibility and complementarity between the different spheres of development. The issue of such development in relation to different environment has, however, the common denominator namely the extent to which the material, psychological, social and spiritual needs of man can be satisfied. Planning for development should provide for judicious development of law, labour and capital, compatible with the unique social, cultural, economic, geographic and ethnic characteristics of the environment.

Understanding Rural Reality and Local Needs

One of the major bottlenecks in the promotion of rural development seems to be the lack of adequate data-base as well as knowledge of the dynamics of rural economy society and power structure. It is essential to have a clear understanding of the rural realities for any rural development planning. Existing literature identifies, among others, the following problems:

(a) low standard of living,

(b) lack of financial resource,

(c) limited knowledge,

(d) social resistance to change, and

(e) the need for institutional reform. In-depth studies done by sociologists and social anthropologists in different parts of the country have succeeded in identifying different facets of the dynamics of rural society in relation to the process of development. In view of the diversities in terms of region, caste, class and other affiliations, it is often problematic to deduce quantitative indicators as well as establish causal linkages in developmental planning.

Thus, the first step is to learn about the society in terms of class and activity-wise population composition of concerned villages. For example, an in a typical village the class composition may be of the following types:

(i) Owners of the means of production (land):

(a) surplus generating class (absentee landlord and supervisory farmer);

(b) non-surplus generating class, who can only produce that consumption requirements (owner cultivator);

(ii) Non-owners of the means of production (land), who cannot even product their consumption requirements (share croppers and landless labourers)

(iii) Artisans (craftsman, weaver, carpenter, potter, blacksmith).

(iv) Traders (vendors, retail traders)

(v) Service-holders

(vi) Professionals

(vii) Other manual workers.

For vetting action programmes for predevelopment, proper identification of their classes and the beneficiaries of each programme is necessary. Further, the needs of particular sections have to be ascertained through detailed investigation. The available knowledge-base for a proper matching a different classes of rural population and local needs with action programmes is extration inadequate and there is need for great emphasis on useful and up-dated activity for accelerating the process of rural development.

Mobilization and Utilization of Rural Resources

Inventory of available resources is an essential pre-requisite before launching any rural development programme. This includes the followiag items:

(i) Manpower resources, *i.e.*, types of people in terms of:

(a) production relation,

(b) per-capita income,

(c) income level,

(d) economic activity, and

(e) education level.

(ii) Ecological resources, *i.e.*, types of land (soil qualities), water supplies (river, canal, lake), habitats, forests, etc.

(iii) Infra-structural resources, *i.e.*, road, electricity, transport, drinking water, irrigation, educational institutions, medical institutions, financial institutions, market etc.

(iv) Economic resources, *i.e.*, type of agriculture (land use, cropping pattern, technology used), fishing, poultry, animal husbandry, insect rearing, orchards, cottage industries, crafts, trades, etc.

(v) Other resources, *i.e.*, animal etc.

After determining the resource inventory, at next stop would be the mobilization of rural resources, so that the requirement of external resources for strengthening a particular activity could be worked out. For pertaining the impact of action programmes. Social that the developmental programmes are based as far as possible on available rural local areas As a matter of fact, a number of developmental efforts during the last three decades had a natural death largely due to hence constraints immediately after the condition of programme period. Assessment planning resourcv potential also helps in the identification of action programmes in the short-run and in the long-run, as well as integration of activities for maximum effect. A number of decisions could be easily taken in the management of such programmes once a proper resource inventory and mechanism for mobilization is available. Appropriate organizational structure for continous information collection and feed-back on resources inventory and mobilization for programme implementation has to be instituted.

Planning and Co-ordination

Going by the experience of last three decades, planning and coordination of rural development programmes seems to be the major problem in the achievement of desired results. While on the one hand, the macro planning exercises have not been able to take account of the local resources, needs, etc.; on the other hand, local and regional planning have not been properly integrated. This to a large extent has been responsible for lopsided results. Any planning for successful action programmes has to take into account not only the resources, needs, and local problems but also proper integration, both vertical and horizontal keeping in view the short-term and long-term implications. Relevant coordination mechanism has to be set-up based on the planning exercise.

In implementing the rural development programmes the following four types of coordination can be envisaged: (a) For any kind of development work related to agriculture, the farmer is the focal point. For cultivation of his own land, he needs the following inputs like; seeds, water, fertilizer pesticides equipments; working capital labour and technical know-how. Thus, they do the production operation and to market an output, a farmer has to maintain coordition with the several agencies for input mobilization suco as seed, pesticide and particular dealer, equipment dealer, irrigation people labour, working capital (bank, money lender) and extension agency. For output distribution he has to maintain coordination with transport people, storage depot (cold storage) and traders. Hence any programme for improving the efficiency of a farmer is dependent on the mobilization of different agencies so that essential services are made available to the farmer in time. (b) Similarly, different agencies involved in the implementation of the programmes such as government departments, financial institutions, and local level organizations should have proper coordination to ensure effective implementation. (c) Coordination across the related programmes such as agriculture, animal husbandry, rural industries, etc. have to be brought about and if necessary integrated to maximize the desired impact on the beneficiaries. (d) Finally, coordination among the developmental agencies, professional institutions, grass-root level organizations and the beneficiaries would be useful for successful implementation of action programmes. Along with the coordination aspect of different agencies, it is important to ensure peoples' participation both at planning and implementation levels.

The programmes usually preclude the association of the rural people and beneficiaries, as often planning and implementation remain the responsibility of the concerned agencies. This in many instances perpetuates the feeling that the developmental activities are the responsibility of government and general agencies. Attempts by many state governments to involve local panchayats in the preparation as well as implementation of action programmes would be useful in bringing about peoples' participation. From the view point of self-sustenance of developmental efforts, participation of people at the stage of planning and implementation would create the desired motivation for necessary follow-up among the beneficiaries and the local level organizations, thereby increasing the chances of success.

Appropriate Organizational and Institutional Structure

Rural organizations play a critical role in establishing appropriate linkages within and across the developmental programmes. In view of the gradual break-up of the traditions economic and social institutions in rural India the necessity of replacement and strengthening of the existing rural organizations has become much more important than even before in ensuring involvement of people it developmental programmes. To support is recent thrust on economic growth in rural areas with social justice, the promotion if adequate institutional network in the new areas stands as a prerequisite.

Broadly, one can categorise rural organisations in-terms of maintenance of the existance activities such as law and order, land revenue health, communication, etc; and institutions geared for developmental activities such as financial institutions, cooperatives and other government and non-government developmental agencies. Although some character in the organizations and their functions have been introduced during the last decision basically the structure and linkages have remained static. While some of them have cutlived their necessity, others are marked overlapping functions and job responsibility without proper direction and personnel. This, in turn, has created the vicious circle in which the effectiveness of these organizations is open to doubt, and coordination among them is never free from confusion. In view of this, attempts have to be made to visualise the type of organization and institutional network needed, along with the planning of developmental programmes. This entails not only be reorganization of the existing institutional structure, to suit the emerging conditions demanded by action programmes, but also a creation of new organizations for future needs of development.

In terms of the existing structure of organizations for the implementation of some basic programmes one can take the land forms measures as a classic case. Although are realised by all concerned that no strategy of rural development can succeed unless serious efforts for land reforms are initiated, not has remained an issue since independence spite various policies and programmes. Report of the Task Force on Agrarian relations of the Planning Commission[1] identific among others, the following reasons for the performance: (i) gaps between policy legislation and between laws and their elementation, (ii) lack of political will, be legal hurdles, (iv) absence of correct up dated land records, (v) absence of assure from below, (vi) inadequate administrate organisation and policy instruments, and some weak spots in the programme, and the deficiencies in reporting system and sanction. These are indicative of the type of subsequences one is going to face unless advisory organisational networks are set up in advance. Since a number of action programmes for rural development in the Six Plan are related to agrarian structure, appropriate institutional integration is a pre-requisite for any measure of success in rural development efforts.

Once the organizations at the level of basic structure in the rural areas are strengthened, the task of the promotional agencies would be easier. Often the practice of creating a number of developmental agencies without any supporting structute, has minimised the impact of such organisations, Absence of proper linkage between the grassroot level organisations and the developmental agencies, in many instances, has proved fatal for programme implementation. For a development agency, an attitude of 'cooperation' rather than 'conflict' with the local organisations for mutual benefit need to be inculcated to avoid pit-falls and tensions in the implementation stage. While planning for the development of particular activities and necessary institutional support, it is crucial to take into account the existing facts on the concerned activity. For promotion of rural entrepreneurship to accelerate the pace of rural industrialisation, it is important to consider the general as well as specific characteristics of rural entrepreneurs in their environmental context. These may be in the nature of :

(a) Relatively low risk-taking and innovative capacity;

(b) Limited technical, business skills and awareness of opportunities;

(c) Lack of effective leadership;

(d) Shortage of financial resources;

(e) Limited marketing net-work, etc.

Therefore, the next step would be to identify the existing potential entrepreneurs of different economic activities at the levels of production and distribution as producer and trader entrepreneurs respectively.[2] Similarly, the trader entrepreneurs could be identified in terms of their activities such as marketing, transport, storage, etc. as well as the level of operations; wholesaler, middleman, retailer, etc. It is only after such identifications and detailed information collection that the relevant institutional network should be designed for meeting the needs of the programme and the beneficiaries. A number of programmes implemented during the last decade for promotion of rural entrepreneurship and rural industrialization, have not been very effective largely due to the lack of proper recognition of this dynamics and common set of assumptions often made about the entrepreneur and his environment. In recent years, District Industries Centres have been entrusted with the task of promotion of rural entrepreneurship and establishment of a network of industries in rural areas under this programme. Care has been taken to ensure proper identification and integration of various activities to attract and stimulate right kind of entrepreneurs in the countryside through adequate staff and resource support at the district level. Although it is too early to assess the impact of this programme, it is seen that a number of District industries Centres in the eastern and north-eastern region states are unable to take off largely due to the absence of appropriate organizational and institutional structure as well as relevant information. This has, in a few cases, resulted in considerable delays in planning and implementation of action plans. Similarly, it is not uncommon to find banks and other financial institutions in the rural areas facing serious constraints in their entrepreneurship promotion divers often caused by inadequate institutional network. Thus, it is essential to re-orient the existing organizational structure as well as establish new ones with appropriate vertical and horizontal linkages, keeping in view the short-term and long-term effect of each programme, to ensure desired results from the developmental efforts.

Issues in Monitoring and Evaluation

As discussed earlier, while planning for particular rural development activity, rates the long term and short-term objectives as well as the general and specific objective are outlined. Often the goals, strategies are implementation structure at microlevel active plans are neither clearly envisaged nor any attempt is made to ensure adequate consistency with micro-level objectives of the programme. Further in addition to the absence of clarity of objectives at the plan formulation stage, appropriate methodology for monitoring and evaluation of projects is rarely incorporated, keeping in view the specific project needs, and its utility in the performance appraisal of particular activities for optimal-utilization of resources. In the process, monitoring and evaluation of projects in a number of instances either remains outside the success of project planning and formulation, or whatever incorporated stays as merely a past exercise left to the subjective judgement of the implementing agency. This often post serious constraints for implementing agencies in visualising the project in totality and the measuring qualitative as well as quantitative progress. In the absence of built-in-feedback mechanism with appropriate time schedule it becomes difficult to ascertain the progress and monitor actual performance agreed planned activities or identification and solution of problems during project implementation. Further actions taken for mid-course corrections, follow-up activities, training etc., for projects are often based on personal experiences, and sometimes decisions taken on such activities turn out to be of minimum significance for the achievement of the action plan. On the other hand, any outside agency involved in evaluating the projects find it extremely inadequate to make proper assessment of the activities. Without spending a lot of time and energy in understanding the dynamics of the project from the beginning to the end from different perspectives.

Going through a cross section of agencies, it is not uncommon to find that the goals, strategies, monitoring and evaluation systems of rural development activities undergo changes depending on the needs of the as well as the donors during project implementation, and immediately after the project period comes to an end. This brings in further complexities in understanding the internal linkages of the project and their impact on the beneficiaries, in a time frame. For instance, be target—achievement matrix of Govt. agencies in assessing the impact of particular programmes, in the absence of any input-output relationship, considerably limits the scope of proper evaluation even at the block head. Similarly, a number of voluntary agencies, following a donor-oriented approach area rural development planning, consider evaluation from the donor's perspective rather than for their own utility and as a part and leve of their effectiveness. Further, the 'village adoption' approaches followed by business houses and other agencies, often 'lack systematic and coherent planning with proper time and resource utilization perspectives, where assessment becomes hazardous and short-sighted. It is often seen that in project formulation and preparation of feasibilities, evaluation and follow up mechanism are either omitted or given a place of secondary importance, resulting in confusion between the ends and means of the project, as well as the effectiveness of the programme. As another level, this has affected the process of developing appropriate methodology for monitoring and evaluation system keeping in view the specific needs of the programmes and the users. Thus, it is essential that monitoring and evaluation systems, with built in feedback mechanism, need to be linked to the planning exercise for effective implementation of the rural development activities so that based on these, key indicators for appropriate system can be developed.

Conclusion

We have discussed here some of the issues specifically relating to the (1) understanding rural reality and local needs, (2) mobilization and utilization of rural resources, (3) planning and co-ordination, (4) appropriate organisation and institutional structure, (5) monitoring and evaluation in the context of management of rural development. In view of the complexities involved in developing appropriate systems for rural development activities, this paper tries to identify some of the basic issues which needs to be tackled by concerned agencies, planners and researchers.

REFERENCES

1. Report of the Task Force on Agrarian Relations of the Planning Commission. "*Two Decades of Land Reform—A Brief Review*," 1973;
2. Chaudhuri, K.K., "Social Recruitment of Rural Trader Entrepreneurs: A Case Study." *Decision*, 3 July 1979.

6

*Rural Industrialisation and Appropriate Technology—Some Thoughts**

D.J. KANVINDE

The cause of village industries was championed by Mahatma Gandhi and development of khadi and village industries became an integral part of the programme of constructive work of lakhs of his followers, but the movement for rural industrialisation has so far not struck deep roots in India. Not that either the planners or the Government were unware of the employment potential of village industries, but though the programmes to sustain and develop rural industries were formulated, they somehow did not get integrated with the overall growth process through carefully worked out linkages. The first Five Year Plan outlined specific measures for assisting village artisans and for the development of village industries and the All-India Khadi and Village Industries Board was set

*The views expressed in this article are those of the author and do not necessarily reflect the views of the State Bank of India or its Associates. Reprinted from *the State Bank of India*; *Monthly Review*.

up in 1953, on the recommendations of the Planning Commission. It was upgraded in 1957 as a statutory body, *viz.*, Khadi and Village Industries Commission, with adequate executive and administrative powers.

In the Second Five Year Plan, on the advice of the Karve Committee on Village and Small Scale Industries, some effort was made to bring about a degree of integration of the production plans of the decentralised sector with the development plan of the country as a whole. The Plan, in fact, tried to entrust the responsibility for producing additional wage goods mainly to the decentralised sector, while laying emphasis on the development of basic and heavy industries. Apart from the emphasis on rural and household industries, another significant achievement of the Second Plan was the foundation that it laid for systematic development of the modern sector of small scale industries and creation of an institutional set-up in the country to assist the development of small scale industries. Some efforts were also made to foster the development of ancillary industries in the small sector aligned to large scale industrial projects. The modern small scale industries sector, no doubt, drew much strength from the industrial development and income generation which took place in India since the late fifties, but by the very nature of things, these were clustered around the cities, where large industries were concentrated and rural areas received little benefit from their development.

The Seminar on Technology for Small Industries in Rural Areas, organised by the Rural Industries Planning Committee of the Planning Commission in March 1962, was another landmark in the field of rural industrialisation. The Seminar was addressed by eminent thinkers and contributions made by Dr. E. F. Schumacher and Dr. D. R. Gadgil to the thinking on this subject were remarkable. Dr. Gadgil, in his paper read at this Seminar, indicated a broad outline of an action plan, which would integrate rural industries with the factory sector, through intermediate technology, in the context of a 'dynamic common production programme.' He also suggested the concept of a 'common utilisation programme,' which envisaged taking stock of the total supply of industrial primary and other materials within the country and planning their allocation to various processes of transformation and industrial use. According to Dr. Gadgil, basic industries, capital goods industries, public utilities, etc., would have to adopt advanced technology to reap the advantages of scale, but for the rest, there was a distinct advantages in organising production on the basis of intermediate technology. The crux of the matter is to prevent unnecessary adoption of processes involving higher technology, when materials can be processed locally, with relatively simpler technology, without any significant difference in the value added,, but in the process, creating much larger employment opportunities in the rural areas.*

Rural Industries Projects Programme

The Government of India started the Rural Industries Projects Programme in 1962, as an instrument to foster the growth of rural crafts and small scale industries and to bring about wider dispersal of industries. In the first phase of the programme, 49 areas throughout the country were chosen by the Government. Each project area covered 3-5 Community Development Blocks and was to be administered by a Project Officer. The project activity was confined mainly to villages and towns with a population of not more than 15,000. The project was envisaged as a package programme, wherein the project staff would (a) provide necessary inputs to small scale units and artisans in the area, (b) counsel them in formulation of schemes, (c) guide them in getting scarce raw materials and in marketing their products and (d) assist them in securing necessary financial assistance from the State Government and financial institutions. Encouraged by the initial success of the programme, it was decided in 1969 to transform the programme into a national programme, with a view to covering the entire country-side in

*For fuller discussion, please see the author's 'Rural Industries—Towards an Integrated Approach'—State Bank of India Monthly Review, March 1973, pp. 83—95.

about 25 years, by taking up 50 new districts in each successive Five Year Plan.

Industrial Policy Resolution of 1977

Industrial Policy Resolution, 1977, laid emphasis on promotion of cottage and small scale industries widely dispersed in rural areas and small towns in line with the priority for employment generation. During the Fourth Plan period, for example, capital investment for providing employment to a worker in khadi and village industries was very low compared to large industries. According to an official estimate, the average investment per worker in khadi and village industries was estimated at Rs. 530, against Rs. 10,000 in the textile industry and Rs. 5-10 lakhs in cement and steel industries. Even between a large scale factory and a small scale factory (with gross investment in plant and machinery of Rs. 7.5 lakhs or less), the productive capital per worker (in 1970) varied between Rs. 26,130 and Rs. 5,240, whereas the difference between the value added per worker was much less, *viz.*, Rs. 5,490 and Rs. 2,665 respectively.

The Industrial Policy Resolution of 1977 laid down that whatever could be produced by the small and cottage sector must only be so produced. A list of more than 500 items was proposed which would be the exclusive preserve of small and cottage industries. The focal point of development of small scale and cottage industries was to be shifted from big cities and State capitals to the district headquarters. In each district, a District Industries Centre was to be set up under the single roof of which all the services and support required by small and village entrepreneurs would be provided. Within small scale industries, special attention was to be given to units in the 'tiny' sector, *viz.*, those with investment in machinery and equipment up to Rs. 1 lakh and situated in villages and in towns with a population of less than 50,000 according to the 1971 census.

District Industries Centres

In terms of the new industrial policy, till the end of 1979, 325 District Industries Centres (D.I.Cs.) had been set up in the country. Each District Industries Centre is headed by a General Manager, who is to be assisted by seven Managers-in-charge of various functions like supply of raw materials, marketing, economic survey and research, equipment and technology, credit, etc. The lead bank for the district is normally expected to depute one of its officers as Manager (Credit) of the D.I.C. The main problem has been that the Managers have not been in position. In many States, the posts have been combined. Consequently, though the DICs. were set up in many districts, their functioning has not yet stabilised—particularly in backward areas.

While efforts were made to give a new sense of direction to the growth of rural industries, the institutional set-up, which the Government was seeking to create at the district level, could not start functioning effectively. The handicaps of tiny industrial units in the form of lack of management skills to study market trends, to adopt production techniques and designs to the changing trends in demand, to maintain proper books of accounts with a view to having a proper control over their finances, etc., are indeed serious. Some of these can be removed by training and assistance from promotional agencies such as the DICs., but the promotional agencies themselves have not been sufficiently developed to cope with the problem of reaching out to lakhs of artisans, spread over thousands of villages, with a package of services, so vital for their sustenance and growth.

Appropriate Technology: Another Dimension

Emphasis on labour intensive technology in official policy by itself would not lead to development of the tiny sector, unless a careful study of the markets for their products precedes anyplanned effort for their development. In the absence of such a study, it would be difficult to sustain any significant growth of the sector. Industrial planning will, thus, have to be based on a realistic assessment of the market forces. A charismatic leader like Mahatma Gandhi can stimulate demand for 'khadi' or products of village industries and thus create a market for them. But when the influence of such idealistically stimulated demand wanes, stocks of unsold goods start accumulating and production activity in the tiny sector cannot continue for long, official efforts notwithstanding.

Further, appropriate technology, which is being mainly defined with reference to the factor-endowment of the country as 'low capital-investment and labour-intensive technology' will also have to be related to the needs of the market. In other words, it should also be 'appropriate' to the 'needs of the market.' If technology of production is so defined as to cover 'degree of sophistication in production, polish, packaging and preservation, etc.,' it would include not only capital and machinery but also input of artistic skills and aesthetics. For example, if the goods are to be produced for an 'elitist' market such as the export market, the degree of sophistication in quality, presentation, aesthetic appeal and packaging will have to be much higher than if they are produced for the local market.

Conversely, if goods are to be produced for the rural market —particularly for the consumption of the rural poor—there need not be such a high degree of sophistication in presentation or finish. On the other hand, the emphasis has to be on low cost of production and consequently on low prices. In fact, trying to sell high-priced, highly sophisticated industrial goods in the rural areas is detrimental to the interest of the rural poor. It is like depriving them of their meagre purchasing power through high-power salesmanship. It should, in fact, be the responsibility of the planners to so organise production as to enable the poor to stretch their meagre purchasing power to the maximum extent, by providing them with essential consumer goods at low prices, even though their quality and finish may be somewhat inferior to the products meant for the urban market. In this context, the efforts of the Khadi and Village

Industries Commission to produce low-cost goods are to be commenced. What is important is that the operations of the Commission need to be integrated in the overall industrial planning of the country. If the product is to be sold to the rural poor, it is not necessary to add to its cost by using high technology, aimed at increasing 'value added by manufacture.' In the ultimate analysis the value added by manufacture will have to depend upon whether the market for which the manufacturing process is intended (i.e. the process of adding 'value' to the basic materials) can afford it. This is another dimension to the concept of 'appropriate technology,' which is of particular relevance to a poor country.

Task of the Rural Industrial Planner

It is, however, heartening that during the past few years, exercises in rural industrial planning are being undertaken either under the aegis of the Rural Industries Projects, or the District Industries Centres or the Integrated Rural Development Projects. In planning for industrialisation of a rural area, say, a district or a Community Development Block, the planner has to take into account (i) resource-base of the area, (ii) skill-base of the area, (iii) population and income levels, and (iv) size and nature of the market for various commodities which can be locally produced.

Let us take an illustrative example of a district which has the following economic features:

(A) Resource Pattern

(i) *Agricultural Production*: rice, wheat, gram, cotton, sugarcane, groundnut, jowar, etc.

(ii) *Forest Produce*: Firewood, timber, bamboo, cane, kendu leaves, etc.

(iii) *Minerals*: Clay, good quality stones suitable for carving.

(iv) *Leather*.

(B) Skills

Traditional cane/bamboo work, bidi-making, pottery, brick-making, stone carving, idol-making, black smithy, copper smithy and artistic metal-work, weaving etc.

(C) Markets

Villages, weekly 'hats' (markets), nearby towns, nearest metropolitan centre, rest of India and export market.

In planning for industrialisation, the rural planner will have to take decisions about: (i) technology to be used, taking into consideration the nature of the market demand and policy of the Government, (ii) the extent of new capacity to be created, (iii) location of industrial activity and (iv) institutional support to be provided to various industrial activities.

Choice of Technology

The most important decision is regarding the choice of technology within the overall constraints of Government policy in this regard. A few illustrations can be given in the field of agricultural processing. Among the local varieties of rice grown, for example, the coarser varieties can be locally processed with relatively crude methods, including even hand-pounding. Superior rice will, however, command an elitist market and would need to be processed better and polished. In the case of cotton, there is not much choice in the matter of technology so far as ginning and pressing is concerned and if local production of raw cotton is large enough, a ginning and pressing factory can be set up. In the case of processing of sugarcane, much will depend upon the acreage under the crop and the quality (sucrose content) of the cane. If the acreage is small, the production can be handled locally in the manufacture of 'gur' or khandsari. If production of sugarcane is large enough, it will have to be sold in the urban market and considering the nature of urban demand, setting up of a sugar factory can be considered, though it would require considerable investment and project planning, which can be taken up either in the private sector or the co-operative sector. In regard to oilseeds, oil-pressing can be undertaken by village ghanis, but if the production of oilseeds is very large, market will have to be found for oil in urban areas. Increased capacity can be in the bullock-drawn 'ghani' sector or in power-driven oil-presses. If the production is much larger, it can be processed through oil mills, which may either further refine the oil or hydrogenate it and in addition, extract oil out of oil-cakes produced in the village ghanis through the solvent-extraction process. Solvent-extraction units, in fact, can supplement the oil-ghani sector by creating more value out of the by-products of the ghani and thus may not exactly compete with these, though competition with ghanis is not completely ruled out.

In the case of forest produce, for example, the choice of technology is not very significant in the case of minor forest produce. In the case of major forest produce, *e.g.*, bamboo and timber, processing is possible in the small scale sector. If bamboo production is not very large, it can be used by local attisans in preparing utility items or even artistic products. The latter would, however, need, not only higher skills but also marketing, effort. If bamboo production is very large, it can be used for manufacture of pulp for paper or rayon, which can be undertaken mainly by large scale industrial units working with sophisticated technology. Timber can be handled with manunal labour or machinery It can be processed into intermediate products such as logs, planks, rounds, plywood, hardboard, etc., in large scale units or in small scale units and there is scope to choose appropriate technique or size. The limiting factor in the short run could be availability of skilled persons, with sufficient entrepreneurial initiative to set up requisite number of small scale units. If a large enough number of such units cannot be set up in the short run, large scale units may have to be considered, because the timber produced has to be processed for the market.

In the ultimate analysis, the choice of technology would depend upon several factors such as the nature and the size of the market, quantity of production needing processing, availability of skills, policy of the Government, etc. But in all these calculations, consideration of the availability of market for production is of fundamental significance because it will decide whether the unit will be liable or not. No non-viable unit can survive for long in a competitive world.

Extent of Capacity to be Created

Creation of new capacity would depend upon the adequacy of the existing processing facility available in the neighbourhood of the centre, extent of additional production needing processing facility, the type of market demand, stability of additional production level, etc. If adequate processing facility is not available to cater to the needs of increased agricuitural production, say of sugarcane, agriculturists will suffer a loss and agricultural development will receive a set-back. At the same time, if the processing facility is created much in advance of the increased production, the manufacturer will suffer a loss due to under-utilisation of capacity.

Location

Location of an industrial activity either in a village or town will depend upon the technology selected, need for infrastructure such as power, etc., adequacy of the hinterland for supply of raw materials, availability of transport facilities to the centre of production as also to the market. For example, while a few simple industrial activities can and should be located in the village itself, larger and more sophisticated industrial units will need to be located at the central villages and towns, where power, trained labour and ancillary services are available and the size of the market demand is large because of the large local or neighbourhood population which visits the town either because it is the main market centre or administrative headquarters.

Institutional Support Necessary

Institutional support will be required to the maximum possible extent in the case of handicrafts which produce artistic products. A major factor in the case of handicrafts is that they are based principally on traditional skills, which are passed on from generation to generation. The skills can be further developed and improved by training and by acquainting the artisans with the new trends in patterns, colour schemes, etc., in vogue in the principal consuming markets. The markets for these can be in the urban areas or in foreign countries.

The problems in developing handicrafts are (i) upgradation of traditional skills, (ii) adaptation of the existing patterns of production to those in vogue in the major consuming centres, for which perhaps a larger investment would be required and (iii) arranging for the marketing of their products. The handicrafts which turn out artwares have a bright future among all the rural industries because machine-made goods cannot easily compete with their products and thus there is no threat of their being rendered "inferior goods." Secondly, since their prices depend upon their aesthetic appeal and not so much on the material or labour content. they can fetch very high prices, provided they reach the discerning buyer. This is why the merchant-exporter makes a lot of profit, but has a tendency to put a very low value on the goods when he buys them. Objective appraisal of value of these articles is difficult, except to a trained eye The merchant-exporters, no doubt, perform an important function of scouting for the right buyer. Many public sector institutions like the All-India Handloom Board, All-India Handicrafts Board, Silk Board, etc., also help in the marketing of handlooms and handicrafts, through sales emporia in the major Indian cities and abroad. The local planner has to establish close contacts with these institutions and pass on the information regarding the trends in the markets collected from these to the local artisans. If Indian handicrafts or works of art can catch the fancy of the foreigners, they can command a vast market. Export markets are, however, subject to vagaries of changes in fashions. Constant watch over the trends in fashions will, therefore, have to be kept and these will have to be promptly communicated to the craftsmen spread through the length and breath of the country. The local industrial planner has to create an institutional machinery through which such a channel of communication can be established between the All-India institutions and local artisans. Thirdly, he will have to ensure that the traditional skills are not only encouraged but also upgraded through training. Fourthly, the artisans will have to be ensured remunerative prices and towards this end, some machinery will have to be evolved to ensure than an increasing proportion of sale proceeds accrues to them and is not appropriated by the middleman—individual or corporate.

A Sample Industrial Development Plan

An industrial plan for the district will be somewhat on the following lines. The purpose of the plan indicated on page 8.4 is to illustrate the influence of the market on technology, scale and location and not to show the type and extent of the industrial activity feasible in the area. Figures of capacity and the number of units have, therefore, not been worked out in detail.

It will be seen from the table that the more urbanised the market, the more sophisticated has to be the technique of production. The more distant the market from the unit of production, the stronger is the need for institutional support. In fact, when goods are produced for the distant market, the producer's knowledge about the trends in market demand is inadequate. He, therefore, has to be constantly kept informed on this point. Hence the need for institutional support.

Industry	*Market*	*Technology*	*Location*	*Infrastructural and Institutional support required*
1	2	3	4	5
AGRO-BASED				
Rice Hulling				
(i) Superior variety	Village/Town/City	Power operated dehusker	Central village/ Town	Power, transportation facility, credit.
(ii) Coarse variety	Village/Hat	Hand operated dehusker	Village	—
Dal Miil	Town/City/Hat/ Village	Dal Milling	Central village/ Town	Power, transportation facility, credit.
Gur/Khandsari	Village/Hat/Town/ City	Gur-pan, etc.	Village	Transport, credit.
Sugar Factory	Town/Country-wide market	Sugar machinery	Town	Power, transportation facility, credit.
Cotton Ginning and Pressing	Town/City	Ginning and pressing machinery	Central village/ Town	-do-
Weaving	Village/Hat/Town/ City	Handloom, powerloom	Village	Yarn supply, marketing, credit.

Oil Pressing	-do-	Power/bullock operated village ghani	Village	—
Solvent Extraction	Town/City	Solvent extraction process	Town	Power, transportation facility, credit.
Soap	Village/Town/City	Simple technique	Town	-do-
FOREST BASED				
Saw Mills	Village/Town	Bandsaw machine	Central village/Town	Power, transportation, credit.
Furniture	Village/Hat/Town	Skill-based	Village/Town	Marketing assistance, transportation, credit.
Bidi-making	-do-	-do-	Village	—
Artistic Wood Work	Town/City/Abroad	-do-	Village/Town	Marketing assistance, transportation, credit.
MINERAL-BASED				
(i) Black Smithy	Village/Hat	Crude technique	Village	—
(ii) Copper Smithy	Village/Hat/Town	-do-	-do-	—
(iii) Artistic Metal Ware	Town/City/Abroad	Skilled based	Village/Town	Metal supply, marketing assistance, credit.

(Contd.)

1	2	3	4	5
NON-METALLIC				
(i) Pottery/Brick Making	Village/Hat/Town	Simple technique	-do-	—
(ii) Ceramic	Town/City	Sophisticated processing—skill based	-do-	Process-training, design-research, marketing assistance, credit.
ANIMAL PRODUCTS				
(i) Tanning	Village/Hat	Simple techniques	-do-	—
(ii) Leather Products/ Footwear	Town	Simple techniques	-do-	Design-research, marketing assistance, credit.

Further, though exercises in rural industrial planning will have to be based on intimate knowledge of the local economy, its resource-base and skill-base, trends in income generation, pattern of market demand, etc., unless these exercises are fitted into the overall planning for the district/state/country, such plans cannot be realistic. Unless the micro-level plans are dovetailed with the meso-level or macro-level plans and linkages with the various projects planned at the higher levels are established, the local plans will not be able to derive advantages from these projects. In the ultimate analysis, so far as the units producing consumer goods are concerned, they will have to be linked with the pockets of demand for various goods created by the processes of income generation released in the economy through the setting up of various projects. Some of these projects would also give rise to the demand for intermediate products, which local units in the small sector can meet.

Further, in respect of many of the major forest products, or primary and other industrial raw materials, it would be necessary to work out a common utilisation programme as suggested by Dr. Gadgil, planning their allocation to various processes of transformation and industrial use. Such a plan will have to be worked out at the macro-level and suitable guidelines issued to the micro-planner to adopt appropriate technology, at the local level, for various industrial units planned to utilise the materials, in keeping with the overall strategy.

To sum up, planning for rural industrialisation has not yet been well developed in the country, but if employment opportunities in the rural areas are to expand—and expand they must, in the context of the growing pressure of unemployment and under-employment—there appears to be no alternative to it. Marketing of products is crucial to the viability of any programme of industrialisation. Selection of labour intensive technology will have to be based on a careful study of the market demand for products. In the credit planning

exercises, bankers are associated with grass-root level planning. If they make available their expertise in examining from the point of view of viability, the projects in which production for market is envisaged, they will be doing a signal service to the development of the rural economy on sound lines.

7

*Productivity as a Function of Social Structure**

OSWALD A.J. MASCARENHAS, S.J.

Introduction

This paper is an extension and application of Johan Galtung's theory of social structure and science structure, and contends that productivity, and development in general, should be a function of the social struture that stimulates it. Historically thus for all types and levels of productivity have made the social structure subservient to it. These are identified as the Model I (conservative), Model II (liberated), and Model III (co-operative) productivity systems that man has lived through. But if productivity should continue to increase in quality and intensity, if technocracy should survive despite industrial democracy, then the entire productivity system should be a function of the enlightened social structure that is currently

*This paper was presented at the Plenary Session of the Fifth Asian Conference of the Asian Regional Training and Development Organization, and Ninth National Convention of the ISTD, November 9-11, 1978.

emerging—the Model IV, radical society—where the producer is the centre, and productivity is his periphery.

This paper is essentially an extension and application of Johan Galtung's theory of social structure and science structure [13]. Galtung presents a new approach to epistemology and methodology of social sciences. He conceives of social science methodology, and methodology in general, as a function of the structure of the society that produces it. The contention of this paper is that productivity in general should be a function of the structure of the society that generates it, and not *vice versa.* Traditionally, productivity has determined the structure of the society. Thus, pristine agricultural productivity made society nature-oriented; pre-industrial productivity which was primarily extractive made societies raw-materials-centred; present industrial productivity which is predominantly fabricative has made people energy-centred; and post-industrial productivity, such as Daniel Bell, [3] envisions it, is currently making people information-centred. Should we reverse this trend, and make society, and its strutcture in turn, determine the type and level of productivity it should engage itself in? How should we redesign the future: by corporations humanizing and environmentalizing the social structures, as Ackoff has suggested [1], or by making the evolving social structure humanize and environmentalize the corporation and its productivity? We need to investigate this reversal process.

Different Modes and Models of Industrial Productivity

We may visualize, for simplicity, four models of social interaction in a firm based on two bipolar dichotomous constructs yielding a 2×2 factorial design of four social structures characterized in Table 7.1.

Every productivity field is a social structure. For every social structure interaction is a starting point. Interaction implies an exchange of value, be it economical, socio-psychological, spiritual or cultural, among the interacting participants in the social structure. These value-exchanges may affect

TABLE 7.1

Modes of Industrial Productivity

	Uniformity	Diversity
Verticality	Conservative productivity	Liberated productivity
Horizontality	Cooperative productivity	Radical productivity

the actors *internally* triggering internal processes that may enrich of impoverish them. The firm itself is an actor, an agent of change, and a field of interaction. Thus when linesmen experience genuine job-fulfilment either because of job-enrichment or job-enlargement or job-rotation or job-innovation, they feel enriched internally.

If this positive value exchange is communicated (feedback) upwards, it may internally enrich the supervisor and his superiors. The value exchange may be obviously external to the actors; such as wage increments, bonus, gratuity, worker security and welfare. But the more important value exchanges are value *in*-changes actors; among sense of employer-employee mutual belongingness, dedication, inter-dependence; identification with firm's problems of demand and supply, factor-conditions and management-objectives; inter-group and intra-group loyalty and team spirit.

There may be negative value exchanges. External ones commonly experienced are; low wages or salaries, job-dissatisfaction owing to monotony, insecurity, non-safety conditions, lack of job-incentives in terms of bonus, gratuity, career-prospects, housing and other perquisites; *internal* ones are exploitation, lack of recognition, promotion and training, and a consequent lack of identification with and dedication to the job and the firm.

The net balance of these positive and negative exchanges, both external and internal, is derivatively productivity loss or productivity gain, and this will differ from firm to firm, from individual to individual. If this difference to the various actors is very substantial then the interaction may be characterized as *vertical* (inequitable); if it differs little or nothing at all, then the interaction is *horizontal.*

In over-vertical structure all kinds of resources accumulate on the top. Physical (economic) productivity may be high, but this is due primarily because of forced or bonded labour conditions wherein workers are constrained to work owing to existence and survival needs. In other words, there may be high value exchange; negative on the part of the workers and positive on the management side, be they external and/or internal. Here vertically is tantamount to exploitation. The actors are predominantly the capitalists and the proletariat. The level of productivity may be high; but it is unproductively productive; in fact it may not always remain high; internal contradictions, may soon bring it low.

In the long run any structure tends to become *uniform* (stationary or similar) or *diverse* (unstable or dissimilar). In the vertical case this change is brought about because of the overwhelming influence of and from the top: while in the horizontal case it is brought about by the well connected, tight, all-actor-interacting structure. When the vertical structure is uniform and frozen (forced stationarity) we have a dictatorial *conservative* social structure of productivity. There is no mobility, either upwards nor downwards nor sideways. Individuals are allocated to their position by seniority and ascription. This is a feudal monopoly (or oligopoly), highly and exploitatively conservative. Productivity may be high; but it is unproductive. Thus top heavy, large and conservative firms congenitally tend to be exploitative and unproductively productive. India does not need this type of productivity; we have fortunately, though painfully, weaned ourselves out of this stage of colonial feudalism.

However, when verticality is blended with, and tending towards, diversity, we seem to have a liberated society. There is vertical mobility, not necessarily by ascription (birth and seniority) but based on talent and dedication. There is also horizontal mobility owning to job rotation, job enrichment and job enlargement. This social structure pays premiums for being creative, innovative, dedicated. However, the recognition of talent is from the top; it is vertical.

Horizontality can combine with uniformity. The result is a *cooperattve* society. The structure is not frozen; but there is no mobility either. The company goal is solidarity between equally interacting participants. There may not be much competition and dominance. Cooperative farming, cooperative dairies, cooperative marketing, cooperative banking, are some examples of this mode of and model of productivity.

Finally, horizotality can blend with diversity to generate a *radically pluralis* productive set-up. There is horizontal mobility as well as vertical; but no movement exploits any other actor in the productive system. There is group solidarity, but it does not constain individual actors from innovativeness, creativity, excellence and adventure. Our present social structures have not yet realized this stage. It is a missing institution in our present socio-economic context. But signs are that we are converging towards it. Having painfully, but successfully, passed through the feudal, capitalist and socialist forms of production-structures, one is bound to arrive at this pluralist-radical fòrm. Perhaps this may be the dominant and most productive structure of the year 2000 [3,4].

This supposes controlled and planned change towards a future. But if as Sir Geoffrey Vickers, the eminent British social scientist, once said, "the rate of change increases at an accelerating speed, without a corresponding acceleration in the rate at which further responses can be made, then this brings us nearer the threshold beyond which control is lost" [26, p. 377]. In fact, there is full scale planning for control the world over. There is heavy centralized national technocratic planning that characterizes the USSR. In France, *Le Plan* has become a regular feature of national life. In Sweden, Italy, Germany, Japan and India governments actively intervene in the economic sector to protect certain industries, to capitalize others, and to accelerate growth. In the USA and UK, as also in India, even local governments come with what are at least called planning departments. But despite all this planning and forecasting of the future the productive system in general is still spinning out of control. The problem is, as Avlin Toffler has put it, not that we plan too little; we also plan too poorly. Part of the trouble can be traced to the very premises implicit in our planning [22, p. 448].

Toffler offers 3 reasons for our poor planning. Our t echnocratic planning, he says, is *econocentric*; it is geared to the maximization of material welfare; economic advance is the primary aim, and technology, the primary tool. Secondly, technocratic planning is *short-range*; except for some oriental countries like China and India, the Western countries focus heavily on the present or with futures near at hand; a 5 or 10-year plan is insanely futuristic; one—or two-year forecasts are regarded as long-range planning. Thus we exploit the present at the expense of the future. This is unproductive productivity. Thirdly, our technocratic planning is *undemocratic*.

"Reflecting the bureaucratic organization of industrialism, technocratic planning was premised on hierarchy. The world was divided into manager and worker, planner and plannee, with decisions made by one for the other. This system, adequate while change unfolds at an industrial tempo, breaks down as the pace reaches super-industrial speeds. The increasingly unstable environment demands more and more non-programmed decisions down below; the need for instant feedback blurs the distinction between line and staff; and hierarchy totters. Planners are too remote, too ignorant of local conditions, too slow in responding to change. As suspicion spreads that top-down controls are unworkable, plannees begin clamoring for the right to participate in the decision-making. Planners, however, resist" [22, p. 449].

Clearly this undemocratic productive system is in the long run crucially unproductive.

A democratic productive system supposes *detachment*, down to every individual, making the structure less connected, but keeping the basic conditions, so that each relation inside the units is horizontal. The 'detachment' predicted between individuals is not to be confused with *isolation* or *indifference*; isolation is self-sufficiency without mutual trust and contact, whereas detachment is self-sufficiency with contact; indifference is unmotivated contact [13, pp. 13-39].

In is assumed that each unit (sub-structure) is still very uniform inside; *i.e.*, satisfied, developed (or developing) and fulfilled in its productive task; but there is enough distance between the units to permit diversity, emulation and growth—and therefore diverse forms of uniformity. While the vertical case with built-in horizontal interaction leads to selective vertical mobility, the horizontal case with built-in detachment leads to selective horizontal mobility. In the first case, the selection is from the top; it is made by others. In the second, the selection is by the individual himself, who moves from one type of productivity existence to another. In the vertical case dis-similarity arises becavse of the need for mobility for replacement. In the horizotal case there is no such need at the *social* level; but there may be a need at the individual level—the need for diversity in individual productive (and training) experience. Some training and development programmes are cautiously emerging in this direction [2, 5, 7, 8, 12].

There is horizontal division of labour, keeping the net benefits from interaction constant; even though all engage in different forms of activity, the assumption (or presumption) is that everybody will know so much about each other and his (or her) work that they can interchange, take over, with ease. This is horizontal, job-rotation; there is no change in rank and no break-down in uniformity.

The verticality in the conservative and liberated productive systems may be economically interpreted as the dimension of exploitation. In Model I people work as groups (individuality lost) and the groups are kept apart; in Model II people work as individuals and even though kept apart are currently being together through trade brought unions.

Structure of Productivity under each Model

Should the structure of productivity be determined by the structure of the society in which it is embedded? This is the fundamental question we must next address ourselves to.

In Model I society all production is hierachized with the feudal lord at the top, and the disciples (workers) under him forming a feudal productive monarchy. The production form is collective; the lord conceives of the product in outline, and the workers exectute it and fill in the details. The workers serve the lord; the product is branded after the lord, but it is anonymous in its origin and production. This is a society where the basic structure is vertical, with the one point at the apex; there is no mobility; the lord does not cease to be the boss until death (or, not even after death, as the spirit of the founder still persists and rules the operations), and the seniormost worker does not replace the lord, but may take over some administrative functions at the most. The next of kin becomes the lord, irrespective of talent and experience. If there is no adequate replacement the system dies, but no disciple can aspire or ever become the lord, unless he were of the lord's family. There is an unquestionable "divine right" of the king; all authority comes from God. One works for God or for the Monarch or the Prince. He may spend his lifetime producing an artifact (an antique today), but it is owned by the Lord. One is reminded of the Mughal period of productivity in India.

The founder (lord) is characterized by much charisma, adventure, entrepreneurship; it is inherited or suddenly received; it is incommunicable (unless by inheritance downwards); it is non-delegatable for the disciples. All forms of monopolies and monopsonies may be classified under this Model I.

Privately owned firms may belong to this category and we have several of them in India as well as the world over. Here the stock is family owned or is sold in a closed tightly controlled market. All the large companies of India that are not on the stock exchange come under this feudal category. However, several of them, either by private initiative or by public injunction, are moving towards Model II society.

In Model II society vertical uniformity gives in vertical diversity; there is competition with an emphasis on individual originality. The tie between the producer and the product is protected and recognized, and in special cases, announced (in product packages). There is subservience to the proprietor and his original charisma; but departures from his pristine spirit is tolerated. Individual talent is not enough; one has to perform and compete, and demonstrate one's talent in action.

Model II society stratifies the production group into classes with horizontal relations within each group, and vertical relations between. "The idea of intersubjectivity at the top is the reflection of horizontality cum vertically" [13, p. 25]. Hence every production charisma and entrepreneurship adventure need not come from the top; it may be originated by one of the production groups collectively or individually. Once originated and accepted by the production (say, research) group, from that point on it is communicated downwards as in Model I society, not for feedback, but for dissemination upwards and downwards. However, because of the basic verticality of the system, productivity is *attributed* only to the top structure even though originated and produced horizontally. However, originators and innovators are rewarded by being moved vertically upwards. The top structure is no more an apex, but may be a group of planners, innovators, venture-managers (say, a board of governors, strategic planning group, joint executive management board, and so on). The boss is *Primus Inter Pares.*

Thus Model II productive society is a more open system than Model I. The product (final) consumer of yesterday may become product-producer of today, and product-innovator of tomorrow, and may eventually join the executive ranks. Vertical mobility is a reward scheme. Horizontal mobility scheme is either a training scheme or a perpetuation of *status quo.* Vertical mobility downwards is a disincentive. Thus Model II productive society is *public*: it is a corporation that is owned by several stock-holders over and beyond the family that originated it.

Authority originates both vertically (by delegation) and horizontally (by individual talent recognition from the top). Since the basic structure of Model II society is vertical, authority (which is premised on verticality) is necessary and structural.

In the Model III *cooperative* society there is basic horizontality. There is no necessary stratification of people and knowledge in this society so that the layer above is inaccessible to the level below. Elitism is out; there is no esotericism either. All are welcome to be producers and consumers. There is no need of a middleman. All production needs collective performance—cooperation from all. There is no major difference between the producer and the consumer. Talent is recognized in individuals but not necessarily searched for nor rewarded as in Model II society. Talent is created through performance; it is not in-born as in Model I and II societies, Talent and production is not a special institution, but an aspect of life. This is not tantamount to egalitarianism—a generalized equality of time and talent across all participating producers. Model III society just makes production/consumption an integral part of this cooperative society. There is no need for professionalization; but there is a persistent call for full participation.

We are reminded of Jewish communes of cooperative farming, Sicilian peasants collectively owning, operating and consuming farm produce, Chinese People's Republic and communes,Indian cooperative dairies, cooperative banking (*e.g.*, Ranchi), and so on, as obvious existing examples of Model III society

The transition from Model I to Model II society, and from Model II to Model III productive form, can be seen as a process whereby the production process has become increasingly public. There is little or no verticality. If middlemen are needed they are ad hoc people in the periphery. All planning and innovative thinking emerges from the group. There is shared inter-subjectivity, shared validation of ideas and experiments, and shared production. What is achieved in Model I society under conditions of individualism and verticality, in Model II society under conditions of collectivism and verticality, is, now in Model III society, achieved under conditions of individualism horizontality. One may originate a brilliant idea or a venture, but it is immediately owned, shared, validated and fructified by the entire cooperative group. The emphasis is not on creative originality but on productive horizontality. There is no room for individual careerism in Model III society. If there is, it is a deviation. Hence it may not appeal to our modern career-oriented youth. There is no vertical nor horizontal mobility. There is only replacement and fresh entries. But, most importantly, there is equity (not necessarily equality) in the structure, participants, operations and consumption. There is no division of labour; everybody participates equally. The source of authority is not God, or the lord, as in Model I society, neither individual talent-success combined with recognition from the top, as in Model II society, but democratic or technocratic consensus (uniformity) development was employee-centred and Authority, if and when needed, is temporal and not professional; it is operational not structural.

Because of its strong emphasis on uniformity, it is doubtful if Model III society would have sufficient elasticity and dynamism to renew itself fundamentally. While in Model I society the charismatic inspiration of the master of the topman brings in production revolutions. and while in Model II society the combination of top-management charisma and middle management genius (innovation in R+D departments) stimulates growth, product differentation and diversification, in Model III society there may not be equivalent regenerative sources of new thinking. and new ventures. Pressure towards uniformity is precisely the weakness of Model III. like exploitation in Model I and II. Little wonder cooperative farming. dairies, cooperative banking, cooperative manufacturing houses made headway progress since their foundation.

Hence is it true that stronger the verticality and exploitation higher the productivity rate (as in the feudalist and capitalist countries, all of which are developed today). while stronger the horizontality and equity lesser the productivity (as in the socialist and communist countries that are developing or underdeveloped today)? Is therefore verticality and exploitation necessary conditions of development and productivity? To answer this we must speculate into the structure and potentiality of the Model IV society.

In Model IV society there is a (convex) combination of horizontality (in structure) and collectivism (in operations). There is a decided emphasis on diversity (over against the uniformity of Model III society). The concern of vertical mobility is replaced by a concern with horizontal diversity. Hence there would be no pressure on horizontal units to produce the same product, but rather pressure to explore different and diverse prodcut possibilities within a general horizontal framework. There need not be an effort to *integrate* these explorations and product-diversifications as in Model III framework; instead there would be ample room for pluralism of production ideologies, multiplicity of productive operations. There is no *unique* conception of productivity nor a unique brand for products. There is horizontal mobility not by assigning, but by self-selection. An individual would move from operation to operation, from one group to another, looking for self-identity and fulfilment.

We do not yet have social structures that come near to this Model IV society. But since the Model I feudal system is come and gone, and since the capitalist Model II society of the West is currently threatened by wars, revolutions, student riots and hijackings, and since the cooperative society of Model III is still experimental in many situations and countries, there seem to be many trends in the world today indicating efforts towards a more equitable and a more horizontal world productivity set-up.

In the Model IV society, where there is no verticality, but pure horizontality, there is no hierarchy that makes one either outshine or subservient to the other; this is a *polycentric* society where every part (or person) is a centre, sufficiently different from and sufficiently identical to the other, so that there is maximum horizontality (equity) cum maximum diversity. Hence each country developed or developing, small or big, each culture and each character, howsoever insignificant, would find place, scope and centrality.

Wither this Model IV society? This maximal horizontality and maximal diversity may be chaotic, anarchic, and disruptive and therefore unproductive! This is confused thinking; a false fear. Hitherto, in the history of human civilization as well as in the history of production, chaos, anarchy, disruption, and any other human (labour) unrest has stemmed from unjust horizontality (overimposing authority, unfair wage structures...) and unfair and low diversity (lack of self-identity in work, little job novelty and enrichment, no job enlargement ..). We need to train ourselves to maximal horizontality and diversity—possibly this was how the human race was born (multiple origin, multiple location and multiplicity of stock, different times and epochs). Possibly the orginal human race was maximally horizontal (enveloping the entire globe of land and sea) and maximally diverse (both in space, time and nature) till cross-civilization and cross culturation brought us together, and then was born invy, avarice and war; then was born verticality (power) and uniformity (control).

Model IV society nostalgically regresses into the pristine state; not to primitivity, but to productivity. In other words, there is room for a dialogue of civilization, cultures, religions, production-plans, commodity markets, commodity futures; much more exhilarating because it spans much larger gaps (diversity) in understanding and producing than "two mirrors reflecting each other in a scientifically homogenized world" [13, p. 245].

Conflict between narrow economic interests and varities other interests could be averted if we accept a broader definition of productivity or efficiency. The company is a socio-technical system [9] which should satisfy both material, human and social needs of stockholders and stakeholders alike. For any measure of productivity to be complete, "it must include the relation between all the material and psychological needs satisfied by the company and all the material and psychological demands made by the company on its stakeholders" [21, p. 6]. Hence a change in the concept and content of productivity is urgent.

Productivity (traditional definition)

$$= \frac{\text{Production}}{\text{Input of production factors}}$$

Productivity (broader definition)

$$= \frac{\text{Needs 'satisfied' 'through the company' operations}}{\text{Stakeholders' contribution to the company}}$$

This new concept of productivity may not be as neatly measurable and quantifiable as the traditional concept [18], but it includes human (social aspects such as job satisfaction, self-respect, opportunities for personal development, security, and so on. If productivity should be a function of social structure of the producers, then an obvious condition is that productivity measure itself should be broadened to include both quantitative and qualitative aspects, both economic and welfare dimensions.

Presently, our productive systems, macro or micro, are slavishly interdependent, not only economically and politically. but also culturally and technologically. Self reliance (one of India's developmental goals) is the negation of dependence and stands for independence in structure, innovation, operation and consumption, and at the same time equitable interdependence in the sense of being open to exchanges of ideas, innovation, technologies, product and people, across national and international boundaries. It is a geocentric society (the whole world converging towards an epicentre (happily tensioned with polycentricism. It is a productive system emerging towards unity (not uniformity) in the midst of rich diversity. It is a dynamic productive system of the year 2000+. Unless our productivity is streamlined to this emerging social structure, it may be counterproductive in the long run; the 'future shock' may be hard to absorb [22]; we may be victims of our own growth technology and output.

Concluding Observations

Any progress induces turbulence and thrives in the midst of opposition. In the past there have been 4 major trends, that have generated turbulence; growth and expansion to meet increasing demand; the deepening interdependence between the economic and the other facets of the society; the increasing reliance upon scientific research and development to meet increasing competitive challenge; and, fourthly, the radical increase in the speed, scope and capacity of inter-human communication [9, pp. 52-56], This turbulent environment will persist and intensify in the years to come since thus far social structures have been made subservient to productivity types. But if we now begin to reverse the trend, and make productivity a function of the changing social structures, then what will emerge from it will be a more enhanced and more humanizing form of productivity—the maximal horizontal maximally diverse productivity of Model IV.

Some of the components and dynamics of this transition are described in Table 7.2. Some essential productivity features will persist through different epochs and through Models I to IV. Thus agro-based productivity will always be there, since mankind will always need food for subsistence. But while in Model I society it is agricultural, it becomes agronomic in Model II society, i.e., pure rural agriculture gets urbanized with economics; it becomes agro-engineering in Model III society with exccssive mechanization, and finally we may either transit to agrotonics (whereby agricultural growth will be electronically stimulated, much beyond our present complex fertilizers, to agriculture yield hundred-fold fruit in one-hundredth time!) or back to (*i.e.*, back to undisturbed, time-free, mother nature) in search of peace and tranquillity.

Some of the entries in Table 7.2 have been suggested by Daniel Bell [3, 4 p. 198]; however, we have expanded this matrix to apply to several features of productivity and to the model types as suggested by Johan Galtung. The cell entries are suggestive idea types; they are never to be taken as mutually exclusive and collectively exhaustive; they are boundary points, and by nature, every socio-economic boundary is a 'break-point'. Thus Model I is primarily a feudal productivity system characterized by reverence to nature and fealty to the feudal lord and is normally confined to demestic areas of the feudal lord. Model II productivity which is dominantly divergent and extractive seeks raw materials abroad; exploits these non-renewable resources; is however home-bound tradition-centred, but extracting in foreign (III world) countries, Model III industrial society is dominantly manufacturing, is energy-dependent and capital-intensive; it intends to optimize over production domains in order to enhance profit (and market share) possibilities; is inner-centred; is international in the sense that it produces abroad in labour-abundant areas for its own use. In the Model IV society the dominant objective of

TABLE 7.2

Productivity dimension	Model I	Model II	Model III	Model IV
Character	Agricultural (5000 BC-1850 AD)	Pre-industrial (1850-1940)	Industrial (1940-2000)	Post-industrial (2000-?)
Mode	Agricultural artifact	Agronomic extractive artifact	Agro-engineering, extractive, manufacturing	Agrotonics (agricultural manufacturing information processing)
Resource	Nature	Raw materials	Energy	Information
Technology	Neolithic	Labour-intensive	Capital-intensive	Knowledge-intensive
Design	Work on nature	Game against nature	Game improving nature	Game between minds

(Contd.)

Training and development	Reverence to nature; fealty to the lord	Exploitation of nature, loyalty to the proprietor	Optimization of production, responsibility to the stockholder, self-enhancement	Optimization of welfare; equity in wealth and opportunity ennoblement of the 'other'
Producer-character	Nature-centred	Tradition-centred	Inner-centred	other-centred
Productivity locus and market	Domestic-national	Foreign	International	Multinational transnational

productivity is informatton. Knowledge is power. It is game between minds. But hopefully these multinational companies will be transnational in their operations and optimize global welfare and distribution. At least tendentially they seem to be other-centred, or at least are constrained to be so by the recent movements in UNO, UNICO, UNCTAD and UNITAR [23, 24, 25]. Recently, multinational productivity is becoming maximally horizontal and optimally diverse-geocentric [15, 16]; though it has a long way to go in fulfiling the emergent features of Model IV society [17]. The evaluation of transnational productivity and training will not be necessarily in terms of return on investment [6], growth in output and market share and other efficiency measures; training and development will be primarily altruistic, in the sense geared not necessarily for the growth of and productivity in the corporation but for the growth and ennoblement of the individual (the other). A seminal approach in this direction is already in practice [5, 8] or being preached [2]. In other words job related training is not enough [7]; it must nurture self-esteem and self-actualization for the individual and for the group he works with, it must redirect the basic thrust of the training function from traditional skill-training to an integrated programme of organizational development cum integral development of the individual [12]. The modern TBO (Training by Objective [10], HRA (Human Resource Accounting [11], ALP (Action Learning Programmes) [22], good as they are, are all corporation-centred; it is time training, and development was employee-centred and then productivity-centred. Perhaps this is the call of Trade Unions today—a call for maximal horizontality.

Today there is a universal democracy of being. Man is come of age. He is grown to be a person and not a mere number on the pay-roll. He is growingly conscientized to his rights, duties, prospects and destiny. The social structure itself is becoming more and more enlightenen and demanding. In a decade or two the whole globe will be enmeshed by communication networks [22] that will make man information-loaded, and humanity will begin to fold upon itself as if to form one collective reflecting and emerging mass (this is the concept of ultra-humanity of Teilhard do Chardin in his *The Future of Man*).' Productivity cannot control this movement. In order to be productive it is best that it is subservient to this emerging social structure; otherwise there will be a premature death of technocracy [19, pp. 447-52] and productivity and an "advent of Nihilism" which Friedrich Nietzsche prophesived in 1888 as a preface to his last book *The Will to Power* [19].

Since Model IV productivity is maximally horizontal, it may stimulate the small-scale industry, the intermediary technology, so that small will be beautiful, and the big, ugly. The government should take an active part in this programme of horizontalizing productivity, perhaps much beyond the lines of the Norwegian Training and Development Programme [14]. India is taking a lead in this direction—it is 'janataizing' productivity. Perhaps Model IV productivity will be pioneered by the East and aped by the West.

BIBLIOGRAPHY

1. Ackoff, R.L. *Redesigning the Future*, John Wiley and Sons, New York, 1974.
2. Agarwal, P.D. "Training—in search of meaning", *ISTD Review*, May-June 1975, Vol. 5, No. 3, pp. 16-20.
3. Bell, D. *The Coming of Post-Industrial Society*, New York; Basic Books, 1973.
4. Bell, D. *The Cultural Contradictions of Capitalism*, New York: Basic Books, 1976.
5. Brijnath, R.S. "From Tradition to Modernity; ITC Experience in Training and Development", *ISTD Review*, May-June 1975, Vol. 5, No. 3, pp. 20-23.
6. Brown, R J. and Somerville, J.D. "Evaluation of Management Development Programmes: an Innovative Approach" *Personnel*, July-August 1977, pp. 28-47.
7. Crompton, H. "Job Related Training is not Enough", *Supervisory Management*, Vol- 28, No. 4, Winter 1977, pp. 19-21.

8. Edwards, P.B. "Upgrading Unskilled Employees", *Training* and *Development Journal*, October 1974, pp. 35-38.

9. Emery, F.E. and Trist, E.L. *Towards a Social Ecology*, Plenum Press, London and New York, 1973.

10. Ely, D.D. "Training-by-objectives, a systems approach to instruction", *Training and Development Jovrnal*. Vol. 29, No. 6, June 1975, pp. 23ff.

11. Frohman, A.L. and Kotler, J.P. "Joining preocess; Issues in Effective Human Resource Development", *Training and Development Journal*, Vol. 29, No. 8, August 1975, pp. 3-7.

12. Gabora, H. "Training in Transition", *Journal of European Training*, Vol. 5, No. 5, 1975, pp. 247-57.

13. Galtung, Johan *Methodology and Ideology. Theory and Methods of Social Research*, Vol. 1, Christian Ejlers, Copenhagen, 1977.

14. Kile, S.M. "Recent Trends in Norwegian Management Training and Development", *Journal of European Training*, Vol. 3, No. 2, 1974, pp. 113-18.

15. Mascarenhas, O.A. *Towards Measuring the Technological Impact of Multinational Companies in Less Developed Countries*, Anno Press Inc., New York Times Co , New York 1980.

16. Mascarenhas, O.A. "Is Multinational Marketing a Generalization of the Domestic?" *Management and Labour Studies*, Vol. 3, No. 1, June 1977, pp. 57-67.

17. Mascarenhas, O.A. "Corporate Environmentalization for Survival", *Management and Labour Studies*, Vol. 5, No. 1, June 1979, pp. 18-30.

18. Mundal, M.E. *Measuring and Enhancing the prouctivity of Service and Government Organizations*, Asian Productivity Organszation, Tokyo, 1975.

19. Nietzsche, F. *The Will to Power*. Random House, New York, 1967 (edition), p. 3.

20. Rewans, R.W. Action Learning Trust. *Journal of European Industrial Training*, Vol. 1, No. 1, 1977, pp. 2-5.

21. Rhenman, E. *Orgunization Theory for Long Range Planning*. John Wiley and Sons, New York, 1973.

22. Toffler, A. *Future Shock*, Bartam Books, New York, 1971.

23. United Nations: *Multinational Corporations in World Development*, Sales No. E. 73. II. Ali, New York, 1973.

24. United Nations: *Pugwash Conferences on Science and World Affairs*, PWG/Code/5, April 5, 1974, Geneva.

25. United Nations: *UNIDO Guidelines of* 1974, UNCTAD reports, TD/B/520, of August 6, 1974.

26. Vickers, Geoffrey. "Ecology, Planning, and the American Dream" in Duhl Leonard J. (Ed.): *The Urban Condition*: New York, Basic Books, 1963, pp. 374-95

8

Communication Among Public Sector Managers

I. J. SHARMA AND SWARANKANTA

I

Introduction

Communication is the vital thread that holds any organization together. This paper attempts to study the various problems faced by the middle managers in the public sector undertakings in India, with special reference to communication. The paper concludes that though there is satisfaction with the level of communication with peers, there are serious gaps and brriers between senior and junior level managers. This, the authors feel, is a fact that must be taken into account at the policy-making level, if any improvement is to be expected.

Much has been said about the mismanagement of our public sector undertakings and the resultant underutilization of the resources. Yet, we find that little justice has been done to the problem, by way of empirical studies, by both its critics as

Reprinted from *Management and Labour Studies*, XLRI.

well as protagonists. Perhaps the whole thing has been ritualized. One need not mention in this context the crucial role played by the middle managers in the success of business undertakings, be they in the private sector or public sector. Their motivation and morale would be the decisive factor in the successful working of an enterprise. They are the linking pins between the senior management and the supervisory cadres on the one hand, and the outside world on the other. They are the transmitters of orders, instructions, complaints, grievances, information and the like. Their central position forces them to bear the brunt of all the pressures coming from different directions. These pressures are increasing day by day, whereas their powers are being eroded, by growing unionization on the one hand, and the tightening of control by top managers on the other. Their vulnerability has forced them to take a militant posture. The unprecedented popularity of managers' associations is only one of the manifestations. Recent writings in America[2] have shown a growing concern towards this problem.

On the Indian scene, most of the work on the problems faced by the Indian public sector middle managers is of a holistic nature, composed of impressions gathered by the various authors during interviews. Prof. Laxminarain[3] has attempted to analyse the problem systematically but has examined only a few aspects of the motivational factors of the managers and even these are oversimplified. For instance, he has asked one simple, all inclusive question on each subject, *e.g.*, on communication the question would read: Do I get sufficient information to do my job properly?

And in order to find out the need gap on information, he has supplemented this question with:

I would like to have information up to . . . . . (this) extent.

In actual life this communication pattern could be divided into various categories, *e.g.*, intergroup, interagroup, vertically, directly with the supervisory or indirectly with the top management, and so on. Thus, there may be a situation where the manager may be dissatisfied in spite of the fact that communication within the group is excellent, because he is very vaguely clear about the organization. The normative value of this work, therefore, is immensely increased because our effort is to pinpoint those areas where the lacuna exists.

Paranjpe[5] has tried to investigate the causes of the flight of technical personnel in our public sector. Although the work is commendable, he seems to have mistaken the wood for the jungle, by assuming that better prospects outside or the lack of promotions within, are the only cause of the flight of technical personnel in the public sector. Our contention is, *inter alia*, our public sector middle managers, especially the technical functionaries, have been an uncared lot. There is a simmering discontent among the ranks of technical functionaries in all the areas of job satisfaction, resulting in their flight from organization to organization.

The present work is a modest attempt to study the various problems faced by the middle managers in the public sector undertakings in India, as perceived by them. Specifically, the problem area covered is their communication problems. The study may help us to pinpoint certain specific blind spots in the managerial policies and organization structure of our public sector units, that need the urgent attention of the policy makers.

The Questionnaire

The questionnaire has been adapted with suitable modifications from Emanuel Kay's 'Crisis in Middle Management'[2]. It is in the form of statements which apply to the position of the job holder who has the choice to tick from 'strongly agree', rated as 5 points, to 'strongly disagree', rated as 1, on a 5 point scale.

In order to maintain consistency, each statement has been cross-checked by another independent in the questionnaire.

The consistency has been further checked by compiling the correlations among the dependent questions.

The Sample and the Methodology

The present report is the analysis of questionnaires filled up by 245 middle managers, employed in 14 central government public sector undertakings which are engaged in the following fields:

TABLE 8.1

Nature of Business	*No. of Firms*
1. Basic metal producer	2
2. Mining and mineral	2
3. Chemicals and pharmaceuticals	2
4. Capital goods	2
5. Trading and marketing concerns	2
6. Consumer goods	1
7. Industrial development, technical consultancy and contract construction.	3
Total	14

Geographically, the subjects were spread over Delhi, Pinjore, Nangal, in the north, and Bhopal, Nagpur, Bhilai and Korba in central India. A large number of managers were contacted personally and the purpose of the research was explained to them. The nature of questions in the questionnaire was also explained to them. In some cases, the questionnaires were filled up by the authors through interviews. In cases where the managers wanted absolute confidence, they filled them up by themselves and returned them to the author by post.

Level-wise, the managers have been classified into two categories :

(a) Lower middle, *i.e.*, those managers who have been employed as executives and are directly in contact with the non-executive supervisory cadres; all these fall in the E_1 and E_2 pay scales in the pubiic sector.*

(b) Middle, *i.e.*, those managers to whom the lower middle managers reported and who in turn executed the plans and policies of the senior management. In no case are they in a position to lay down the policies, which is a privilege of senior management.

The age-wise break-up of our sample is given below:

TABLE 8.2

Age Group	*Middle Managers*	*Lower Middle Managers*	*All Managers*
20-25	—	4	4
25-30	—	35	35
30-35	2	49	51
35-40	14	46	60
40-45	19	31	50
45-50	18	14	32
50-55	10	3	13
Total	63	182	245
Mean age of managers (years)	44.08	35.77	37.91

*In order to maintain uniformity of pay scales, the Bureau of Public Enterprises has divided managerial pay scales into eight categories, ranging from E_1 to E_8, the former being the starting executive of the scale.

Function-wise, our sample represents managers from production, maintenance, research and development, marketing, personnel, general administration and finance. The first three have been grouped into technical functionaries, the subsequent three into administrative or non-technical functionaries. Finance has been treated separately because of its peculiar role in the public sector. Their number-wise break-up is given below:

Technical functionaries	125
Non-technical functionaries	95
Finance functionaries	25
Total	245

During the data collection, it was felt that the intensity of problems varies among the functions. Hence, an effort is made to test the significance of difference by X^2 technique between the technical and non-technical functionaries. Because of the nature of the sample finance functionaries have been left out while testing this significance.

II

Communication

Communication is considered to be the vital thread that holds the organization together. Through this process, ideas and informations are converted into decisions, plans and policies and are executed through orders and instructions. An unrestricted and smooth flow of information is, therefore, a *sine qua non* for the survival and growth of any organization, which has to continuously adapt to the changing conditions within the business, as well as the outside world. Communication has been traditionally divided into horizontal, vertical and diagonal categories, depending on the flow of information relative to the chain of command. Alternately, it is also termed as formal or informal, depending on the relationship of the communicators.

The difference, however, is blurred in actual practice because a manager in a given situation operates in a highly complicated communication grid, getting information from various sources and transmitting it into numerous channels. The efficacy of the flow of information must be taken in its net result, *i.e.*, to what extent the flow of information helps the managers to discharge their duties to their satisfaction, rather than the formal trappings of the source. With this end in view, we asked the managers six questions each referring to the specific sources of information and the adequacy to which he receives it.

Group Communication

The first statement reads:

> 'I receive sufficient specific information relative to my immediate job to do it properly.'

The question relates to the communication within each work group. The responses to this statement are set out in Table 8.3 In reply to this statement we find that about 62 per cent of the total managers have shown satisfaction, 29 per cent, dissatisfaction and the remaining 9 per cent are non-commital. Level-wise the middle managers have shown less satisfaction than the lower middle managers. This is natural because the job requirements of the lower middle managers are more structured and the information needed is more specific. Both these elements are loose in the case of the middle managers. Besides, he has to depend on multiple sources for information as compared to the lower middle managers. They also suffer from the men-in-the-middle syndrome. The difference, however, is not worth overstressing because of its statistical insignificance. Similarly on average terms, although the technical functionaries are less satisfied as compared to the non-technical functionaries, who sit in the corporate headquarters and have easy access to the source of information, the difference is not significant.

TABLE 8.3

Statement: I receive sufficient specific information relative to my immediate job to do it properly

Class of Managers	*Per cent of Managers Saying*					*Total*	*Mean*
	Strongly disagree	*Disagree*	*Don't know*	*Agree*	*Strongly agree*	*N*	*Scores*
Middle Managers	15.8 (10)	20.63 (13)	4.76 (3)	36.51 (23)	22.22 (14)	100 (63)	3.29
Lower Middle Managers	10.99 (20)	21.43 (39)	4.95 (9)	44.51 (81)	18.13 (33)	100 (182)	3.37
Technocrats	16.0 (20)	20.0 (25)	4.0 (5)	40.8 (51)	19.2 (24)	100 (125)	3.27
Generalists	6.32 (6)	24.21 (23)	4.21 (4)	42.11 (40)	23.16 (22)	100 (95)	3.52
Finance Functionaries	16.0 (4)	16.0 (4)	12.0 (3)	52.0 (13)	4.0 (1)	100 (25)	3.12
All Managers	12.24 (30)	17.14 (42)	4.9 (12)	42.45 (104)	19.18 (47)	100 (245)	3.27

Level-wise differences not significant (X^2=4.23).
Function-wise differences not significant (X^2=5.158).

In order to verify the authenticity of the foregoing analysis, we posed the managers another statement, *viz.*

'Communication within my work group is good.'

The responses are analysed in Table 8.4. We find that an overwhelming majority, *i.e.*, about 75 per cent, have shown satisfaction with intragroup communication. In all the cases, be it the middle managers or the lower middle managers, the technorats or the generalists, a larger number have reported satisfaction as compared to the preceding question However, there are significant differences in the satisfaction of the middle managers and the lower middle managers and the technocrats and the non-technocrats. The lower middle managers and the generalists report more satisfaction with the group communication as compared to the other categories. The finance managers have finished as the least satisfied. The junior managers seem to have developed a strong common bond among themselves and cross communication within themselves seems to be flowing freely as compared to all other categories. As for the finance functionaries we may only point the need of better intergroup communication. Perhaps they are looked down upon with suspicion by their colleagues. Statistically, both level-wise as well as function-wise the differences are significant.

Vertical Communication

Our next question examines the managers' perception of the understanding of his problems by the top management. The statement reads:

"Top management is usually well informed about the problems and difficulties at my level."

It was expected that the response to this statement would be highly unfavourable because, psychologically, it is very difficult for the subordinates to convince themselves that their superiors understand their problems very well. True to expectation, we find in Table 8.5 that among all the managers, 27.75

TABLE 8.4

Statement :Communication within my work group is good

Class of Managers	Per cent of Managers Saying					Total	Mean
	Strongly disagree	*Disagree*	*Don't know*	*Agree*	*Strongly agree*	*N*	*Scores*
Middle Managers	6.35 (4)	20.63 (13)	7.94 (5)	38.1 (24)	26.98 (17)	100 (63)	3.59
Lower Middle Managers	7.69 (14)	11.54 (21)	3.3 (6)	60.44 (110)	17.03 (31)	100 (182)	3.68
Technocrats	8.0 (10)	15.2 (19)	5.6 (7)	52.8 (66)	18.4 (23)	100 (125)	3.58
Generalists	4.21 (4)	14.74 (14)	00 —	57.89 (55)	23.16 (22)	100 (95)	3.81
Finance Functionaries	16.0 (4)	4.0 (1)	16.0 (4)	52.0 (13)	12.0 (3)	100 (25)	3.40
All Managers	7.35 (18)	13.88 (34)	4.49 (11)	54.69 (134)	19.59 (48)	100 (245)	3.65

Significance of difference: Level-wise significant (X^2=11.65 df. 3) at 0.05 level.
Function-wise significant (X^2=6.26 df. 2).

TABLE 8.5

Statement: Top management is usually well informed about the problems and difficulties at may level

Class of Managers	*Per cent of Mangers Saying*					*Total*	*Mean*
	Strongly disagree	*Disagree*	*Don't know*	*Agree*	*Strongly agree*	*N*	*Scores*
Middle Managers	28.57 (18)	19.04 (12)	4.76 (3)	33.33 (21)	14.29 (9)	100 (63)	2.86
Lower Middle Managers	27.48 (50)	23.08 (42)	9.34 (17)	32.42 (59)	7.69 (14)	100 (182)	2.69
Technocrats	34.4 (43)	24.8 (31)	6.4 (8)	28.8 (36)	5.6 (7)	100 (125)	2.46
Generalists	21.27 (20)	21.27 (20)	10.64 (10)	32.98 (31)	13.83 (13)	100 (95)	2.97
Financè Functinaries	20.0 (5)	12.0 (3)	8.0 (2)	52.0 (13)	8.0 (2)	100 (25)	3.16
All Managers	27.75 (68)	22.04 (54)	8.16 (20)	32.65 (80)	8.98 (22)	100 (245)	2.72

Significance of difference at .05 level : Level-wise differences not significant (X^2=7.336 df 3).
Function-wise differences significant (X^2=2 .01).

per cent have shown a strong disagreement with the statement, against only 8.98 per cent showing strong agreement. Nearly 50 per cent of the sample has shown dissatisfaction with the upward communication. However, for the first time we note that the middle managers, as compared to the lower middle managers, have recorded more satisfaction on upward communication, though the difference is not significant. The explanation could be found in the fact that the organizational gap between the middle managers and the top management is lesser as compared to the lower middle managers. As such, they get a better feedback of upward communication from top managers than the lower middle managers do. Functionally speaking, we find that the finance managers have recorded the highest mean satisfaction as compared to others, whereas the technocrats have finished last on this score. Once again, we find the differences significant between the technocrats and non-technocrats. The reason for the finance functionaries' satisfaction is obvious because, as a staff department, they have access to the highest authority in the organization, since the system of public administration, each public penny that is spent must be accounted for and duly sanctioned. Naturally, therefore, even the minor finance functionary is revered by the senior officers. As a result, the finance functionaries develop close relationships with the top management and hence do not face the problem of transmitting their problems upward.

Having revealed a serious gap in the upward flow of communication, we proceed to corroborate it with the fact that the downward flow of communication is as halting as it is upward. Communication is a two-way process. If we understand others, we go by an assumption that others also understand us. Similarly, in the opinion of the middle managers if the top management understands their problem, it is fair to assume that they also know about the top management's thinking as it relates to their activities. With this background in mind we confronted the subjects with the statement:

"I receive sufficient specific information about the company as it relates to my activity."

The responses are analysed in Table 8.6. Our hypothesis is substantiated as we find that the response to this statement is fairly close to the response to the preceding question for all the managers taken together or each category of managers taken separately.

We find that more than half of the managers in our sample feel that neither the top management understands their problems nor do they properly convey the top managerial policies to the middle managers. Besides, the technical functionaries appear to be the bitterest critics of the vertical communication. They nurse a feeling that they are not being taken into confidence by the senior management. The dissatisfaction among the lower middle managers may be explained due to the organizational distance.

Job Understanding and Appraisal

An elementary cannon of a sound organization is the clarity of role specifications. The incumbent must be very clear regarding the role expectations of his immediate superiors. It is in the light of these expectations that the performance of the manager concerned is likely to be evaluated. Role ambiguity causes much stress and frustration in any organization. In order to check the one-to-one communication between each subordinate and his superior, we posed our respondents a statement on job understanding:

"I have a clear understanding of what my manager expects of me on my job."

The object is to check if the manager concerned is clear about his duties and obligations. Surprisingly, from Table 8.7 we find that 41.63 per cent of the total sample is absolutely clear and 43.27 per cent fairly clear about what his senior expects of him at the job.

TABLE 8.6

Statement: I receive sufficient specific information about the company as it relates to my activity

Class of Managers	*Per cent of Managers Saying*					*Total*	*Mean*
	Strongly disagree	*Disagree*	*Don't know*	*Agree*	*Strongly agree*	*N*	*Scores*
Middle Managers	28.57 (18)	19.05 (12)	4.76 (3)	31.75 (20)	15.87 (10)	100 (63)	2.87
Lower Middle Managers	27.47 (50)	21.98 (40)	10.43 (19)	31.32 (57)	8.79 (16)	100 (182)	2.72
Technocrats	33.6 (42)	24.0 (30)	7.2 (9)	28.8 (36)	6.4 (8)	100 (125)	2.50
Generalists	23.16 (22)	20.0 (19)	11.58 (11)	29.47 (28)	15.79 (15)	100 (95)	2.94
Finance Functionaries	16.0 (4)	12.0 (3)	8.0 (2)	52.0 (13)	12.0 (3)	100 (25)	3.32
All Managers	27.76 (68)	21.22 (52)	8.98 (22)	31.43 (77)	10.61 (26)	100 (245)	2.76

Significance of difference at .05 level : Level-wise not signicant (X^2=4.098).
Function-wise significant (X^2=13.01).

TABLE 8.7

Statement I have a clear understanding of what my immediate manager expects of me on my job

Class of Managers	*Per cent of Managers Saying*					*Total*	*Mean*
	Strongly disagree	*Disagree*	*Don't know*	*Agree*	*Strongly agree*	*N*	*Scores*
Middle Managers	4.76 (3)	3.17 (2)	3.17 (2)	42.86 (27)	46.03 (29)	100 (63)	4.22
Lower Middle Managers	3.85 (7)	9.89 (18)	2.75 (5)	43.41 (79)	40.11 (73)	100 (182)	4.06
Technocrats	7.20 (9)	12.0 (15)	3.2 (4)	37.6 (50)	40.0 (125)	100	3.91
Generalists	— —	4.21 (4)	3 16 (3)	47.37 (45)	45.26 (43)	100 (95)	4.33
Finance Functionaries	4.0 (1)	4.0 (1)	— —	56.0 (14)	36.0 (9)	100 (25)	4.16
All Managers	4.08 (10)	8.16 (2)	2.86 (7)	43.27 (106)	41 63 (102)	100 (245)	4.06

Level-wise differences not significant (X^2=1.288 df. 2).
Function-wise significant (X^2=9.243 df. 2) at .05 level.

Thus job understanding, an ideal element of bureaucracy, is present in our public sector. The middle managers and the non-technocrats are more clear regarding their job specifications *vis-a-vis* their other counterparts. Since the middle managers are much older and have spent more time in the organization concerned, they are apt to know better about what they are supposed to do in the organizations, as compared to the lower middle managers, who are young and have less experience. On the other hand, generalists, because of their corporate posting are better posted about their role specifications as compared to the technocrats, who work either in isolation, or, in many cases, in ministerial jobs which are hardly suitable to their background and training.

Role clarity by itself cannot guarantee effective performance by the subordinates. In fact, the acid test of any leadership function is the attribute of self-exemplification in it. An effective manager should play the role of friend, philosopher and guide for his subordinates. In order to check the leadership attributes among the managers, we confronted them with the statement :

"My manager has given me specific help in improving my present job."

From the contents of Table 8.8, it becomes clear that only 60.82 per cent have shown agreement with the statement and others have either disagreed or abstained from committing themselves.

At the same time, it could not be considered as a problem area because our question does not examine whether the superiors failed to help the manager concerned when he needed the guidance. Besides, the narrowness of the role and the over-definition of the job may lead to the redundancy of the leadership function. As for the differences between the middle managers and the lower middle managers, we find that the lower middle managers have given a more favourable certificate

TABLE 8.8

StatementMy manager has given me specific help in improving my present job

Class of Managers	*Per cent of Managers Saying*					*Total*	*Mean*
	Strongly disagree	*Disagree*	*Don't know*	*Agree*	*Strongly agree*	*N*	*Scores*
Middle Managers	14.28 (9)	9.52 (6)	19.05 (12)	41.27 (26)	15.87 (10)	100 (63)	3.35
Lower Middle Managers	769 (14)	21.42 (39)	8.79 (16)	37.91 (69)	24.18 (44)	100 (182)	3.49
Technocrats	14.89 (19)	15.63 (20)	9.38 (12)	41.41 (53)	18.75 (24)	100 (125)	3.34
Generalists	4.34 (4)	23.91 (22)	14.13 (13)	33.69 (31)	23.91 (22)	100 (95)	3.48
Finance Functionaries	— —	12.0 (3)	12.0 (3)	44.0 (11)	32.0 (8)	100 (25)	3.96
All Managers	9.39 (23)	18.37 (45)	11.43 (28)	33.78 (95)	22.04 (54)	100 (245)	3.46

Level-wise differences significant ($X^2 = 11.69$).
Function-wise differences significant ($X^2 = 12.517$).

to their superiors, *i.e.*, middle managers, who in turn have not commented equally well about their superiors, *i.e.*, the senior management. If we look at the function-wise break-up, we find that about 60 per cent of the technocrats have shown satisfaction towards their superiors, against about 57 per cent of the generalists. However, qualitatively, the latter category has shown a better appreciation of the superiors role as compared to the technocrats. The finance people have the best world for their officers. The differences are significant, both function-wise as well as level-wise.

Communication: Some other Considerations

Having discussed the communication problems in general, we now proceed to test the hypothesis that the age factor in general, and the length of experience in a given firm inparticular, equip a manager better in terms of communication skills. The coefficient of correlation (a) between age and communication scores is 0.11 and (b) between length of service with the present firm and communication works out to 0.15. Thus, we find both our prepositions rejected as the correlations are very weak in both cases.

Conclusion

We reach the conclusion that the middle managers are fairly satisfied with the communication within their peers and colleagues. They are generally very clear about their duties and obligations, albeit, the middle managers and the technocrats are somewhat less satisfied as compared to their counterparts. However, there hangs a haze between them and the senior management. Neither is the senior management able to transmit their thinking to the middle managers effectively, nor are the middle managers able to put their problems properly before the senior management. Beyond mentioning the organizational distance arising from the gigantic size and status bottlenecks as the possible causes of this fact, we are not in a position to commit ourselves. But the situation deserves the immediate attention of the policy-makers as we observe that the managers' associations in the public sector are growing militant in the absence of proper effort on the part of the senior management to develop effective two-way communication. It is also recommended that the jobs of the managers are made more challenging so that the superiors could earn the respect of their subordinate by helping them. Extreme bureaucratization seldom provides the superiors with opportunities to exemplify.

We also note that intergroup communication is better among the lower middle managers and the generalists *vis-a-vis* their other counterparts. On the other hand, vertical communication is better among the middle managers and the generalists *vis-a-vis* others which is due to their position in the organization. Considering the plight of the technocrats on all the accounts, we feel that special efforts should be made by the senior management and the generalists to bring the technocrats into the organizational mainstream.

Last, though not of least significance, is the organization design. To be successful, each organization must be tailor-made to make a match between the needs of an enterprise and its environment.[4] However, the foremost endeavour of the government has been to lay down a 'straight jacket pattern' of organization structure and personnel practices for all its units.[1] The trend, though seemingly irreversible needs the serious attention of our policy makers.

REFERENCES

1. Ishwar Dayal. 'Managerial Prospectives, *Economics Time*, April 27-28, 1981.
2. Kay, Emanuel. *The Crisis in Middle Management*, New York : AMACOM, 1971, and Kaufman, H. G. *Obsolescence and Professional Career Development*, New York: AMACON, 1974, have raised this issue. Significantly, both the studies have been sponsored by the American Management Association which seems to have been seized with the issue where as the issue has escaped the attention of the Indian academic world.

3. Laxminarain. *Managerial Compensation and Motivation in Public Enterprises*. Bombay : Oxford & I. B. H., 1973. His background paper at the Seminar on 'Organization in Multiunit Public Enterprises' held at Akbar Hotel, New Delhi, makes an interesting reading of the structural problem of some units.

4. Mintzberg, H. 'Organization Design.' *Harward Business Review* (Jan-Feb. 19 1) : 103-1016.

5. Paranjpe, H.K. *The Flight of Technical Personnel in Public Undertakings*: New Delhi: I.I.P.A., 1964.

9

*Management of the Family Planning Programme; Its Performance in the Seventies**

BALDEV R. SHARMA

Introduction

This paper begins with a brief history of the family planning programme in India since its inception in the early fifties. The author shows that by the end of the sixties the programme was ready for the take-off. However, two independent happenings in the last decade—mass vasectomy camps and the emergency—seem to have caused a setback to the programme as the quick and substantial gains produced by the said happenings were soon negated by subsequent unfavourable public reaction. These

*The author is grateful to Mr. G.S. Das for his help in locating and organizing some of the data used in this paper. Professors B.R. Dey, Ashok Maggu, and Michael Vanjour gave much of their time and provided useful tips to handle statistical analysis of data. The author is most grateful to all of them for their valuable help. However, the author alone is responsible for interpretations of the data and conclusions drawn therefrom.

conclusions are reached on the basis of in-depth analysis of programme performance in the seventies, using State as the unit of analysis and number of sterilizations as an index of performance. The author concludes that for effective management of the family planning programme we must emphasize education and voluntarism as the main planks of any future strategy.

India was the first country in the world to have adopted (in 1951) a national policy aimed at checking population growth. Today there are 66 countries that have organized family planning programmes at the government level covering 92 per cent of the world's population. A policy adopted by the government does not guarantee an effective programme as there is often a lag of several years between the adoption of the policy and the beginning of effective work. But a national policy does indicate the government's recognition of the seriousness of the population problem. The Second Five-Year Plan argued the problem this way:

> "Given the overall shortage of land and capital equipment relatively to production, as in India, the conclusion is inescapable that an effective curb on population growth is an important condition for rapid increase in income and the level of living."

India has only 2.4 per cent of the world's land area, which accommodates 14.8 per cent of the world's population with only 1.5 per cent of the world's income to sustain this population. The average rate of natural increase of Indian population during the period 1961-71 was 2.48 per cent per year. It is estimated that, if the population continued to grow at the current rate, it is likely to double itself by the year 2015. By using an index scale with 1970 equal to 100, it is calculated that the population of India will be 205 in the year 2000 and 422 in 2030, that is, more than four times its 1970 size. Thus the fertility trends during the next two decades can have major implications for the socio-economic development of the country. Let us look at some examples.

Although India's national income increased by 51 per cent during the period 1960-75, the increase in *per capita* income during the same period was only 1.2 per cent, which is due largely to the 35 per cent increase in population during the said period. Similarly, the number of unemployed persons is reported to have increased from 3.5 million in the early fifties to over 12 million in the mid-seventies despite the fact that 25 million or so new jobs had been created during the intervening period. It should be clear from these examples that the astounding growth of population of India has in the past tended to retard, if not neutralize, the development programmes of the country.

During the last three decades, attempts have been made to bring about a reduction in birth-rate with the aid of massive educational propaganda and provision of family planning services throughout the length and breadth of the country. These efforts are aimed at reducing population growth to a level considerably lower than the rate of economic development. Specifically, it was decided to bring down birth-rate to 30 per thousand by 1978-79 and to 25 per thousand by 1983-84. These targets have remained unattained so far despite spectacular achievements reported during the emergency in the years 1975-76 and 1976-77. In fact, the programme is understood to have run into serious trouble in some parts of the country where coercive methods were used to achieve unrealistic targets. The family planning movement has yet to pick up after the setback caused to it during the emergency.

This paper attempts to have a critical look at how the family planning programme was managed in the seventies. Family planning in India has all along been treated as part of health, which is a State subject. Hence it is proposed to use State as the unit of analysis in this paper. Through inter-State comparisons over the last eight years, it may be possible to explain variation and to identify trends which may help in the formulation of a future strategy. To achieve an all-India focus, efforts were made to include in the study as many States and union territories as possible.

A Brief History of the Programme

During the First Five-Year Plan (1951-56), family planning activities consisted largely of (a) giving advice to people in government hospitals and rural medical centres, (b) conducting field experiments on different family planning methods (c) collecting systematic information on the medical, technical and motivational aspects of family planning and (d) printing of educational materials. A sum of Rs. 1.45 million was spent on family planning activities during the First Plan period.

Further emphasis was given to the programme during the Second Five-Year Plan (1956-61). The number of service clinics was increased from 147 to 4,165 and the scope of research was extended to include, besides bio-medical, demography, communication, attitudes, and other fields. Sterilization as a family planning method was introduced during this period. Central and State Family Planning Boards were set up during this period for giving guidance and laying down policies. Expenditure on family planning activities went up to Rs. 21.56 million during the Second Plan period.

It was during the Third Five-Year Plan (1961-66) that the family planning programme was really placed on a firm footing. The overall emphasis was shifted from the clinical approach to the extension approach. This shift involved (a) intensive education, (b) provision of facilities nearest the homes of the people, (c) advice to people on the largest possible scale and (d) widespread popular effort in every rural and urban community. The use of IUD was introduced for the first time in 1965. The organization structure was modified twice, first in 1963 and then again in 1965, to sub-serve the new approach. A sum of Rs. 248.60 million was spent on the family planning programme during the Third Plan period.

The years 1966-69 are referred to as the Inter-Plan period. During this period, the United Nations carried out two evaluations of the family planning programme in India. The Planning Commission too conducted two evaluations of the programme. Based on the findings of these studies, suitable modifications were made in the programme which led to greater enthusiasm for the programme throughout the country. Perhaps the most significant decision of this period was the introduction of compensation for those undergoing sterilization. The term "incentive" was not yet applied to this payment. Instead, it was called "compensation" for meeting out-of-pocket expenses of the acceptors. The total expenditure on the programme during this period was Rs. 704.64 million.

During the Fourth Five-Year Plan (1969-72), the family planning progamme was declared as one of the matters of highest national priority. An effort was made to consolidate the structure and components of the programme initiated in the preceding years. Also, additional efforts were made to cater to those sectors, areas and segments that were likely to produce optimum results. In the last year of the Fourth Plan (1973-74), a heavy cut was imposed on the finanical resources allocated for the programme. Despite this, however, more acceptors were enrolled during this Plan than during all the previous Plan periods put together. This extraordinary performance was made possible to some extent by the mass vasectomy camps organized all over India during 1971-72 and 1972-73 with conspicuous success. During the intensive vasectomy campaign between September 1972 and March 31, 1973, over two million sterilizations were performed in mass vasectomy camps held in 207 districts throughout the country. Soon thereafter, the practice of organizing mass vasectomy camps was dispensed with for fear of being counter-productive. A sum of Rs. 2,844.33 million was spent on the programme during the Fourth Plan period.

The financial outlay for the programme for the Fifth Five-Year Plan (1974-79) was Rs. 4,973.57 million. During this period, the strategy of delivering an integrated package of family planning, health, nutrition and MCH services was more vigorously pursued. The year 1974 was observed, as the World Population Year and India, as a member nation, decided to utilize this opportunity to give further impetus to her own population programme. The most impartant happening of this period was the declaration of emergency in the country and the unprecedented impetus that it gave to the family planning programme, overshadowing the level of performance of all previous years and Plan periods.

On April 16, 1976 (towards the middle of the emergency period) was announced a comprehensive National Population Policy. The new policy envisaged (a) raising the age of marriage from 15 to 18 for girls and from 18 to 21 for boys, (b) compulsory registration of marriages, (c) freezing of representation in the Central and State legislatures on the basis of the 1971 Census until the year 2001, (d) earmarking of 8 per cent of the central government assistance in the State Plans against performance in family planning, (e) higher priority and adequate outlay for girls' education and child nutrition, (f) introduction of population values in the education system, (g) involvement of all Departments/Ministries of the government in the promotion of the family planning programme, (h) higher monetary compensation based on parity in the case of sterilization, (i) introduction of group incentives and (j) a new multi-media motivational strategy.

The implementation of the above-mentioned measures backed by the unprecedented powers exercised by the government during the emergency resulted in the all-time record high performance of 8,660,564 sterilizations in a single year (1976-77). The year ended with changes of far-reaching consequences for the nation. The 30-year hold of the Congress government was replaced by the Janata government, which announced the termination of all forms of compulsion and coercion in the implementation of the family planning programme and reiteration of the government's commitment to the promotion of family planning on a purely voluntary basis. The name of the programme was changed from family planning to family welfare, which reflected the new government's concern to promote the total welfare of the family and the community. The government's commitment to the programme is contained in the Statement of Policy dated June 29, 1977, which emphasizes that although the approach will be educational and wholly voluntary, there will be no slackening of the efforts in implementing the programme. The Child Marriage Restraint (Amendment) Act, which raises the minimum age of marriage to 18 years for girls and 21 years for boys, was passed in 1978. An infringement of the provisions of this Act has been made a cognizable offence.

To sum up, through successive Five-Year Plan periods the government has been spending ever rising sums of money to promote the cause of family planning in India. However, in terms of both expenditure on the programme as well as the efforts put in, the last two Plan periods stand out as most crucial. The most significant happening during the Fouth Plan (1969-74) was the decision to organize mass vasectomy camps which led to the phenomenal increase in the number of sterilizations. Similarly, the most important happening during the Fifth Plan (1974-79) was the declaration of emergency and its influence on family planning performance.

About the Data

It was decided to use only sterilization figures as an index of family planning performance in different States and union territories. Being a terminal method, sterilization is by far the most effective and reliable method of limiting family size. Also, during the first seven years of the family planning programme (1956-62), sterilization was almost the only method advocated by the government for limiting family size. IUD insertion and free supply of conventional contraceptives were introduced much later. Even after the introduction of other methods and the advocacy of the so-called "cafeteria" approach, seterilization has continued to remain the dominant method of family planning in India. As shown in Annexure I, of all couples effectively protected till the year 1977-78, about 89 per cent had been protected through sterilizations, 4 per cent through IUD insertions, and the remaining 7 per cent through conventional contraceptives. It may be concluded, therefore that sterilization has been and continues to be mainstay of the family planning programme in India.

The basic information on which this paper is based is taken from official sources of the Government of India, Ministry of Health and Family Welfare. For one or more of the reasons given below, the following States/union territories have been excluded from the purview of this study:

1. Andaman and Nicobar Islands,
2. Arunachal Pradesh,
3. Chandigarh,
4. Dadra and Nagar Haveli,
5. Goa, Daman and Diu,
6. Lakshadweep,
7. Manipur,
8. Meghalaya,
9. Mizoram,
10. Nagaland,
11. Pondicherry,
12. Sikkim, and
13. Tripura:

   (a) Non-availability of data for each of the eight years selected for this study.

   (b) Relatively small population and, therefore, negligible contribution to the family planning programme.

(c) Geographical isolation or remoteness of the State/ union territory from the mainland.

Although the number of States/union territories excluded from the scope of this study is relatively large, their exclusion is unlikely to have a serious impact on the outcome of the study. This is because these 13 States/union territories together account for only two per cent of all the sterilizations performed in India from the inception of the programme to date and about two per cent of the total population of the country. It is proposed to examine the record of performance of the family planning programme in terms of the number of sterilizations performed in the selected States/union territories during the period 1970-71 to 1977-78. This time period was chosen for two reasons. First, State-wise data are not available for the earlier years. Second, this period covers the last four years of the Fourth Plan and the first four years of the Fifth Plan. These two Plan periods are, as already indicated, most crucial in the history of the family planning programme in India.

The Findings

Annexure II gives the number and rate of sterilizations performed in each of the 18 States/union territories selected for this study together with the all-India rate of family planning performance. A glance at the last two rows of Annexure II will show that the overall performance of the country as a whole is by and large similar to that of the selected 18 States/union territories. For ready reference, the State-wise and year-wise rate of performance has been summarized in the accompanying Table 9.1 As seen in this table, there are major differences among the States in terms of overall rate of performance during the 8-year period under study, For example the sterilization rate among the States varied between 1.77 and 7.53 per 1000 population.

Differences are also observed in the rate of performance over the years for the country as a whole, the lowest and the highest rate being 1.48 and 14.33 per 1000 population respectively. More signficantly, fluctuations in the rate of performance

TABLE 9.1

Number of Sterilization per 1000 Population

Sl. No.	*State/Union Territory*	*1970-71*	*1971-72*	*1972-73*	*1973-74*	*1974-75*	*1975-76*	*1976-77*	*1977-78*	$\bar{X}$ *of 8 Years*
1.	Maharashtra	4.93	7.62	11.59	3.58	4.34	10.93	15.11	2.15	7.53
2.	Andhra Pradesh	5.18	6.23	7.53	3.10	2.81	3.46	15.71	2.62	5.83
3.	Haryana	2.17	4.54	5.30	1.59	5.68	5.19	19.62	0.51	5.57
4.	Gujarat	3.55	10.79	3.45	2.09	5.27	5.09	10.32	3.56	5.52
5.	Delhi	1.92	2.44	2.73	1.93	2.18	4.45	26.42	1.05	5.39
6.	Tamil Nadu	1.75	6.07	6.79	2.53	4.45	5.99	12.36	2.18	5.27
7.	Himachal Pradesh	1.29	1.62	1.67	1.68	1.89	4.61	27.28	0.46	5.06
8.	Orissa	4.44	3.88	4.02	2.37	2.90	5.16	13.07	3.17	4.88
9.	Madhya Pradesh	2.14	2.23	7.28	1.00	1.50	2.40	20.93	0.73	4.78
10.	Kerala	3.19	6.93	4.05	2.21	2.67	6.58	9.24	3.09	4.69
11.	Assam	1.16	2.70	3.86	1.28	2.35	8.58	12.81	0.75	4.19
12.	West Bengal	1.67	1.64	4.92	0.58	1.17	4.18	17.47	0.69	4.04
13.	Karnataka	1.60	1.90	4.45	2.16	1.95	3.74	13.10	2.81	3.96

14. Punjab	2.30	2.89	4.14	1.49	2.50	3.57	9.24	0.84	3.37
15. Bihar	1.48	2.38	4.47	0.50	0.54	2.69	10.99	0.62	2.96
16. Rajasthan	1.18	1.28	2.72	0.94	1.35	2.99	12.41	0.41	2.91
17. Uttar Pradesh	0.88	1.72	3.82	0.31	0.54	1.34	8.64	0.13	2.17
18. Jammu and Kashmir	2.36	1.35	2.26	0.83	1.04	1.87	3.54	0.93	1.77
X of 18 States/UTs	2.40	3.79	4.73	1.68	2.51	4.60	14.33	1.48	

*Information presented in this table has been taken from Annexure II.

ANOVA TABLE

Due to	*SS*	*Degree of freedom*	*MS*	*F*	*P*
States	277.2447	17	16.3085	$F_{17,117}=2.4766$	$P<.001$
Time	2,205.4330	7	315.0519	$F_{7,119}=47.8454$	$P<.001$
Error	783.6108	119	6.5850	—	—

appear to be extremely erratic. To determine whether the observed variations over time and among State are statistically significant or not, two-way analysis of variance was computed, the results of which are presented in the ANOVA table.

It is clear from the above ANOVA table that family planning performance in India has varied significantly both over the years and among the States. To find out which of the two factors explains greater variation, it was decided to use the following test:

$$F7,\ 17 = \frac{MS\,(\text{Times})}{MS\,(\text{States})} = \frac{315.0619}{19.3189} = 16.3085\ (P > .001)$$

We can say on the basis of the above test that variation in family planning performance due to the time factor was significantly greater than variation due to States. Before going into the factors that might explain fluctuations over time, let us first look at the inter-State differences in terms of family planning performance.

Table 9.2 summarizes the results of 153 difference of means tests (t-test) between every two of the 18 States/union territories. The States have been listed in the table in ascending order in terms of family planning performance. Thus, Jammu and Kashmir ranked the lowest, Uttar Pradesh next to the lowest, and so on. On the other hand, Maharashtra randked the highest among all States, its performance being significantly higher than that of every other State. A closer look at Table 9.2 will show that after excluding Maharashtra, the remaining 17 States can be classified into three homogenous groups as follows:

State/UT *Low Performance States*	*Sterilizations per 1000 populations*
1. Jammu and Kashmir	1.77
2. Uttar Pradesh	2.17
3. Rajasthan	2.91
4. Bihar	2.96

Average Performance States

5. Punjab	3.37
6. Karnataka	3.96
7. Best Bengal	4.04

High Performance State

8. Assam	4.19
9. Kerala	4.69
10. Madhya Pradesh	4.78
11. Orissa	4.88
12. Himachal Pradesh	5.06
13. Tamil Nadu	5.27
14. Delhi	5.39
15. Gujarat	5.52
16. Haryana	5.58
17. Andhra Pradesh	5.83

Highest Performance

18. Maharashtra	7.53

Table 9.3 shows in a summary from the results of 28 (*t*-testes comparing the difference of means between every two of the eight years. Had there been a steady and significant increase in the rate of family planning performance in the country from one year to the next, we would have found the sign (+) in practically every cell of Table 9.3. A close look at this table will show, on the other hand, that the performance has been fluctuating over the years. Even after a lapse of several years, performance rate has sometimes remained more or less the same (as indicated by the sign "ns"), while in some other cases it went down (as shown by the minus sign)! This is indeed surprising considering the fact that in every succeeding Plan period financial allocations for the programme have been constantly rising and public awareness about the need for smaller families has been increasing.

TABLE 9.2

Showing Results of Difference of Means Tests (t-Test) Between States

	Jammu and Kashmir	*Uttar Pradesh*	*Rajasthan*	*Bihar*	*Punjab*	*Karnataka*	*West Bengal*	*Assam*	*Kerala*	*Madhya Pradesh*	*Orissa*	*Himachal Pradesh*	*Tamil Nadu*	*Delhi*	*Gujarat*	*Haryana*	*Andhra Pradesh*	*Maharashtra*
	1	*2*	*3*	*4*	*5*	*6*	*7*	*8*	*9*	*10*	*11*	*12*	*13*	*14*	*15*	*16*	*17*	*18*
1. Jammu and Kashmir	X	ns	ns	ns	*	**	**	**	**	**	**	**	**	**	**	**	**	**
2. Uttar Pradssh	ns	X	ns	ns	ns	*	*	**	**	**	**	**	**	**	**	**	**	**
3. Rajasthan	ns	ns	X	ns	ns	ns	ns	ns	*	*	*	**	**	**	**	**	**	**
4. Bihar	ns	ns	ns	X	ns	ns	ns	ns	*	*	*	**	**	**	**	**	**	**
5. Punjab	*	ns	ns	ns	X	ns	ns	ns	ns	ns	*	*	*	**	**	**	**	**
6. Karnataka	**	*	ns	ns	ns	X	ns	ns	ns	ns	ns	ns	ns	*	*	*	*	**

7. West Bengal	**	*	ns	ns	ns	ns	X	ns	ns	ns	ns	ns	ns	ns	*	*	*	**
8. Assam	**	**	ns	ns	ns	ns	ns	X	ns	ns	ns	ns	ns	ns	ns	ns	*	**
9. Kerala	**	**	*	*	ns	ns	ns	ns	X	ns	ns	ns	ns	ns	ns	ns	ns	**
10. Madhya Pradesh	**	**	*	*	ns	ns	ns	ns	ns	X	ns	ns	ns	ns	ns	ns	ns	**
11. Orissa	**	**	*	*	*	ns	ns	ns	ns	ns	X	ns	ns	ns	ns	ns	ns	**
12. Himachal Pradesh	**	**	**	**	*	ns	ns	ns	ns	ns	ns	X	ns	ns	ns	ns	ns	**
13. Tamil Nadu	**	**	**	**	*	ns	ns	ns	ns	ns	ns	ns	X	ns	ns	ns	ns	**
14. Delhi	**	**	**	**	**	*	ns	ns	ns	ns	ns	ns	ns	X	ns	ns	ns	**
15. Gujurat	**	**	**	**	**	*	*	ns	ns	ns	ns	ns	ns	ns	X	ns	ns	**
16. Haryana	**	**	**	**	**	*	*	ns	ns	ns	ns	ns	ns	ns	ns	X	ns	*
17. Andhra Pradesh	**	**	**	**	**	*	*	*	ns	ns	ns	ns	ns	ns	ns	ns	X	*
18. Maharashtra	**	**	**	**	**	**	**	**	**	**	**	**	**	**	**	*	*	X

Notes: (1) The States are listed in this table in ascending order in terms of family planning performance, Jammu and Kashmir being the *lowest* and Maharashtra being the *highest*.

(2) Figures regarding the overall $\overline{X}$ performance of the States were taken from the last column of Table 9.1.

(3) Symbols used in the table may be read as: ns = not significant; * = $P < .05$; ** = $P < .01$.

TABLE 9.3

Showing Results of Means Tests (*t*-Test) Between Years

Year	*1970-71*	*1971-72*	*1972-73*	*1973-74*	*1974-75*	*1975-76*	*1976-77*	*1977-78*
1970-71	X	ns	(+)	ns	ns	(+)	(+)	ns
1971-72	X	X	ns	(−)	ns	ns	(+)	(−)
1972-73	X	X	X	(−)	(—)	ns	(+)	(−)
1973-74	X	X	X	X	ns	(+)	(+)	ns
1974-75	X	X	X	X	X	(+)	(+)	ns
1975-76	X	X	X	X	X	X	(+)	(−)
1976-77	X	X	X	X	X	X	X	(—)
1977-78	X	X	X	X	X	X	X	X

Notes: (1) Family planning performance of each year is based on the $\overline{X}$ of 18 selected States/union territories and is taken from Table 9.1 (last row).

2) The table may be read horizontally from left to right. The sign (+) means that, compared with the base year shown at the beginning of each row, there was an *increase* in the level of performance during the year shown in the column heading. The sign (—), on the other hand, means a *decrease* compared with the base year.

(3) Sign (+) or (−) also indicates that the observed increase/decrease in $\overline{X}$ performance over the base year was found to be statistically significant ($P<.01$). The sign "ns" means that the observed difference in means *not* statistically significant.

That programme performance has fluctuated during the last eight years is neither erratic nor accidental. In the following pages of this paper I propose to examine more closely the factor(s) that might explain these fluctuations. As already noted, two important happenings took place during the seventies which had a direct bearing on the performance of the programme. These were (1) the organization of mass vasectomy camps during the years 1971-72 and 1972-73 and (2) the declaration of emergency during the years 1975-76 and 1976-77. The observed fluctuations in programme performance appear to be the direct result of these two happenings.

If the eight years under study are divided into two time periods, such of four-year duration, we obtain the following picture:

Part I: Mass Camps

1970-71: Pre-Camps Year
1971-72: First Year of Camps
1972-73: Second Year of Camps
1973-74: Post-Camps Year

Part II: The Emergency

1974-75: Pre-Emergency Year
1975-76: First Year of Emergency
1976-77: Second Year of Emergency
1977-78: Post-Emergency Year

If we now revert to Table 9.3 (read with Table 9.1 last row), we shall observe that compared with the $\widetilde{X}$ performance of the base year 1970-71, performance in the first year of the camps increased by almost 58 per cent, although the observed difference was not statistically significant. During the second year of the camps, the increase in the rate of programme performance was of the order of 97 per cent and statistically significant. When at the end of 1972-73 it was decided to discontinue with the practice of holding mass vasectomy camps, performance fell

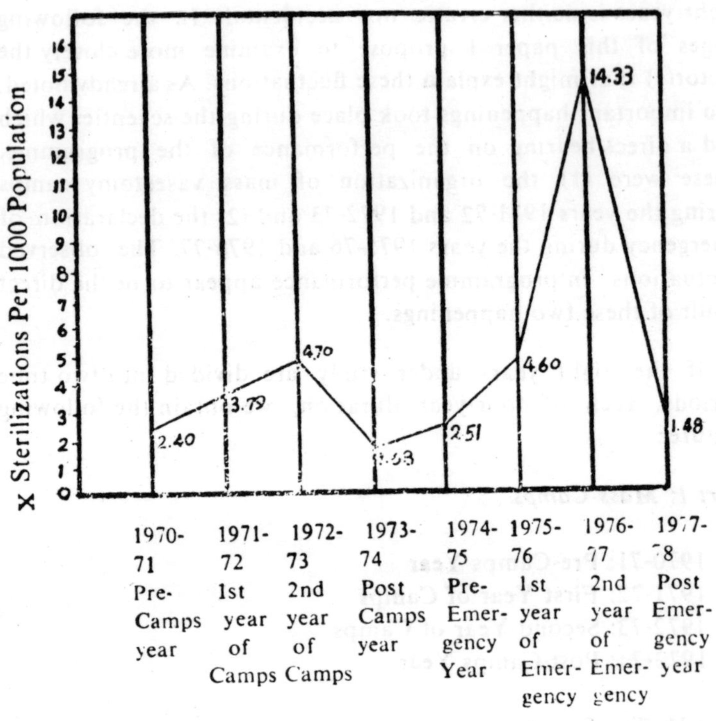

Note—For the level of significance of differences in $\bar{X}$ performance, refer to Table 3

Fig. 9.1—Showing X Sterilizations per 1000 Population during the Period 1970-71 To 1977-78

drastically. In fact, the rate of performance in the post-camps year (1973-74) was lower than that of the pre-camps year (1970-71) by 30 per cent, although this difference was not statistically significant.

The trend just described for the first four-year period repeated itself in exactly the same manner during the second four-year period. Compared to the performance in the pre-emergency year (1974-75), that of the first year of emergency (1975-76) increased by about 83 per cent and of the second year (1976-77) by 471 per cent, both increases being statistically significant. As had happened in the case of the camps, performance during the post-emergency year (1977-78) fell drastically. In fact, the level of performance in 1977-78 was the lowest during the eight-year period, 38 per cent lower than that of 1970-71. Fig. 9.1 summarizes these findings.

As already indicated, family planning programme began in India in 1956. During the first nine years of the programme 1956-64 the annual rate of sterilizations remained less than one per thousand population for the country as a whole. During the next five years (1965-70), there was a considerable improvement, the annual sterilization rate ranging between 1.37 and 3.59 per thousand population. Using data for *all* the 14 years (up to and including 1969-70), an attempt was made to forecast the annual rate of performance in the selected 18 States during the seventies. As performance during the first nine years of the programme was extremely low, the forecast based on the experience of the said 14 years is bound to be *conservative.* It is reasonable to expect that as the programme gets going and people's awareness about the need for smaller families increases, the rate of programme performance should rise higher and higher with each passing year. However, in making the forecast no allowance has been made for the snow-ball effect.

Table 9.4 and the accompanying Fig. 9.2 show year-wise the expected rate of programme performance for the selected 18 States during the seventies. Had there been no mass vasectomy camps and no emergency, we would have expected performance according to the dotted line in Fig. 9.2. Because of the said two happenings, however, the actual performance during the seventies was highly fluctuating as shown by the solid line in Fig. 9.2. If we compare the expected with the actual number of sterilizations shown in Table 9.4, the gains and losses can be summarized as below:

TABLE 9.4

Showing Expected and Actual Rates of Programme Performance During the Seventies for Selected 18 States/Union Territories

Year	*Population of selected 18 States*	*Estimated sterilizations per 1000 population*	*Expected No. of sterilizations*	*Actual No. of sterilizations*	*Goin/Loss vis-a-vis the expected number of sterilizations*
1970-71	540,536	2.9998	1,621,500	1,329,914	−291,586
1971-72	552,011	3.2621	1.800,715	2,187,336	+386,621
1972-73	563,588	3.5244	1,986,310	3,212,856	+1,135,546
1973-74	575,270	3.7867	2,178,375	942,402	−1,235,973
1974-75	587,018	4.0490	2,376,836	1,353,850	−1,022,977
1975-76	598,547	4.3113	2,580,516	2,668,754	+88,238
1976-77	609,315	4.5736	2,786,763	8,259,023	+5,472,260

1977-78	619,871	4.8359	2,997,634	926,497	—2,071,137
1978-79	638,231	5.0982	3,253,829	1,029,499*	—2,224,330
Total			21,582,478	21,819,140	+236,662

*Data in terms of the actual number of sterilizations performed during the year 1978-79 are not readily available. The figure shown here is based on the information given in *Centre Calling*, Vol. 14, No. 3, March 1979 for the period April 1978 to December 1978 (9 months) which was proportionately increased by multiplying it by 4/3.

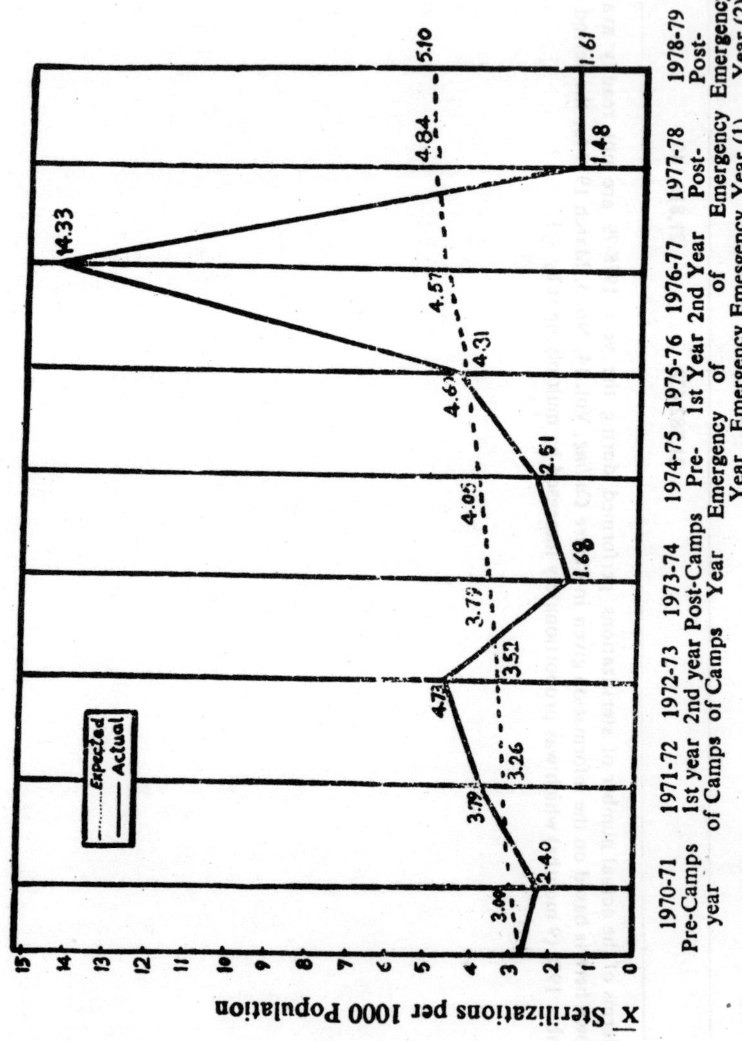

Fig. 9.2—Showing Expected and Actual Number of Sterilizaitions per 1000 Population for Selected 18 States/Union Territories

	Number of Sterilizations
1. *Gain* due to additional sterilizations during 1971-72, and 1972-73 (*Camps*)	+1,522,167
2. *Loss* due to poorer performance during the next 2 years (1973-74 and 1974-75)	—2,250,950
3. *Gain* due to additional sterilizations during 1975-76 and 1976-77 (*Emergency*)	+5,560,458
4. *Loss* due to poorer performance during the next 2 years (1977-78 and 1978-79)	—4,295,467
Total	+ 2 6,662

The preceding profit and loss account may give the impression that the country is, on the whole, still a gainer. That this is not so should be clear from Fig. 2, which shows that the worst is not yet over and that it is likely to take still more time before programme performance approximates even the conservative estimate depicted by the dotted line. By the time that happens, the spectacular gains of emergency would be totally wiped out and the country would have suffered further losses due to continued poor performance of the programme. The loss to the country has so far been discussed only from the point of view of number of sterilizations. What about the huge sums of money spent on family planning during the seventies. Let the following figures speak for themselves:

Expenditure on Family Planning		*Millions*
1. First 3 Plans put together (1951-66)	Rs. 271.61	Rs. 976.25
2. Inter-Plan period (1966-69)	Rs. 704.64	
3. Fourth Plan (1969-74)	Rs. 2,844.33	Rs. 7,985.61
4. Fifth Plan (1974-79)	Rs. 5,141.28	

Conclusion

To sum up, although family planning programme had started early in India, it had a relatively slow start and its accomplishments during the first decade (1956-66) were quite modest. However, by the mid-sixties the programme gained momentum and so during the Inter-Plan period (1966-69) rapid strides were made in terms of programme performance. As the programme entered the decade of the seventies, it was ready for the take-off. However, two independent happenings of the decade (mass vasectomy camps and the emergency) seem to have caused a servere setback to the programme. Despite the fact additional expenditure amounting to several billions of rupees was made during the seventies, programme performance has failed to make any real gain. On the contrary, performance during 1977-78 and 1978-79 is the lowest since the mid-sixties.

Needless to say, the said two happenings had one thing in common—compulsion—although its manifestation was more blatant during the emergency than in the course of the mass vasectomy camps. On each occasion compulsion which led to quick and substantial gains for the programme. However, those gains were short-lived and were soon negated by the setback caused to the programme arising from the unfavourable, if not hostile, reactions of the population. This negative sentiment is reported to be one of the factors responsible for the results of the 1977 general elections.

If the preceding explanation for the fluctuating performance of family planning programme in the seventies is accepted, then the lessons are not difficult to draw. As stated in the Statement of Policy dated June 29, 1977, there should be "no room for compulsion, coercion or pressures of any sort.' Therefore, effective management of the programme demands that we must emphasize education and voluntarism as the main planks of

any future strategy. Such an approach takes longer to yield results but, as shown in this paper, quick and short-term gains are unlikely to help in achieving the overall objectives of the family planning programme in India.

ANNEXURE I

Number of Couples (in '000) Effectively Protected Through Different Family Planning Methods During the Period 1966-67 to 1677-78*

Sl. No.	Year	Number and Percentage of Couples Effectively Protected Through							
		Sterilizations		IUD Insertions		Conventional Contraceptives		All Effectively Protected Couples	
		No.	%	No.	%	No.	%	No	%
1	1966-67	2,164	59.40	1,247	34.23	232	6.37	3,643	100
2	1967-68	3,849	69.31	1,466	26.40	238	4.29	5,553	100
3	1968-69	5,280	72.97	1,475	20.38	481	6.65	7,236	100
4	1969-70	6,402	74.21	1,470	17.04	755	8.75	8,627	100
5	1970-71	7,379	74.98	1,481	15.05	981	9.97	9,841	100
6	1971-72	9,143	77.35	1,500	12.69	1,177	9.96	11,820	100
7	1972-73	11,729	81.86	1,400	9.77	1,199	8.37	14,328	100
8	1973-74	12,062	80.90	1,342	9.00	1,505	10.10	14,909	100
9	1974-75	12,779	83.00	1,357	8.81	1,260	8.19	15,396	100
10	1975-76	14,742	81.84	1,492	8.28	1,780	9.88	18,014	100

11	1976-77	22,057	86.50	1,569	6.15	1,873	7.35	25,499	100
12	1977-78	21,997	89.30	975	3.96	1,660	6.74	24,632	100

*Data for the first 11 years regarding the number of couples effectively protected through different methods have been taken from *Family Welfare Programme in India Yearbook*, 1976-77 (Table E-1, pp. 91-129), Similar information for the year 1977-78 has been taken from the *Yearbook* for 1977-78 (Table E-1, p. 91).

ANNEXURE II

Number of Sterilizations Performed (both Vasectomies and Tubectomies) and Population Figures for Selected States/Union Territories for the Years 1970-71 to 1977-78

Sl. No.	*State/Union Territory*	*1970-71*	*1971-72*	*1972-73*	*1973-74*	*1974-75*	*1975-76*	*1976-77*	*1977-78*
1.	*Andhra Pradesh*								
	Sterilizations*	225,064	275,869	339,767	142,778	131,559	165,163	760,275	128,785
	Population+	43,437	44,286	45,140	46,870	46,870	47,712	48,408	49,084
	Rate per 1000++	5.18	6.23	7.53	3.10	2.81	3.46	15.71	2.62
2.	*Assam*								
	Sterilizations	17,301	41,578	61,109	20,822	39.387	147,545	226,161	13,547
	Population	14,921	15,374	15,830	16,291	16,754	17,203	17,655	18,108
	Rate per 1000	1.16	2.70	3.86	1,28	2,35	8.58	12.81	0.75
3.	*Bihar*								
	Sterilizations	83,073	136,247	260,883	29,782	32,394	165,537	685,636	39,065
	Population	56,266	57.301	58,346	59,396	60,456	61,484	62,402	63,294
	Rate per 1000	1.48	2.38	4.47	0.50	0.54	2.69	10.99	0.62

4. *Gujarat*								
Sterilizations	94,537	294,675	96,723	59,997	154,757	153,023	317,113	111,803
Population	26,640	27,317	27,998	28,684	29,376	30,046	30,714	31,365
Rate per 1000	3.55	10.79	3.45	2.09	5.27	5.09	10.32	3.56
5. *Haryana*								
Sterilizations	21,707	46,453	55,508	17,063	62,112	57.942	222,738	5,935
Population	10,015	10,241	10,469	10,698	10,929	11,154	11,355	11,551
Rate per 1000	2.17	4.54	5.30	1.59	5.68	5.19	19.62	0.51
6. *Himachal Pradesh*								
Sterilizations	4,459	5,642	5,893	5,988	6.811	16,832	100,740	1,710
Population	3,454	3,493	3,533	3,573	3,613	3,654	3,693	3,732
Rate per 1000	1.29	1.62	1.67	1.68	1.89	4.61	27.28	0.46
7. *Jammu & Kashmir*								
Sterilizations	10,867	6,338	10,841	4,056	5,502	9,502	18,351	4,926
Population	4,607	4,703	4,799	4,895	4,990	5,087	5,186	5,285
Rate per 1000	2.36	1.35	2.26	0.83	1.04	1.87	3.54	0.93

(Contd.)

	1	*2*	*3*	*4*	*5*	*6*	*7*	*8*
8. *Karnataka*								
Sterilizations	46,748	56,778	135.453	66,967	61.690	120,671	430,0[illegible]9	93,932
Population	29,245	29,842	30,443	31,051	31,662	32,254	32,836	33,404
Rate per 1000	1.60	1.90	4.45	2.16	1.95	3.74	13.10	2 81
9. *Kerala*								
Sterilizations	68,017	151,111	90,389	50,389	62,151	156,622	213,974	76,400
Population	21,307	21.804	22,305	22,811	23,319	23,812	24,242	24,662
Rate per 1000	3.19	6 93	4.05	2.21	2.67	6.58	8.83	3.09
10. *Madhya Pradesh*								
Sterilizations	89,129	94,948	317,791	44,545	68.433	112,163	1,002,[illegible]81	35,932
Population	41,568	42,610	43,658	44,715	45,759	46,811	47,880	48,919
Rate per 1000	2.14	2.23	7.28	1.00	1.50	2.40	20.93	0.73
11. *Maharashtra*								
Sterilizations	248,170	391,765	609,391	192,050	238,160	611,588	862,480	125,378
Population	50,313	51,437	52,570	53,711	54,861	55,975	57,072	58,137
Rate per 1000	4.39	7.62	11.59	3.58	4.34	10.93	15.11	2.15

12. Orissa								
Sterilizations	97,267	86,714	91,879	55,252	68,971	125,040	322,984	79,776
Population	21,905	22,366	22,833	23,301	23,763	24,232	24,709	25,188
Rate per 1000	4.44	3.88	4.02	2.37	2.90	5.16	13.07	3.17
13. Punjab								
Sterilizations	31,114	39,900	58,169	21,220	36,460	53,083	139,905	13,048
Population	13,530	13,787	14,048	14,313	14,584	14,860	15,142	15,418
Rate per 1000	2.30	2.89	4.14	1.49	2.50	3.57	9 24	0.84
14. Rajasthan								
Sterilizations	30,464	33,726	73,376	25,970	38,071	86,257	364,763	12,386
Population	25,712	26,326	26,946	27,570	28,198	28,808	29,399	29,973
Rate per 1000	1.18	1.28	2.72	0.94	1.35	2.99	21.41	0.41
15. Tamil Nadu								
Sterilizations	72.030	254,696	290,277	110,095	197,760	270,691	566,708	101,267
Population	41,131	41,943	42,761	43,584	44,413	45,217	45,868	46,501
Rate per 1000	1.75	6.07	6.79	2.53	4.45	5.99	12.36	2.18

(Contd.)

	1	2	3	4	5	6	7	8
16. Uttar Pradesh								
Sterilizations	77,959	154,615	348,302	28,543	50,722	128,729	838,071	13,131
Population	88,213	89,713	91,224	92.747	94,280	95,766	96.986	98,171
Rate per 1000	0.88	1.72	3.82	0.31	0.54	1.34	8.64	0,13
17. West Bengal								
Sterilizations	73,948	74,306	227,610	27,545	56,417	206,424	882,591	35,699
Population	44,225	45,221	46,?32	47,277	48,336	49,419	50,526	51,653
Rate per 1(00	1.67	1.64	4.92	0.58	1.17	4.18	17.47	0.69
18. Delhi								
Sterlizations	7,759	10,364	12,136	8,968	10,563	22,510	138,517	5,705
Population	4,047	4,247	4,447	4,650	4,855	5,053	5,242	5,426
Rate per 1000	1.92	2.44	2.73	1.93	2.18	4.45	26.42	1.05

Overall Rate

All 18 States/UTS	2.40	3.79	4.73	1.88	2.51	4.60	14.33	1.48
All India	2.43	3.91	5.47	1.62	2.28	4.40	13.37	1.47

*Data regarding total number of sterilizations performed in each State/Union Territory are taken from the following sources:

(a) *For years* 1970-71 to 1973-74

Family Welfare Planning in India Yearbook, 1974-75, Table D-8, pp. 60-61.

(b) *For years* 1974-75 *to* 1976-77

Fomily Welfare Programme ni India Yearbook, 1976-77, Table D-8, pp. 82-83.

(c) *For the year* 1977-78

Centre Calling, Vol. 13, No. 7, July 1978.

+Population figures (shown here in '000) are taken from *Family Welfare Programme in India Yearbook*, 1976-77 Table A-4, pp 22-23.

++"Rate Per 1000" was computed by dividing total number of sterilizations given in the first row by the population figures given in the second row.

10

The Boards of Directors—An Inside View

HITEN BHAYA

This article is a panoramic scanning of various kinds of Boards of Directors in India. It sheds light on the divergence between from and content amongst all species of Boards, without neglecting to lay stress on shades of differences within such broad spectrum duality. Thus, the Boards of State Government public enterprises seem to be a shade less effective than their already ineffective counterparts in Central Government enterprises because of the inclusion of MLA's in the former. The chameleon-like role of the Chairman is delineated from a number of vantage points. It appears that most Chairmen lack the art and science of managing human groups—including both inside subordinates as equals in the Board, and outside part time, non-official Directors, as purveyors of objective analysis. The Boards of foreign companies in India seem to be the most purposive amongst all varieties. The dilemmas of ministry and trade union representatives on Boards are captured in terms of their primary moorings, and their need to identify with enterprise-level imperatives. The problems of representatives of financial institutions on the Boards of assisted companies constitute another class by itself. In the author's opinion, all such issues merit further research.

I. Form v. Content

The responsibilities, tasks and the procedure of working for the Boards of Directors of joint stock companies have been well laid out in the relevant statutes and in the respective Memorandum and Articles of Association. These are the formal boundaries in which a Board of Directors is to selection and discharge its responsibilities to the various constituents, the shareholders, of employees, the clients, the debtors and the creditors.

But, like all organised structures, there is a great deal of difference between the from and the content and it is the reality of the content with which we are more concerned from the point of view of Management Science. A more scientific study of the actual functioning of the Boards of Directors is perhaps an area to which attention could be drawn. The purpose of this article is to stimulate such interest. Based as this article is, on purely subjective experience the limitations are obvious. The observations made in this article therefore, need further validation through objective studies and if passive research.

To start with, although the form and the legal entity of the Board of Directors is the same or all companies registered under the Companies Act they differ substantially in composition, in their ambits of decision-making, and in their approach towards their responsibility to the various constituents. For example, whilst the Boards of most private companies are the ultimate authorities in decision-making, the Boards of public enterprises are not so in many matters. But the statutory responsibilities of both are alike. Again Boards of subsidiary companies or linked companies or the Boards of national branches of multi-national companies registered as Indian companies have each a different decision-making scope. It would be interesting to have a study comparing the areas where such Boards are, in fact, the final decision-making authorities and the areas where they are only recommendatory bodies.

II. The Pregnant Agenda File

The scope of the Board's decision-making authority affects the style of functioning of the Boards. The Boards of public sector enterprises for whom many areas of decision-making are reserved by the Government formally and many more informally, would be greatly concerned with the acceptance of their views and recommendations by the Government and a speedy decision. Their agenda notes therefore tend to be exhaustive and discussions dilatory, as all possible reactions on the part of the Government and the possible consequences of non-acceptance of their purposals by Government on the company have to be written out and debated. The presence of Government representatives in such Boards can help limiting the discussions provided they can give definitive opinion on behalf of the Government. Most often such definitive opinions can be given by them on the negative side easily but rarely on the positive side. The agenda papers of Government companies are therefore notoriously bulky running into several supplementary volumes and more are placed on the table.

The agenda itself is large because delegation is limited at every level. Personnel matters occupy a very large proportion of the agenda of such enterprises becuase almost every personnel matter becomes a policy issue, concern with precedents and uniformily being predominant in the public sector. It State Government undertakings where delegation is even more severely limited, the agenda is full of administrative trivial. Inevitably the result of such crowded agenda is that large corporate issues which need presentation review and deliberation are often totally ignored or relegated to reports and statistics to be read at leisure. More so, because the same grounds would be gone over agenda during review sessions with the adminis trative Ministry who, in reality, assume the role of the super

Board. Non-official members of public enterprise Boards have often resented their extremely limited rcle and area of using contribution.

Ministers and secretaries of Government are not chairmen or directors in the public enterprises under their control by a decison of the Lok Sabha as far as the Union Government is concerned, Members of Parliament are also excluded generally from such Boards. In the enterprise under the control of the State Governments, however, this practice continues and it is not unconcerned to find Secretaries and Ministers as chairmen of public enterprises. Members of the Legislative Assemblies are often in such Boards. Needless to say that the process of decision-making will be quite complex and different in the presence of political persons from that in a purely professional Board.

Boards of private sector companies, in contrast, have a shorter and more business – the agenda. The agenda items are also different in character with financial and legal matters occupying an important place. There is more of presentation of information and more than information sharing. Very often, on important issues informal consultation would have already taken place and a tentative dicision arrived at which is then formalised at the Board. In contrast, decision alternatives is the public sector are more open-ended. this prevalent atmosphere is more democratic and discussions are not stifled. This, of course, is also conditioned by the style of the Chairman, and it is not entirely uncommon to the Chairmen of the Boards of public enterprises who control the agenda and the public rigidly and generally get the Board to these the decision they planned for.

III. The Chairman and the Board

The composition of the Board and the personalities of the Board members, their preference, areas of interest, equation with other Board members and with the Chairman and the Managing Director are factors with determine the dynamics of decision-making in a Board in a very large measure. Of course, the preeminent force is the chairman and the Managing Director. There is a difference between a Board which is composed by the Managing Director himself and such where there is a part-time Chairman It is not unusual to find the part-time Chairman sometimes usurping the role of the Managing Director where the latter is weaker in personality or competence and unable to cope with corporate crisis. It is the Chief Executive's role that is the crucial one.

From the Chief Executive's point of view the objective of every Board meeting is essentially to get certain decisions approved or disapproved as he plans, to tentatively feel the mind of the Board before issues are presented for decision, and to inform the Board on matters and developments to the extent he feels prudent to do. A successful Board meeting therefore depends a great deal on the clarity in the mind of the Chairman and the Managing Director, the home work done and the manner in which the meeting is conducted. It can be generally assumed that it is only the Chairman and the Managing Director who have taken the pains of going through all the agenda items carefully, and that the other Board members will have read or have views on certain matters only and not on all. In most cases these can be anticipated. Nevertheless, Board meetings may not always run on a predetermined course.

Some Chairmen allow discussions in the Board to be digressive and tangential with cross-conversations freely taking place. Such Boards cannot become very effective decision-making Boards. Some Chairmen may however selectively allow certain items to be defused like this, on which decisions are really not sught for. The more successful Chairman creates an atmosphere of free exchange of opinion to develop but knows when to bring it to a conclusion. This gives the Board members, particularly the non-officials, a sense of participation and positive contribution, even though in effect the contributions may not make much difference to the decision. A successful Chairman develops this skill and the intuition to anticipate the predispositions of the various Board members and deal with their responses adroitly. There are also some Chairmen who distinctly give the impression to other Board members of bulldozing. A resentment then builds up gradually which may either result in non-participation or a negative stance on the part of some Directors.

The Chairman's weight and power coefficient as perceived by the Board members is also an important factor. Ideally this power would vest in the Chairman not so much by the authority of his position but by the respect that he earns by virtue of his knowledge, conduct, personality, standing in the company and in the industry. But this may not always be so. An additional additional source of power arises from the equation of the Chairman with the controlling interests—in the case of public sector enterprises with the Government and the Minister; in the private companies from his equation with the controlling group or owners as well as his standing with the industry and the Government.

IV. The Composition of Boards

The composition of Boards vary widely. In companies which are closely held or family-owned, the Board consists largely of family members and other allied interest groups, and it is not uncommon to find grandfathers in the late seventies along with grand-sons in their early twenties on the same Board. It is not also uncommon to find in such companies that the decision-making power rests with a senior member of the owning group who may not even be on the Board. He may or may not attend Board meetings, but certainly sees that his decisions are endorsed. Where he attends the Board meeting informally he is the real Chairman.

In more professionally managed companies, particularly the Indian branches of foreign companies, the Boards are usual small and consist of a few functional director along with the Chairman and the Managing Director and a few others who are in the Board for their standing in the industry in Government service. Such Boards by their very nature are purposive, business like and deal with corporate issues and policies which have been well processed within the organisation. The latter includes the parent organisation who have the real say on issued that really matter. Boards of centrally owned public enterprise are also designde more or less, in the same model *viz.*, send functional heads who are given a service in the Board along with a representation of the administrative ministry and Ministry of Finance. A few non-officials are included representing either senior industry experience in the private sector, or so interest groups like national trade union leaders or other public enterprise of executives,

The three groups *viz.*, the company officials, the government officials and the non-officials, play distinctly different roles. The company officials are sponsors of proposed pertaining to their area and are expected generally support the Chairman and Managing Director. It is essentially a protagonist as well as supportive supplementary. It is not uncommon however, the functional director may hold a different roles from that of the Chairman. It becomes entirely a matter of the normal work relationship of the Chairman and the Managing Director with such directors as members of his team within the enterprise. Where there is good relationship and the chairman recognises the role of his colleague as director, as distinguished from his organisational role, the functional director can present his point of view in a constructive manner. Where this relationship does not exist, then the role can become negative. In some cases, an authoritarian Chairman asserts his hierarchical organisational relationship and stifles any price of dissidence. It can then cause tensions which would be carried into the organisation.

It has been observed in the case of multi-unit Boards where the chief executives of the units are represented, that the units are large enough to justify a local Board by themselves, formal or informal. In such cases the common reaction of the chief executives of the units is to have a Board of which he would be the Chairman, but not his departmental colleagues. Perhaps at the unit level to differentiation between the organisational relationship and the role of the subordinate as the equal colleague in the Board is more difficult to achieve. It is easier achieved in the Headquarters of the corporate body away multi-unit management.

The role of the government representative to the Boards of public enterprises has often been discussed and written about. The only Team of the Administrative Reforms Committee on Public Enterprises had given the views on this issue at great length. Here by the duality of the roles *viz.* as a director of the Board and as an official in the ministry becomes blurred. In fact, the primary view of a government official predominates in therefore, he can influence the course of decision-making to the extent he is aware of the likely government view on the issue, but he is unable to commit the government. Therefore, the decision remains virtually reserved for the government. He can and usually does perform a facilitating role in processing the decisions at the government level. But, this is by no means certain. The personality factor comes into play depending on whether he takes a very rigid, bureaucratic, non-committal view or a more positive facilitating and supportive stance. Levels of such government representation and the equation between the Chairman and the ministry therefore are important factors in the Board dynamics of the public enterprises.

The role of the part-time directors vary according to the interest of the individual and the manner in which the Chairman and others utilise the part-time director. It also depends a great deal on the manner in which such part-time directors are selected and the purpose they are expected to serve. In the public enterprises this is the prerogative of the minister to be exercised in consultation with the Chairman. These appointments also require approval of the Appointments Committee of the Cabinet. A recent press report indicates that all these appointments should also go through the Prime Minister's Secretariat. The part-time directors can play a very important role, particularly if they are specialists, on issues where their expertise can help good decision making. But, by and large, it appears that part-time directors, who have their own permanent interests and are not able to attend all Board meetings regularly, are not a vital part of the decision-making process of the Board. Consequently, they do perfrom many inconsequential roles, such as, quorum filling. Where Boards are 'packed' many part-time directors are expected to perform a nodding role to the Chairman's proposals. There are some who exercise the right to information or sank postponment of discussions on the ground of short notice, some perform a pure decorative role lending grace to the Board by their presence. To keep such Board members in good humour is a task of a Chairman, because of the possibility of retoring decisions, or damaging the image of the company by such members out of a feeling of being treated lightly.

Very few companies have representatives of trade unions on the Board. Much has been written on the subject. It is natural that such member would be constrained to take a stand on issues affecting the workmen, and also feel compelled occasionally to strongly express his dissatisfaction with the management at Board meetings. But he can be a usefull member of the Board because of many insigns he can bring into the Board which may not be available to the professional executives Here again, the contribution depends much on the personality of the individual but, as a duality of role is involved, the primary role becomes dominant one as in the case of government representatives.

The issue of government representation of the representation of financial institutions on the Board of private companies has assumed a great deal of importance because of the interventionist role of the government in the case of companies which become sick or where mismanagement comes to the notice of the government. For the last few years, there had been many case of irregular accounts and defaults. The question of effectiveness of the representatives of financial institutions on the Board of these companies has been raised and the government has enjoined upon the representatives as well as the representative of the financial institutions to take the more active and watchful role. In practice, however, this is difficult to achieve. By the very nature of a Board's function as an any body, it can only act on the information and knowledge available to it. Much great knowledge and information as to the realising of the situation are available with the Managing Director and those who are intimate connected with the organisation. The past time directors therefore have a very difficult task to anticipate and detect the right point of intervention at the Board. Apex financial institutions like the IDBI, for instance, the often faced with the delicate task of replacement of the key persons in the Board of company, when reviews and reports available with the financial institutions call for the intervention. It is extremely difficult of achieve this within the framework of the Company Law and other statutes. It need considerable skill in negotiation, manipulation and pressurisation to bring about the desire change. Such intervention, apart from the complications it creates, indirectly involve the financial institutions in the responsibility of managing the company—a task close beyond the normal role of financial institutions or a bank.

"Even today it is moot question whether appointment of a director or two (by the financial institutions) serves any real purpose and one has to ask whether and how a large cadre of knowledgeable and public-spirited professional directors can be assembled and put in place.........There is resistance not only to observing the financial norms precribed by the financial institutions, but even more to active involvement in major decisions and perhaps most to the threat of conversion of loans into equity. A practical way has to find out of this dilemma with perhaps greater awareness of each others seeds........ and greater professionalisation of management everywhere" (*Reserve Bank of India Bulletin*, Sept.-Oct. 79' page 725).

The position of the government directors under section 408 is not dissimilar. In such componies, usually a good many members of the earlier management continue and the government director has always an uneasy feeling of not knowing exactly what is happening unless the issues come to the surface and are brought before the Board formally.

Since Board meetings cannot be held subsequently, some companies adopt the device of a Committee of Directors which meets have frequently and can take immediate decisions, later ratified by the Board. In the use of section 408 companies this device the make for more uneasiness on the part of the government directors, apart from the permate the expenditure increases on account of sitting fee for the local members of the Board who form the Committee of Directors.

This is a trying task for the chairman, particularly when dividends are reduced or not declared. As long as dividends are maintained even from Reserves it is possible to keep back from the shareholders unfavourable trends and lapses, fairly successfully. A certain amount of heckling is part of the ritual and it is the Chairman's adroitness which can make the AGM a happy finale for the financial year or otherwise. There are, of course, other important issues of appointment of directors, adoption of accounts and the appointment of auditors. Normally these are routine, but in a particular company or in a particular year these may become tactical problems. In such cases considerable planning and preparation is necessary, otherwise unpredictable things may happen. In contrast, the Annual General Meeting of public enterprise companies are non-events lasting less than an hour.

A resent trend, following the curb on managerial emoluments, is, for directors to step down and become executives. If this trend continues, then a qualitative change is very likely to come about in the functioning of the Boards. Senior executives of a company, who have earned a seat on the Board and the prestige and perquisites that go with it in the normal course of events, would not now be on the Board but can they or will they really relinquish the roles which they played and continue to play in the organisation as top management and top decision-makers? This is hardly likely. If this becomes a widespread phenomenon, the Boards of Directors will have largely part-time directors, except the Managing Director, or will be packed with dummy directors, and a decision-making body will be evolved informally outside the formal Board. The implications of such a change in the structure at the apex of the company form can be far-reaching. Recently, a financial institution, whilst considering the application for assistance from a very well-established company, noted that the unit cancerned had no Managing Director. The person performing the Managing Director's functions was called the President, but had no seat on the Board The reason was obvious, but the Chairman of the financial institution felt that the company could be persuaded to have a more orthadox structure whereby a director of the Boad was in fect the chief executive with clear operational responsibility for the company. An officer of the financial institution who was on the Board of another unit under this group of companies which had, actually, a Managing Director narrated then his experience. He mentioned that the person who virtually presided over the Board meetings and took the decisions was not the Managing Director but a senior family member of the group, and it so happened that in some meetings even the Managing Director was not present.

V. Conclusion

The foregoing only validates the point with which I started this article that the content is more important than the form, and the reality of the working of a Board of Directors is quite different from what a reading of the Companies Act and the formal definitions would lead one to conclude.

The Board of Directors is a mechanism for reaching decisions which ultimately govern the fortunes of a joint stock company and all those who have relationships with the company. It is, therefore, a crucial instrument in the organisation and management of a firm. It has some degree of legal entity and is charged with responsibilities some of which are statutorily defined. Nevertheless it is a body of men and women and therefore act and operate within the dynamics which develops in any group. There are variables which are, to some extent, controllable or predictable because there are certain parameters and processes which govern the formation and functioning of this group; then are also corporate objectives which are measurable, and accountable. But there are many unknown variables in the form of individuals, their trends, motivations, preceptions and skills which are not predictable or controllable to any degree of precision. There are variations also in structure and composition according to the species of which they belong, such as, private limited companies, public limited companies, which owned by the Centre or the State Governments, jointly owned, closely held or share widely dispersed foreign controlled or family controlled, and so on. There are developments to indicate that there are economic and other forces at play which may bring about significant changes both in the form and content. This important organism, therefore is a worthy object of study and research of management scientists.

11

Boards: Form and Substance

N.K. ROY

The author is of the view that although in form and in law the Board is the company, in substance it is very different. The legal framework is entirely negative—only dont's and no do's. The Board minutes are far too abstracted to provide the researcher with any insight into the decision-making process. Company Chairman—especially, retired bureaucrats—are an euphemism for Company's public relations or liaison officers in Delhi. The role of the Chief Executive or Managing Director as a team leader with a unifying touch and a visionary acumen has been stressed. The irony of pussy cat mentality of Board members is also mentioned. The imbecility of public sector Boards also draws the writer's attention.

To write on the functioning of Boards of Directors in India is as hazardous a task is writing on the functioning of the government. There is, first, the problem of segregating form from substance; and, second, and more difficult, the identification of the power structure, the policy motivations, and the many undefined influences that determine the exercise of authority.

I. The Boards and The Law

The appointment and powers of the Board of Directors are prescribed in the Companies Act. Section 291 of the Act says specifically that subject to the provisions of the Act and the memorandum and articles of association of the company, the Board of directors of a company is entitled to exercise as such powers, and to do all such acts and things, as the company is authorised to exercise and do. If the government is the country for practical day to day purposes, subject only to provisions in the country's constitution; the Board is then the company, subject to the Companies Act and the company's constitution.

The specific constraints on the powers of the Board as prescribed in the Act are largely financial in nature. Powers to raise capital and loans, to invest and to dispose of assets to lend to a director, to remunerate a director or a close relative, to appoint a sole selling agent, to award a contract to a party in which a director is interested—these are some of the examples. Inevitably these provisions constitute a set of 'DONTS.'

Because of the 'negative' nature of the law—as of all laws, by and large—certain interesting practices develop. First, wherever the Act authorises delegation of duties, there is delegation, almost universally, to a Managing Diector or to a Committee (composed not necessarily of Director only), and the actions of the Managing Director are covered by appropriate ex-post-facto resolutions of the Board, Second, the Board minutes, which are subject to legal and audit scrutiny, are brief; the detailed logic behind decisions remains hidden in internal reports and notes presented to the Managing Director or to the Committee.

If, therefore, one were to attempt an evaluation of the management from the Board minutes, it will be futile. One will have to probe deeper into the working of the management or the Committee,

II. The Board Chairman

The role played by individual directors in a Board is determined largely by the way the Board is constituted. Some of the Board members may be wholetime executives, with overall responsibility for specific areas. Others may be non-executive directors—'outsiders' in common pariance—who represent specific interests, such as lending institutions or the government. A few outsiders may be there as nominees of the controlling interests or majority shareholders. The mc st common example of the last type of director is the Company Chairman, whose primary function in practice is to act as the company's chief public relations man at Delhi—the seat of the country's government. Many companies find the placement of their titular chief there of much practical value. (The number of top bureaucrats who, after retirement from government, today adorn the chairmanship of companies and are placed in Delhi will illustrate the point. In most cases their familiarity with the industry or its technology or its economics is minimal in company meetings their functions are limited to announcing dividends and hosting luncheons; the Chairman's statement made in the company's annual accounts is usual the handiwork of the company's staff).

This pattern is not universal. The public relations type non-executive chairman is seen mostly in 'foreign' companies incorporated in India, even after dilution of foreign capital in terms of FERA, and there are only a few exceptions. In established Indian companies with the controlling interest in certain families, the chairmanship is held by a family man who will have been involved in the business for a long time and may also be the Managing Director.

III. The Board and the Managing Director

The leadership in the Board is provided by the Managing Director. Major matters of policy on the direction of the companys growth, the adoption of new technology, the share of market to be secured, the financial viability of investment proposals, the procurement of finance, the appointment and placement of key management personnel: these are examples of matters that the Board has to decide, in addition to overseeing the committees of managers and technical staff under them, generally carry out evaluations and suggest choices between alternatives. But the initiation of proposals is the duty of the executive directors alone, who have distinct responsibilities. A full evaluation in the context of the total company interests requires a coordinating authority and a drive which is provided by the Managing Director. The extent to which individual directors take a total view individually is a matter that requires research. Some general observations are however permissible. A Managing Director with drive, imagination and great personal tenacity dominates the scene and often takes the company to great heights. But the nature of the job is such dictatotial tendencies, with intoterance of other views and pernicious shortsightedness, may sitence other views in the Board. The typical executive directors, keen on making further personal progress in the company, may be unwilling to antagonise the chief executive and may carry on as a yes-man, with disastrous consequences to the long-term interests of the company.

It is not that there are no remedies to such situations. In family managed companies, the play of family interests may provide a corrective. In other companies the chief executive is the nominee of the controlling interests, such as a foreign group, and these interests do not as a rule repose sufficient confidence in, or maintain contact with, other directors. There have been cases in which a foreign group have realised the mischief caused by a chief executive with a long tenure and have forced a change. But the change has occured too late for the good of the company.

The extent to which individual directors understand each important matter on the agenda is however a matter of some

doubt. Prof. Parkinson's famous satire on business decision making—*The Pursuit of Progress*—will be borne out as realistic by the experience of many who have sat on Boards. The time spent on a ten million rupee investment proposal may be less than that spent on the purchase of a one thousand rupee worth of ordinary equipment, because while only one or two may understand the first proposal, the second proposal is within the "point of vanishing interest" (Parkinson's phrase) of every one.

Public sector companies are a class by themselves. The Board's powers here are severely hamstrung by bureaucratic and political interference. Both technical and financial powers of the Board are subject to clearance by a number of ministries; the management of personnel by the Board is rendered almost impossible, again by ministrial interference, the direct access of unions to ministers, often the leadership of unions by MPs and MLAs; and there is the continuous exposure to inquiries by Parliamentary Committees, the Bureau of Public Enterprises and other public bodies. The ways in which these external influences impair initiative and decision making in the public sector are found in Mr. Bagaram Tulpule's observations on his experience at Durgapur Steel Plant ("Amidst Heat and Noise—Durgapur Recalled", AIMA). It is no wonder therefore that many public sector units today are unable to attract talent for executive positions; the authorities are recognising a 'management crisis' but are yet to spell out solutions.

IV. Conclusion

Ideally the Board of Directors should be constituted of professional men, with some years of experience in the industry, competence and skill in their specialised fields certainly, but also full identification with the total company interests. This is the kind of management that has worked wonders in countries with a longer history of industrial development than we have. The extent to which company directors in India satisfy these criteria could be an area of major research. The 'qualifications' of directons which the Company Law Department recognises are vague and inadequate. The Boards function within the four corners of Company Law. The extent to which they function as instruments of progress, the qualities and style of functioning that make the companies go forward, are worthy of a deeper investigation.

This short note is based on the author's personal experience, which is necessarily of a limited nature, and on the experience of friends who have confided in him but where must, necessarily, remain unnamed.

12

Managing A Board of Directors

N. L. HINGORANI

This article emphasises harmonious team working as the keynote of managing Boards. Board members, even if they happen to represent different interest groups, must not harbour nations similar to those of parliamentary opposition benches. Many a times Board members face the dilemma of personal convictions not matching with those of the group or organisation they belong to. Nor should the nominating organisation by pass its nominee director and settle issues directly with the concerned enterprise. The author also observes that Boards usually become a 'decision-taking body, whereas 'decision-making' is done by a sellect few only. The so-called professional directors rarely display any sense of involvement in or enduring commitment to the organisation. The author suggests that directors should belong to four broad groups: a core managerial group, a group which will not stake its reputation with a mismanaged organisation, a group representing major shareholders, and a group representing lenders. The presence of organisation's senior executives on the Board tends to reduce the tenor of discussions to the level of routine, operational matters. Agendas, minutes, and reporting to shareholders all leave much scope for improvement in candour and authenticity.

I. Missing Harmony in Boards

A Board of directors of a company is impected to be a homogenous group, elected by shareholders, reconciling diverse interests. Usually, the Board comprises members known and near to the effective managerial group turning a substantial part of share capital. However, there are always compromises on account of various interest groups especially among managerial, shareholder and lender groups. This is more so in larger and older companies where shareholdings are widely diffused and growth is achieved mainly through borrowings. It is extremely important that no member of the Board should have a feeling of 'belonging to opposition.' Once the idea of opposition digs in, the working of the Board becomes unpleasant, complicated and dragging. There would be differences of opinion right from the recording of minutes to the validity and sufficient of information supplied to the members, as also to day-to-day actions of shop floor managers. There is no bar to a Board member's access to company act and the data could be misutilised. Such actions lead to open hostility, affecting the working of me company adversely. It is for the managerial group in the Board to see that this sense of opposition does not get created. If it has been created it must get resolved immediately. Time and again group takeovers, internal fights and voting inside the Boards have created a management impasse which could not be resolved without changing the Board membership for differ or worse, for the sake of maintaining internal harmony among the members on the Board.

Among the Boards with internal harmony one could always discern a greater degree of consultation irrespective of the intererest group represented by individual directors. However, there are structures who as individuals do not consider it proper for themselves to endorse a number of decisions, despite their personal acceptance because of their representative capacity on the Board. Either their mandate is not clear or the decision is too big for their competence. Getting clearance from their controlling organisation could be formal or informal. So long as it remains informal, there is usually on problem. However, if formal reference as resorted in the controlling or even promoting organisation has to take a view, may be down the line or up the line, and the decision becomes a matter of detailed review when would results own time. There are bound to be uncomfortable questions from and differences of opinion strong those who are neither involved in the management of the company, nor kenw enough about various aspects of the company. Once again, if too many things are referred to outside the Board management at Board level becomes increing and many matters in the interest of the company are just not brought up because these would need outside reference and approval.

II. The Decision Process

There is another aspect of cross interesting on the Board. Many a management groups would get their issues and problems clears with the nominating organisation direct without taking the director into confidence. On the other hand, the nominating organisation is not in a position to keep its nominee informed. The obvious result is a misunderstanding at the Board meeting where the representative director could be toeing different line of action. This is general avoidable if the management of the companies so desires. It is in the interest of the companies to follow the path of creating greater and better understanding among the Board members.

Fear of leakage of information in sensitive negotiations sometimes makes it incumber upon a small group of directors involved negotiations to keep back the information from the Board. This would be specially true in say, labour negotiations, take own bids, investment negotiations appoinment to top management positions, etc. In success cases the management cannot avoid a situation of presenting an accomplished fact to the Board of directors, with virtually no option for deciding otherwise. However, the impact of such a situation can be greatly softened if most of the Board members are kept informed informally and their views, if any collected and kept in view while negotiating. Known risks of leakage should be clearly avoided. Experience and tact greatly heps in these issues. The board is a 'decision-taking' body leaving the 'decision-making' to others, and mainly to a few from among the Board.

III. The Composition of Boards

In view of the importance of the decision-making process it is very important to carefully look at the composition of the Board. There have to be a few directors personally involved in the working of the company with some motivation. It could be lure of money, ego satisfaction, or mere prestige. Unless and until there is total involvement of some directors beyond mere salary-servant relationship, it would not be possible to manage a company dynamically. A Board cannot have members totally dispassionate and uninvolved, sitting in judgement on the results of the company. Such directors are sometimes called professionals but their interest in the company ends each time with the meeting of the Board getting over. In many weak companies there is a majority of such professionals who fail to give any direction to the company but keep on questioning the working of the company and suggesting restrictive conditions. This definitely proves to be demoralising for the operating executives, and the company loses all policy guidelines as well as sense of direction. There are many enquiries into the causes of failures, instead of a purposeful direction towards better working. This is a sure way of driving a company towards closure, and some times it could help when closure is really desired.

A suggestion is made about personal involvement through equity stake. Most of the managements holding equity in companies are not very badly affected by loss of dividend, or even capital value of equity held by them. In comparison to the total equity on one side and their personal incomes on the other, owned equity and dividends do not carry much meaning to them except as a venicle providing control over the management of the company. Thus, it is the managerial remuneration and other trading arrangements that interest the management financially. Closure is the biggest threat to such managements. 'When it comes to the crunch they would prefer to sell off their interest or even walk out of the management, rather than take responsibility for closure and face many problems under the law as directors of a non-working company. It is not queer to find a number of companies working for years without declaring dividend and even sustaining continued losses. Such companies, when held by a large number of shareholders with no control, lead to suffering and losses for the shareholder only.

While making a choice for Board membership it is essential to have a core managerial group that would take the initiate and fulfil the traditional ownership-management function, irrespective of their own holding. It should be possible to identify the owners of the company as known to the outside world. It is equally important for this group to watch its own interest as owners and take all appropriate action against its own dislodgement. The second identifiable group in the Board should be that of persons who would not easily stake their reputation with companies not likely to succeed. These individuals, though not well-versed with the affairs of that company, would always strive to provide some direction when things appear to be going wrong. It is a great moral check on the owner group. Any such director leaving the Board should be a clear indicator of the affairs of the company. The third group should represent the major shareholders in the event of owners not being major shareholders themselves. With widely diffused holdings a minority shareholding group as directors would also serve the purpose. The basic idea is to watch the general direction in which the company is moving, and to provide support to the management in achieving the growth path. This support proves very helpful in achieving credibility on the market and raise funds much more easily. In the event of the company being heavily debt financed it becomes essential to have a fourth group, that of lenders. Every lender with stakes currently higher than all others must safeguard his own interest in the context of various styles of management in various companies. A lender needs a bridge with the company for getting appropriate information and proper feel about the company. Not that the lending decisions would get altered, but the debt would get better supervised and growing confidence can be placed in the management of the company for all future dealings. Lenders are not there to manage but to help improve at least the financial stability of the company.

In forming a Board the various groups suggested could always be supported by professionals with technical, legal, financial, administrative and other related expertise to fill the need of such qualified persons as are not available in the other groups suggested. The over-riding consideration has always to be of providing a harmonious Board that would primarily safeguard the interest of the company. The size of the Board in this context becomes crucial. The size of a board usually varies from 7 to 12 directors. Allowing for absentees, there would generally be 4 to 8 members present. These members form the core of the Board. In larger companies with diverse ownership the number of directors is 15. All state/government directors are in addition. A Board could thus have more than 20 members. In such large Boards the avenues for discussion get reduced. Same would be the case with attendance of say 3-5 directors. An attendance of 7 directors could be considered good for a meaningful participative discussion. However, some directors would not just discuss anything. An allowance has to be made for their presence also. It has become a common practice to invite one or more operating executives to the Board. This practice is taking firmer roots with restrictions being applied to remuneration on directors acting as executives of companies. The function of these executives is usually to assist the Chairman with information on various agenda items or questions put by board members. However, with the present of executives the accent of discussions is on operating issues and day-to-day problem rather than policy issues or issues of strategic importance.

IV. The Board agenda and Minutes

The agenda for Board meetings is sent to the members generally a few days in advance. From the management point of view it contains routine items and other items. Routines items may relate to production, sales, finance banking, share transfers, etc. On the non-routine side would be capital expenditure periodic profits, donators and charities budgets, annual accounts, etc. Most of the items are for reporting on which stray queried could be raised. There is a possibility of some discussion on capital expenditure and profit position. Accounts are generally signature without a discussion and all enabling resolutions passed. The agenda items never contains policy issues for the Board before the every matters such as personnel policy, dividend policy, marketing policy, borrowing policy, to give some examples, do not get concretised in a discussion ahead of the problem. The discussion does take place when the company is faced with a problem. It usually centres around past corporate experience, and does not crystallise into a policy paper. Some companies do have a corporate planning cell but the issues handled deal more with day-to-day matters rather than policy. Barring in a few companies, the Boards hardly perform any monitoring function beyond looking at the physical targets of achievement and their fulfilment. Explanations offered for non-fulfilment by the executives are generally accepted by the Board, despite information to the contrary being also available at other places in the agenda or in past agenda papers. There is a general tenor of sympathy with the executives irrespective of their immediate past performance. Moreover, achievement of targets, specially the profit target, bars all questions. In the event of companies being in financial difficulties, discussions mostly centre around the means of financing continued shortage of funds on an ad hoc basis. The chairman of the meeting usually goes over each item and takes up time elaborating on each item. Most of the time of the meeting is taken up by these elaborations. Another style adopted is calling an agenda item and taking for comments. Only those who have and the papers in great detail and have been attending meetings regularly can comment in the agenda. There would be very few such members. From among them only some would like to make a comment. A brief accussion could arise only when something to specifically brought to the notice of other mambers by a member commenting on the agenda. The matter may become serious only if some senior members of the Board supports such comments. Nominee directors financial institutions, (specially employees of the institution) raise many points and comments which do not interest other members. However, these are respected in the meeting without much follew-up action, except where the matter relates to procedures or additional information, which it does most of the times.

Recording of discussions in the minutes is usually restricted to the decisions of the meeting. Sometimes, comments made by members which would support the management point of view also get recorded. Observations reflecting adversely on the management are either not recorded, or get cleverly recorded unless and until a member insists on specific words to be recorded, or missing comments to be put on record. This is rather unusual but does happen once in a while. The chairman of the meeting foces a hard task when minutes get challenged or amended from time to time.

V. Information Sharing

Professional directors, who become chairmen, really like to share as much information with the members as possible, at the meeting itself. Besides, given elaborate explanations on the agenda items, a lot of informal information gets shared at the meetings. There is generally an anxiety to take the Board fully into confidence and thus share responsibility appropriately. This also helps him in seeking the assistance of individual Board members on specific tasks, he would like to get done through individuals having rapport with the concerned outsiders, were they would be more effective as person or as croressional experts.

In reporting to the shareholders all directors age to the putting up of as good a picture as possible depending on the circumstances of each company. The directors' report is drafted by the executives. Usually, last year's report is picked up and the pattern is followed. If the results are better all adverse factors are pointed out and no specific helping factors generally get enunciated. On the other hand, if the results are worse all adverse factors get emphasised without plantifying any of them in relation to the operations of the company. In a way a lot of similarity could be discerned among these reports despite the diversity of the nature of operations. Rising prices, higher interest rates, labour, power, transport, etc. would always be quoted as adverse factors irrespective of the fact that some must have helped in improving the operating results of the company. The entire emphasis is on ruppee profits. All directors become signaturies to these reports. It is difficult for each director to evaluate the propriety of the report.

The chairman's speech to the shareholders is his personal document reflecting mostly his personal views. In some cases directors get the crucial copy of the report after it gets published in the press. The views need not be subscribed to by individual members of the Board. Much is not said about the company's operations in this speech. But sometimes, the personal views prove to be pretty embarrassing for the members of the Board as these are identified with the company by outsiders as well as executives working within the company. Any philosophical statement, say, on industrial relations or taxation policy could be deemed as a policy statement of the company and likely to get quoted in discussion and every in negotiations.

VI. Conclusion

A Board by itself being a collection of diverse persons with varying interests, postage a number of problems to be tackled at the Board level itself. But, being a self-management unit, everything gets resolved within as group. Anything going outside for resolution really indicates the weakness of the Board and that of the company as a unit of management. Managing a Board is not the problem of an individual who chairs the Board, but that of all the members of the Board who are equally important, and only one of whom happens to be the chairman but not the leader. A Board is thus a peculiar unit management, without any time or functions divisions but with all the responsibility.

13

The Functioning of Boards of Directors in India

G. LAKSHMINARAYANAN

The author argues in this arcticle that both workers and management should cease to regard the results of employee participation merely in the negative sense of non-strike or non-lockout. The contributions made by nominee directors from financial institutions to the Boards of assisted companies are worthwhile, in many cases, for adoption even by non-assisted companies. The author highly commends the excellent management information system supporting the Board meetings in public enterprises. The participation by civil servants in such Boards has also been found to be of a very high order. The evaluation made of Boards of foreign companies has not been complimentary though the author thinks that the Chairmen of Boards should be persons other than the Chief Executive. And such Chairmen should be like Speakers who speak sparingly.

I. Corporate Management on Trial

"The typical well-orchestrated board meeting with the quick agenda, followed by some report of general interest on the operation of the business, followed by lunch, all on light schedule, induces an atmosphere of compliance and noninquiry that may be dangerous."[1] This, in the land of free enterprise and corporate supremacy. Yet, 'body corporate' is mankind's most innovative concept, with perpetual succession and a common fluel—until dissolved by liquidation or struck out of the Register maintained by the Register of Companies. It is an emergence from the limitations of proprietary/partnership practically unknown to one another subscribing to a common purpose, with liability of each of them limited to the share they own. A company is distinct and separate from the shareholders as well as those who control it. The company's property belongs to itself and not to the individuals who constitute it, The human agency through whom a company acts any by whom its affairs are managed are called directors, and collectively the 'Board of Directors'. A director has power to bind the company when acting as a Board, but has no power whatever individually unless specially authorised by the Board. Legally, the Board of Directors can exercise all the powers of the Memorandum and Articles of the company. The shareholders cannot usurp the powers that the Articles of the company vest in the Board of Directors any more than the Boards cannot usurp the powers that Articles vest in the general body of the shareholders.

II. Intent and Reality

That is the intent, but what is the reality? "Private enterprise is under attack..............Each month brings a new tide of sensational disclosures. Demands for reform are growing. Government agencies are readying new controls. Business leaders are challenged to stand up and speak against the misdeeds of their peers..............One issue often raised through all this is 'What about the boards of directors? They have the responsibility for managing their corporations according to law. Chief Executive Officer acts only through powers they delegate."[2] In India 334 large-scale industries each enjoying credit facilities of Rs. 1 crore and more with outstanding bank credit of Rs. 983 crores were deemed 'sick' as of September 1978,—a disquieting increase from 270 units with Rs. 774 crores bank credit a year before. The very size of the credit units must have taken the operations of these industries through the scrutiny of their respective Boards, and periodic viability tests of the credit institutions concerned. Undoubtedly, external developments beyond the control of the corporate managements must have cast their shadow, but the Boards of Directors are not mere passive spectators. A team of experts of the Central Government which probed the working of a State Electricity Board has allegedly found the Board guilty of violation or occounts, massive diversion of resources and misuse of Rural Electrification Corporation loans.[3]

III. A Measure of Change 1948-49 to 1976-77

The community has vital stake in the corporate enterprise,—not merely the magnitude of savings invested in the corporate sector, but its scope in initiating "a process of development which will raise living stardards and open out to the people new opportunities for a richer and more varied life. Factory establishments accounted for mere 6.6 per cent of India's national income for the year 1948-49, and hardly 1.8 per cent of the country's working population was engaged industry. India entered an era of planning economic development with a view to correcting the imbalance through rapid industrialisation with emphasis on the development heavy industries and expansion of employment opportunity. During the uninterrupts operation of the first three five year plan 1951-52 to 19)5-66 the public sector out reached the staggering level of Rs. 15 200 crores and private sector investment Rs. 9090 crores.[4] Institutional agencies were created to facilitate such massive investment—Industrial Finance Corporation of India (1948). Industrial Credit and

Investment Corporation of India (1955), and Industries Development Bank of India (1964). Simultaneously, a chain of national laboratories and research institutions were set up and the Atomic Energy Commission (India) began sponsoring research in nuclear science. Institutes of Technology were established Kharagpur, Bombay, Madras and Kanpur, as the premier Indian Institute of Science challenge of modern era Likewise management science which is the very core of economic advancement received a welcome charter; courses in business management were introduced in several universities and three All-India management institutes were established, the Indian Institute of Mınagement Ahmedabad in association with the Harvard Business School, the Indian Insitute of Management Calcutta with the assistance and a similar institute at Bangalore. And, the corporate structure is the chief instrument of this profound transformation. In 1977-78, twenty nine years since 1948-49, mining and manufacturing contributed 24.3 per cent of net domestic product, Rs. 17,897 crores out of Rs. 73,389 (at current prices).[5] The following table illustrates a statistical measure of structure of industries in 1976-77.[6]

	Factories (Numbers)	*Employment ('000 employees)*	*Productive capital (Rs. Crores)*	*Value of output (Rs. Crores)*
Public Sector	3,713	1.579	13,121	7,506
Joint Sector	1,408	383	1,615	2,570
Private Sector	76,167	4,687	8,503	24,015
Total	81,277	6,649	23,239	34 091

IV. Professional and Academics on Boards

1967 was an eventful year in Indian corporate history. Corporate banking in India remained 'Commercial' for decades and was oriented to the collateral concept in its lending operations. Bulk of its lending found its way therefore to men with property leaving the rest of the people untouched by the bles-sing of bank credit. Government therefore introduced the theme of 'social control', and as a corollary brought about a sea-change in the composition of corporate bank Boards. An amendment to the Banking Regulation Act, 1949 laid down that not less than fifty-one per cent of the total number of the Board of Directors shall consist of persons, who—(a) shall have special knowledge or practical experience in respect of one or more of the following matters, namely—accountancy, agricul-ture and rural economy banking, coöperation, economics, finance, low, small-scale industry (Section 10-A), and that every Chairman of the Board of directors of the banking company shall be in the whole-time employment of such company (Section 10-B). Chartered Accountants, economists, manage-ment specialists, academics, small-scale industrialists. co-opera-tors and agricultural experts were brought on to the Boards of these core-institutions in the financial sphere. The new composi-tion brought about a profound change to the approach and activity in the banking sphere. The nationalisation of fourteen major banks in 1969 gave a further fillip to this process, and the wind of change began blowing into other sectors of corporate business as well. Many an enlighlened enterprises voluntarily welcomed a broader composition of Board member-ship, credit planning, performance budgeting, industry-profiles and the like got an entry into the banking threshold and these, in turn, brought about a market change in their policy and perspective.

V. Employees as Directors

"The State shall take steps, by suitable legislation or in any other way, to secure the participation of workers in the manage-ment of undertakings, establishment or other organisations engaged in any industry" so runs Articles 43A of the Directive Principles embodied in the Constitution of India. In a memo-randum to the High-powered Expert Committee on Companies and MRTP Acts, the Indian National Trade Union Congress stated that workers by virtue of the investment of their labour are equal partners in the establishment and therefore should have equal representation with the shareholders on the Board. They also asked for place a for workers from the lowest shop-floor level to the highest decision making level. It was the Nationalised banking sector again that heralded this induction. Section 3 of the Banking Companies (Acquisition and Transfer of Undertakings) Act 1970 lays down that the Central Government shall constitute the Board of a nationalised bank to include one Director from employees of the bank who are workmen. and one Director from the employees of the bank who are not workmen; the representatives of both the segments have been occurying their places on the Boards of the fourteen nationalised banks for many years. with one may say, satisfactory experience, although contradictory opinions have been aired from time to time. The State Bank of India, though brought to public sector in 1956, had this consummation only later, following the amendment of the State Bank of India Act in 1977. A representative each from the workmen and non-workmen staff were inducted to the Board in April 1978 and the Board functions as a cohesive team. There have been interruptions in the functioning of the nationalised banks as well as the State Bank of India. But one could not hope for uninterupted working of banks in an atmosphere surcharged with strife, merely because employee representatives participate at the highest decision-making level. The Central Government have reserved two places in the sixteen member Board of the Life Insurance Corporation of India. one from among Class I and Class II employees, and another from Class III and less IV employees, but they have not yet joined the Board obviously for want of agreement on the selection process. In any case, the employee director concept has not percolated to other segments of the corporate sector. Even the High-powered Expert Committee (Sache Committee) appears to be halting in it recommendations in the matter of employee represention on the Boards. The Committee estimates that some 1177 companies employee 500 to 999 workers each, and another 1640 companies employ 1000 or more workers each, and recommends in the first phase employee representation on the Boards of companies with 1000 and more employees but even on this it is indecisive. The Committee refers to two-tier management structure in Germany, the management board consists of senior executives and the higher supervisory board where alone employee the represented. The Committee further observe that the white paper on Industrial Democrate presented to the U K. Parliament prefers two-tier system, whether or not employee are to have representation on Board law (Para 11-25). There appears to be considerable misgivings on the part of academics as well. C.K. Johri opines that the idea of workers participation in management "has remained an attractive political wish that is difficult to translate into a concrete goal backed by the legislative and administrative means of practical implementation."[7] K.K. Chaudhuri examines the recent experience in worker participation through Works Committees, Joint Management Councils, Workers' Directors etc. and concludes that "As against all these attempts towards participation, it is well known that the formal consultative institutions......have hardly found acceptance among managements and employees or fulfilled the objectives for which they were promoted."[8] Despite such harsh criticisms,—perhaps because of that,—corporate managements in India as well as workers' organisations should accept the challenge and move towards an era of employee participation from the lowest to the highest level. And, both sides should cease to think merely of forging conditions of non-strike and non-lockout as the reward for worker participation. This concept should be seen in a larger perspective as demonstrating the worth-whileness of participation of the two segments in the mighty corporate enterprise whose franchise is beyond the confines of management and labour. The establishment of the Joint Consultative Council of Management at the Tata Iron and Steel Company in 1959 is a landmark in industrial relations, and despite temporary aberrations this concept has stood the test of time. Later in the same year, the Chairman of the Kannan Devan Planters' Association went on to say" our future depends on the extent to which we can convince public opinion in the widest future of the worth of our enterprise to the community. If we cannot show to our own workers that we are giving them a square deal, there is little hope for our activities in any larger sphere." Can there be a more forceful exhortation?

VI. Nominee Directors

Man is a traditional 'animal'. Change takes time, as witness the misconception on the role of nominee-directors appointed by the financial institutions and the convertibility clause that goes with certain specified types of assistance. The IDBI Chairman's statement (September 29, 1979) has this to say on the convertibility clause: "Despite all clarifications given, as well as assurance that the clause is neither intended for back-door nationalisation nor as an instrument to wrest management control, the Clause continues to act as a damper to investment". Since its inception, the IDBI has disbursed assistance to the extent of Rs. 2776 crores upto June 1979 which is expected to catalyse investment of the order of Rs. 9100 crores. The term-financing institutions have collectively disbursed total assistance of Rs. 5045 crores upto 31st March, 1979. In this promotional endeavour, the financial institutions provide not only financial assistance. but act as friend, philosopher and guide in the entire spectrum of promotional collaboration. Finance-wise the major contribution comes from sources other than the promoters, one or the other financial institution acting as the lead institution. The minimum contribution expected from the promoters ranges from 10 per cent to 20 per cent of total project cost, the percentage going lower on a slab basis for projects costing more than Rs. 25 crores. In the context of the predominant interets of institutions, far in excess of that of promoters, the Industrial Licencing Policy Enquiry Committee recommended both the convertibility clause and the appointment of nominee—directors and the Government of India had issued guidelines for the implementation of the recommendations in the year 1971, and the financial institutions have been systematically nominating directors on the Boards of assisted companies. As at end of 1976, the IDBI, IFCI and ICICI had 638 nominees on the boards of assisted companies. 161 of these were non-officials.[9]

The financial institutions clearly spelt out the role of their nominees in their appointment letters. With a view however to focusing on ihe importance of the matter, the Management Development Institute—this Institute has been set up under the auspices of the IFCI—organised a seminar in January 1975 "to consider and articulate the role and responsibilities and functions and obligations" of nominee-directors. It was reaffirmed that nominee-directors' role was "like any other director, to further the company's objectives which should by and large converge with the interest of the financial institutions and shareholders. The nominee-director should perform this role normally without interference in the day-to-day working of the company, by supporting all measures for the promotion of productive efficiency within the framework of government policies and by active participation in policy formulation on important aspects of the company's operations."[10] Apart from "the maintenance of law-and-order duty" for ensuring fulfilment of various statutory obligations by the assisted companies, the nominee-directors are to help in decision-making and foster a balanced regard to the clairs of the nominating institutions, the company shareholders, the workers and the community. He is to promote examinator by the Board, policy issues relative to saes purchases, investment, appointment of key personnel, preparation and review of periodic capital and performance budgets. He is to help inducting a competent professional management team and the setting up of an appropriate review end monitoring system. In fact, the objectives and practice are so salutary that the nominee-director is a source of strength to the company. One could go so far as to commend that the practices that Institutions call upon their nominees to foster may well be useful even to many non-assisted companies which have not adopeed such wholesome practices.

VII. Boards of Public Sector and Multi-National Companies

As of 31 March 1978, 49179 companies limited by shares were at work in India, 8186 public limited companies with Rs. 2905 crores paid-up capital, and 40993 private limited companies with Rs. 8514 crores paid-up capital. Of these, 745 were Government companies, 300 public limited with Rs. 725 crores paid-up capital and 445 private limited with Rs. 7802 crores paid-up capital 473 foreign companies were operating in India as on 31 March 1978, 265 of them incorporated in UK, and 80 companies incorporated in USA.[11]

As of 31st March, 1977, 145 Central Government undertakings were at work with an investment (equity and loan) of Rs. 11,097 crorcs. They had Rs. 14,542 crores turn-over. By their very nature, the composition of the Boards of Government of companies is largely from within the company, civil servants nominated by the Government, and others nominated by Government, financial institutions. One characteristic feature of the functioning of these Boards is the excellent managemen information system and the clarity and depth of their presentation to the Board. Minuting again is of high order, salien points raised by each director are carried and point-by-poin notes on follow-up action are placed at the next meeting Participation by civil servants nominated to the Boards is profound, they are well-informed, progressive and contribute to setting the proper tone at Board Meetings, quite contrary to popular misconceptions. It happened many years ago that a Government nominee was confronted with a decision on granting credit facilities for a substantial amount to a basic industry which then was not in a happy financial situation. The management of the unit had also a political angle. The matter was discussed all length, he agreed that the decision was to be taken purely on business principles. But this had its echo shortly thereafter, in that a query was raised whether he should not have consulted the Government in advance. He firmly held that his role as director of the institution was diffcrent from his duties as Government servant and had he to combine the roles, he would do justice neither to the Government nor to the institution. And this exemplary stand was warmly upheld by the highest authority in the ministry.

However, it has also happened in some Government companies—such instances are fortunately not many—that forward planning in regard to future investments on participated cash surpluses has not been timely, and in fact some companies with low-cost investment and consequent heavy caeh build up have been slow to plough back long further investment activity and convert idle cash resources into promising investment in existing or allied sectors. This is a wastage of scarce resources, and public sector companies should be alerted about investment avenues and consequent higher return to the exchequer.

The functioning of the Boards of multi-nationals and their Indian associate companies has its special features too. In one large industry in which three foreign collaborators participate (all three from the same foreign country) all the three companies have appointed the same executive of the Indian company as their alternate director, and in fact when he wrote to the three companies on a matter requiring consultation, they promptly advised their alternate to seek advice in future from any one of them only, so that he would not have to face the possible situation of conflicting advices from the three companies. They wrote that the one company to whom the alternate diector would write in the future would decide if any consultation was called for with the other two, and in that event it would be taken care of at their end. Just four Board meetings are held by the company in a year, in accordance with the minimum requirements of law. There are no committees of the Board either. Paper-work for Board meetings is fair, but generally not as detailed as in the case of Government companies. But the multinational companies and their associate companies have generally two prominant features: the eye on profit, and timely meeting of obligations. But the eye-on-profit approach could lead to distortton in the company's strength and stabilty, as excessive concern for profit could detract from farsighted investment goals and consequent erosion of the company's future viability. In fact, it did happen so even in respect of a reputed company. Successive chief executives seconded byt he foreign company so outbid each other in registering higher profit, that its investment in plant was almost becoming obsolete/non-competitive, and the company had to reverse this trend through seeking soft-loan modernisation.

VIII. Private Sector—Parameters of Assessment

Evaluation standards of the private sector Boards has necessarily to be different from public sector as well multi-nationals/ associate companies. Public sector companies are closely controlled by the Government—perhaps over-controlled, their capital and performance budgets are reviewed in depth and corrective action when needed is swift and decisive. Further, Government companies are geared more to social costs and social benefits, and parameters of public sector companies are markedly different from those of public limited companies in the private sector. As in the case of Government, public sector companies cannot go bankrupt, but there is no such certainty in the private sector. Multi-nationals and their Indian associates too have special fields of activity, usually in the essential and high-profit areas. Performance assessment of these managements cannot therefore be the same for appraising the functioning of the Boards of private sector bodies corporate. There is so much of a gap between the shareholder-owner and the Boards of directors who exercise the powers of the company that, should the company go sick, the shareholder has virtually no remedy even if he loses his share capital. It is in this class of companies therefore that the functioning of the Boards has a wider impact, economic, social and political. How to make the Board effective has been the million dollar question even in economically advanced countries. Myles L. Mace makes a brutally frank point when he says that the old concept that the stock, holders elect the Board, and the Board selects the management, is fiction. It just does not apply to to-day's large corporations. The Board does not select the management; the management selects the Board Mr. Kenneth R. Andrews says "The revival of the board of directors as an important instrument of corporate management has been on the agenda of unfinished business for a long time." "Yet the first principles of effective management are still first principles and cannot be repealed...... The job of managing a modern corporation is too demanding and too complex........someone must always be in charge. The challenge is how to ge, the best of both worlds, the energy and decisiveness of a strong chief executive and the balancing involvement of a thoughtful and informed board of directors", says Louis W. Cabot.[12]

IX. Conclusion

Necessarily, the health of a body corporate—from the community's, from the workers' and from the shareholders' standpoint—has to be the joint responsibility of the top management and the Board. It is the Board's primary responsibility to determine policy lay down the goals, in consulation with and the concurrence of the chief executive. Having done so, it should be unsparing in ensuring performance of task laid. And, it is the chief executive's responsibility to conduct the enterprise to reach the goals set, and in that domain, the directors shall have no entry. Thus set, one would lay down that the Chairman of the Board shall be a person other than the chief executive. The chief executive cannot report to himself. Then again, the majority of the Board members should be from outside, so that they rise from the immediate preoccupations of the executives, and perceive matters from a broader spectrum. The subject matters coming up to the Board should be selective, important, well documented and submitted to the directors sufficiently in advance. The management should not irrevocably commit itself to any particular approach, but must keep an open mind. The discussion should be free and as largely participative as may, and to this end the Chairman himself should foster meaningful participation, and often put himself in the position of the Speaker, the one who speaks least and who speaks last. An eminent professional chief executive of a major industry nominated on the Board of an important public institution remarked that it was always a pleasure to hear his chairman speak, but that the Chairman would always speak and the directors never. That, of course, may be an exceptional case, but the moral is not out of place. Again, while the corporate sector as a major force in the economic and sector welfarc of the community has a duty to bring to bear the highest of professional and eithical standards always, one could be proud that despite aberrations here and there, the well organised and well conceived segment of the corporate sector has fared admirably well, and with continuing refinements will set for itself yet higher standards of conduct. To the still errant, one may perhaps say with Richard Hildreth in a lighter vein!

> "You set up a National Bank to watch the other banks; but who watches the watcher? Where there is but one watchman in a city albeit the same be a most 'grave and ancient watchman.' Yet does it generally happen, that he betaketh himself soon after twilight to the watch-house, and there most quietly and severely sleepeth out his watch till his coat be stolen, or the city is set on fire with the candle from his own lanthorn. When it is burning and the engines are already at work, he opened his eyes at last and bawls fire! as lustily as though he had been the first to make the discovery. Is it not far better to dismiss the watchman, and so arrange things that it shall be for the interest of the rogues to watch and betray each other's roguery."[13]

REFERENCES

1. Chandler, Marvin, "It's time to clean up the boardroom." *Harvard Business Review Sept.-Oct.* 1975.
2. Cabot, Louis W. on an 'Effective Board'—*Harvard Business Review* Sept.-Oct. 1976.
3. *The Economic Times*, 16 Sept., 1979.
4. *India, 1979*, p. 201.
5. Centre for Monitoring Indian Economy, October 1979—Table 7.4.
6. *Ibid.*, Table—12.1.
7. 'Worker Participation in Management: Style and Substance—*National Labour Institute Bulletin* Jan.-Feb. 1979.
8. 'Idea and Reality of Workers' Participation on Management in India—*Economic and Political Weekly*, Nov. 1979. M. 118.
9. Roy, R.K. *Prajnan*, Jan.-Mar. 1977.

10. Madan B.K. *Role of Nominee—Directors of Financial Institutions*, page (vi).

11. *India, 1979*, pp. 192 and 196.

12. 'The President and the Board of Directors', *Harvard Business Review* Mar.-Apr. 1972.

13. Richard Hidreth, History of Banks, 1837.

14

Social and Value Perspectives of Effective Management

T.A. MATHIAS, S.J.

Given the economic and social realities of the Indian scene, what should be industry's response ? This paper considers the various views on the social responsibility of business and whether profits should belong to the shareholders only or be used to better social and national life in a variety of ways. Enumerating the areas of social responsibility, the author concludes that if the social responsibility of business houses is to be meaningful, it must have worker support, which can be ensured through effective communication.

The economic and social realities of the Indian scene can be summarized as follows: a vast land, with large resources in many important areas, but with some important gaps, an enormous, growing, increasingly conscious, highly individualistic population; a reasonably well-developed industrial infrastructure with, however, critical shortages in key areas such as power; a rising GNP and per capita income which is most unevenly distributed, resulting in a situation where a majority of the population live in grinding poverty and a minority in relative affluence.

Business and Social Concern the Negative View

What should be industry's response in this situation ? One view expressed with great force by on less a person than Nobel Prize Economist. Milton Friedman, is that business has nothing whatever to do with solving the social problems of the country. The only responsibility of a manager is to ignore the political, social, economic conditions of the society in which his business operates and to concentrate single-mindedly on the one objective of maximizing profits. "The responsibility of a manager in business," he says, "is simply to conduct the business in accord with the owner's desires which generally will be to make as much money as possible, while conforming to the basic rules of society."[3] And again "Concern for corporate social responsibility is fundamentally subversive of a free society. There is one and only one responsibility of business: to use its resources and engage in activities designed to increase its profits, so long as it engages in open ann free competition without deception or fraud."[4]

Friedman's position still represents the thinking of a certain number of managers and heads of business enterprises, though the massive weight of history and public opinion is turning the tide against them.

Milton Friedman is an intelligent and articulate person who justifies his stand by a number of considerations:

1. The manager is the agent of the owners in a free enterprise system.
2. The owners are exclusively the shareholders. They alone have the right to dictate policy and they are interested only in profits. They may agree to some lessening or diversion of profits, if, in the end, this will bring in greater profits.

3. Social responsibility is against the interests of owners and even of society itself whose real demand from business is efficiency.
4. Corporate social responsibility is subversive of a free society because:
   (a) It is a private intervention into a public concern which is the affair of politicians, not businessmen. The latter, moreover, do not have the competence to deal with such problems.
   (b) By taking over the State's responsibility, corporations are inviting State intervention in their own affairs and thus promoting the ultimate destruction of free enterprise through socialism.
   (c) Corporate social resposibility, *i.e.*, acting without a direct profit motive, dullens the pure competitive instinct which is essential to a free market.

To put the whole thing in a nutshell, let me quote Friedman again:

"Business cannot solve society's problems until the solutions are made profitable for business or unless government imposes such penalties for non-compliance as to affect profits."[5]

An example of such an attitude is the US auto industry which went on turning out millions of high emission and high petrol consumption cars, even when the public were aware of pollution and the need for conserving oil. The industry went even fureher and mounted a high power advertising campaign to persuade the public to continue buying such cars—all because they brought in more profit per unit. It was only when consumer groups like "Nader's Raiders" and conservationists got active and government finally intervened with pollution and petrol consumption standards that GM, Ford, Chrysler began complying.

This prompted Harold M. Williams to say: "Business in its daily conduct reflects a disconcerting insensibility to changing public demands and expectations. The lethargic response of the automobile companies and the oil companies to matters of pollulion and safety are leading examples. As contrasted to industry's leadership in technology, business habits and conservatism dictate that it merely be responsive and be dragged, heels dug in. into the new social values, rather than providing innovative leadership. Business responds in a piecemeal fashion and only to the critics who have enough power (*e.g.*, government or boycott lobbies) or enough nuisance value (Ralph Nader) to enforce their demands. Our managerial conscience is not yet challenged or disturbed."[8]

The Positive View

On the other hand, we have an increasing number of social scientists, politicians and businessmen themselves who take a completely different stance from the one put forward by Friedman. It can be stated in the following words: "Successful business today can no longer operate in isolation from the social. economic, political and ethical realities of society. Enlightened business houses all over the world have given deep thought to the problem of fitting business into its right placein society. Today, any business has to care more for society and for social values than it has ever done before and profit maximization can no longer be the only or even the major goal of business. In the 1980s, business will be spending as much of its decision-making time on the society surrounding it as on the organization itself. In fact, it has been predicted that social concerns will even take precedence over company concerns." This highly enlightened and forward looking statement is taken from a paper prepared by three TISCO managers.[2]

The case for social responsibility so ably stated above does not rest merely no emotional arguments. It has solid philosophical, ethical and even business reasons behind it:

1. Business must contribute to the solution of social problems, because like education, it is a sub-system of the whole social system called society. As a sub-system, business benefits from a healthy, just, contented society where peace prevails, and where the masses have growing purchasing power to buy manufactured goods. It is only in such a society that business can have any sense of security.

2. "No man is an island" said the poet John Dunne. Still less is any organized economic activity an island. Just as business and businessmen expect others to respect their rights, so also they must be sensitive to the rights of the community.

3. Property has an essentially social purpose, not an individual purpose; *i.e.* it must serve primarily the interests of the whole society. The only justification for the private ownership of productive property is that it contributes more effectively to the greater good of the community, by ensuring competition and providing incentives for more efficient production. If, therefore, private enterprise is permitted to exist it is because of a general acceptance on the part of the people of its usefulness for the attainment of their personal, social and national goals. Private enterprise will continue only so long as this perception persists. If, therefore, business should consistently show itself insensitive to the needs of society, we may expect rising demands for government controls and even government takeover. As a matter of fact, therefore, it is lack of social responsibility that is subversive of a free society and that invites government's intervention and finally promotes socialism.

4. Modern business wields enormous social power which affects the lives and future of millions of citizens. Corporation like General Motors are almost a state within a state. In our own country, a company like Tata Steel has an impact on the lives of millions of

people through its employment policies, its pricing policies, its policies in regard to raw materials, etc. Now where there is power, there must also be responsibility. Otherwise, we have no real order in society, but only the illusion of it. If power and responsibility are divorced, then onty pure competition and the interplay of market forces, *i.e.*, "might is right" or the law of the jungle prevails. This is an intolerable state of anomie in modern society.

5. Finally, social responsibility is really good business. SR is good PR It projects the image of a responsible, reliable, trustworthy company. This image inevitably reacts favourable on customers, investors, workers. The latter feel proud to be associated with such a company and wish to contribute to its growth. Anybody here present can think of examples from the Indian scene of companies which are publicly perceived as highly responsible and others which are not. The workers of the former kind of company would be the first to resist attempts by the government to nationalize the company, as the workers of TISCO and TELCO recently demonstrated: while workers of the latter type of company are likely to view any takeover attempt with favour. This happened in the case of the privately owned coal mines.

Social irresponsibility and exclusive concentration on profits also damages a firm in another way. It inhibits foresight and timely adaptation to new requirements imposed by circumstances, government regulations or consumer preference. An excellent example is the American auto industry which kept on producing big, gas-guzzling cars, even when oil was becoming scareer and more costly. In the meantime, European and Japanese companies were concentrating on small, fuel-saving vehicles. Now that oil is scarce and petrol is rising beyond $1 a goallon, and the government requires the production of small vehicles, the American auto industry finds itself behind the rest of the world and unable to stand up against European and Japanese competition. It will take them another three years to catch up.

Expressions of Social Responsibility

It is interesting to conduct a poll among the public on what they consider to be the social role of companies chiefly the large industrial concerns.

In 1966, 1971, 1976, at intervals of 5 years such a poll was conducted in the USA by Theodore V. Purcell.[6] The question put to a representative cross section of the American public and their answers are indicated in the table below:

QUESTIONNAIRE

"Do you think (READ LIST) is a problem that business and companies should give some special leadership to, or not?"

	Should give leadership		
	1976	*1971*	*1966*
	%	%	%
Controlling air and water pollution	92	89	69
Eliminating economic depressions	88	83	76
Rebuilding our cities	85	84	74
Enabling people to use their creative talents fully	85	85	73
Eliminating racial dircrimination	84	81	69
Wiping out poverty	83	81	69
Raising living standards around the world	80	74	43

(Contd.)

Finding cures for disease	76	70	63
Giving a college education to all qualified	75	70	71
Controlling crime	73	64	42
Cutting down highway accidents	72	67	50
Raising moral standards	70	64	48
Reducing threat of war	68	61	55
Eliminating religious prejudice	63	52	37
Cutting out government red tape	57	50	34
Controlling too rapid population growth	44	43	17

Note: Substantially the same responses were obtained from Indian respondents when the questionnaire was administered by the author.

From these answers, the following conclusions may be drawn:

1. There is a continuous growth in the number and the proportion of people who believe industrial firms should be involved in a variety of national and social tasks which are only remotely connected and sometimes pot connected at all with their primary function, *viz.*, to produce goods efficiently.
2. The public are inclined to expect from larger firms almost the same responsibility as from government itself.

These observations may be flattering to the executives of companies, but they are also frightening to many who believe they have neither the time, the competence, nor the finance to perform the functions expected of them.

It is interesting to probe into the reasons why people have such high expectations of business firms. I believe they are as follows:

1. People see in large companies a reservoir of high skills, managerial ability and vision which they believe should be placed at the disposal of the community in other ways than merely in producing goods. This, of course, is a compliment to managers, but it also places a grave responsibility on them to respond to public expectations.
2. Ordinary people believe companies are making much more profits than they actually declare. They would like to share in these profits, at least indirectly, by having the companies help in the solution of social problems which will make life easier for all.
3. People have a subtle, though inarticulate, feeling that the profits made by firms do not belong exclusively to the shareholders, but at least partly to the public as well.

To Whom Do the Profits of a Firm Belong

This brings us to the question of the disposal of the profits made by a business. To whom do they belong and to whom should they be distributed ? The classic capitalist theory holds ownership of the means of production, the buildings and the machines, confers on the shareholders exclusive title to the profits which should be entirely distributed among them, after allowing for depreciation, building up reserves and paying the employees. The Marxist theory, on the other hand, holds wtih equal force that the profits belong entirely to those who work in the industry. It is they who transform the raw material and confer value added to it and thus enable the production of profits. Hence the profits should be entirely distributed among the workers, including, of course, the working managers. At most, some rent may be paid to the owners of the factory, depreciation allowed for and reserves built up.

One thing is certain: no modern government tolerates the view that the profits made by a business belong entirely to the shareholders. That is precisely the reason for the imposition of various corporate taxes that take away a goodly proportion of the profits which are then used or supposed to be used for the general welfare of the community. Governments have a further tendency to impose on businesses varous public responsibilities like rural welfare, funding of education and medical services. Enlightened modern business houses also obviously hold a similar view. How else can one explain the involvement of the Tatas, the Mafatlals, ICI and other important business houses in rural welfare, disaster relief and other national needs. The philosophy behind this view has been well expressed by J.R.D. Tata in a speech made at Bombay House on the 40th anniversary of his Chairmanship of TISCO. I quote:

> "All of you here know that we are very, very actively considering what we can do to play a more effective role than we have in the past in helping the people not only in our town, the families of our employees, but also a very large number of people who reside in hundreds of villages over a radius of say, fifty miles, around Jamshedpur. This is one thing that, I believe, will not only be of importance to the people of the villages—if Tatas are able to assist them in developing them selves, in developing themselves, in developing industry, supplying goods and their requirements through Jamshedpur. helping them even in their agricultural pursuits—but it will also help us to improve our relationships further and make people realize that companies like ours and not only producers of materials and makers profit, but also factors and elements which play a productive and effective role in improving the standards of living of those who need it in the country."[7]

This statement of the eminent and humane Chairman of Tata Steel is the diametric opposite of the view expressed by Milton Friedman. I leave it to the readers to decide which is more in harmony with the modern concept of the industrial corporation and its role in the nation, which view expresses values that really respond to the needs of the time in which we live. It should be noted that Mr. Tata sees wide social involvement of his company in terms of what is good for the company in the long run. He realizes that narrow concetration on profits, refusal to be socially involved unless compelled by government or by public pressure is not only a negative value attitude but could also ultimately be counter-productive.

Though Mr. Tata is not a manager himself, he would probably agree with this statement made by Berle in his book 'The American Economic Republic': "The management of large companies should become a purely neutral technocracy, balancing a variety of claims by various groups in the community and assigning to each a portion of the income."[1]

Areas of Social Responsibility

1. Production

In the use of materials, a socially responsible management will endeavour to help the national economy by readily using those raw materials which are plentifully available in place of those that are scarce and have to be imported, such as aluminium in India in place of copper for cables. The firm will endeavour to use the minimum amount of energy compatible with its requirements. While deciding upon manufacturing processes, the prime consideration will not be cost reduction, but the safety of the workers. Where some danger is inherent, the company will make sure that workers are provided with adequate protection, given special pay to compensate for the danger and particular care to forestall it. Finally, in disposing of wastes, the firm will ensure that minimum damage is done to the natural environment particularly in regard to water and air. To ensure that the maximum is done in all these lines, a responsible firm will engage in serious research and development. spending whatever is necessary for the purpose.

All of us can quote examples from India and abroad where firms have been guilty of gross and culpable neglect in all these fields, simply because they were unwilling to incur the additional expense required. In several cases, nothing was done until the government stepped in to stop operations or the courts forced the firms to pay costly damages to workers. In one case in the USA a firm introduced a rule that any women worker getting pregnant would be dismissed, because management had discovered that a particular process was liable to cause injury to the unborn child. Though the process could have been replaced at the cost of some extra expenditure, the management preferred to forbid pregnancies. Finally, on appeal from the women workers the company was forced by the courts to stop operations until the whole process was changed; and several dismissed women had to be taken back with compensation.[9]

2. Marketing

In the area of marketing, there is great scope for the exercise of responsible management which recognizes the rights of the consumer. Such areas are truthful advertising, fixing of reasonable prices, not taking advantage of being an innovator or a monopoly holder to gouge the consumer; passing on savings to the consumer; ensuring that competition is fair, not cut-throat, so as to destroy smaller firms. Thus the management implicitly recognizes the competitors' right to exist, and refuses to practise the law of the jungle. A responsible management will also not join price-fixing cartels at the expense of the consumer.

3. Employment

Socially responsible management will pay a fair, living wage, if possible, even a family wage; even where labour is abundant. Thus they recognize that every man has the right to earn from a full day's work, enough to maitain himself and his family in a decent human standard of living. In a country like India, it is surely also the responsiblity of employers to adopt procedures, which will maximize employment, while not adding unduly to the cost of production. Other areas of social responsibility in employment are the question of providing opportunities to disadvantaged and under-privileged groups such as scheduled castes and tribes, the handicapped and minorities. In the US no firm can receive orders from the Federal Government unless it proves that it is a 'fair-practice employer', *i.e.*, that it makes special provision for ethnic minorities and women. In India there is also the vexed question of giving priority in employment to 'sons of the soil.' This is an extremely difficult point to settle in concrete, since after all the whole country is supposed to be one and the Constitution guarantees to every citizen the right to work in any part of the country. However, two points may be made: where the State in which an enterprise is situated is particularly backward, economically and educationally, there is surely a case for some preference for local people. Secondly, for unskilled work, there seems to be a good case for using local labour. Where skills are required without which the company's operations would suffer, it is difficult to deny a firm's right to employ the best available talent. Even here, however, in a backward state, a firm should make special efforts to build up and train local workers.

A socially conscious management will also recognize labour's right to form unions and to strike for better conditions of work and higher salaries. I am aware this is a delicate subject in India, owing to the apparent irresponsibility shown by many unions, their heavy politicization and the already high wages drawn by organized labour which places them in a privileged bracket of the Indian population. Management should perhaps conduct serious talks with labour organizations and help in the formulation of an Industrial Relations policy by the government which will recognize the rights management, labour and the public.

4. Accountability

A socially responsible firm would acknowledge its accountability to its shareholders, to the community, and to the government.

Hence the need for truthful annual reports and for honest payment of taxes, without even using legal evasion, *i.e.*, profiting from unintentional loopholes in the law. On the other hand, the responsible firm will make sure that its finance managers know the law and make the most of the concessions and rebates permitted by it.

The socially responsible management recognizes that taxes are one means of involving business in the development of the country. Of course, it is the democratic right of every businessman to seek to alter tax laws when they consider them to be unfair or unwise. However, so long as the laws are on the statute book, management has a duty to pay them.

Here we shall not speak about such gross practices as bringing of officials, supporting political parties in return for favoured treatment not accorded to others and other malpractices that are so common on the Indian scene. It is the wholesale indulgence in these practices that has undermined the public's faith in the integrity and national concern of private business. Of course, it would have to be said that the politicians are as much to blame as business people and that it becomes extemely difficult for an honest company to survive in such an atmosphere. Neverthess, there are bright examples of integrity in spite of difficulties and most such firms have not lost, but rather gained by their upright policies.

5. Social Audit

In the last ten years as the concept of social responsibility of business has gained increasing acceptance all over the world, the question has arisen of the means by which top management the public and the government could be kept informed of the firm's performance in this field. Different solutions have been proposed to ensure this. In several important firms, one member of the Board is assigned the special duty of keeping in touch with all the firm's activity in this field and the results produced. He them keeps the other Board members regularly posted on the subject. In one large multinational firm based in Calcutta, the Chairman himself has taken on primary responsibility for this task. Needless to say this firm has shown itself extraordinarily responsive to its social responsibilities. Now several authors and businessmen have suggested the institution of what they call "Social Audit." Just as the company's finances are scrutinized by qualified auditors, and the Board and the stockholders are given detailed information; so also there should be qualified social auditors, men of outstanding competence and repute, who will present a detailed report on the money spent on social projects of every kind, the results produced, the areas where improvement are called for, etc. Several of the leading Tata companies like TISCO have adopted this procedure.

Attitude of Workers

What is likely to be the attitude of a company's workers if the firm spends a fair part of its profits on social projects such as disaster relief, rural uplift, if it takes great care to economize on the use of energy, switches to more easily available raw materials, cleans up effluent gases and liquids, all of which cost money and therefore presumably reduce the bonus that the worker is likely to receive ? There are some who maintain that workers are even less idealistic than the management and therefore they will strenuously object to such policies, I am not so sure of this, provided one important requisite is fulfilled there is a good climate of Communication in the enterprise.

Given such an open climate of communication it is more than likely that workers will appreciate the need for the company's involvement in social activities, provided, of course, they are themselves paid a fair wage.

An open climate of communication is so important that it is really impossible to exaggerate its central place. In a study of the operations of the giant Bank of America conducted **six years ago, the consultants came up with the following statements:**

"For individual well-being, effective performance and employees profits, must see themselves as part of a thriving, socially conscious organization, as people contributing to its growth and influencing its policies.

"This will not happen without a climate of communication that encourages trust, openness and candour in everyday relationships between management and employees."[10]

This conclusion is not surprising, considering that communication is really not a technique but a culture a value and a creed. It indicates management's belief that employees are not elements in the production process, cogs in the wheel, but partners in an enterprise. Communication is probably the field in which Indian managers have most to learn, because it goes against the entire hierarchical structure of Indian society. This explains also why we Indians, who are otherwise so intelligent and capable, find it extraordinarily difficult to deal with large bodies of men and get them to work in harmony for the attainment of a comman purpose.

No wonder communication is said to be the keystone to Managerial Effectiveness.

REFERENCES

1. Berle, A.A. *The American Economic Republic*, 25.
2. Chatterjee, Mitra and Singh. "The Role of Business in the Changing Environment," *Management and Labour Studies* 5, No. 2 (December 1979), 135-44.
3. Friedman, Milton. "The Social Responsibility of Business is to Increase Profits", *New York Times* September 13 (1970).
4. *Ibid., Capitalism and Freedom*, Chicago University Press, 1963, 133.
5. *Ibid.*, Art. cit.
6. Purcell, Theodore V. *Management Review* (May 1976), 28.

7. Tata, J. R. D. *TISCO News* 26, Nos. 6 and 7 (October 1978), 15 and 16.

8. Williams, Harold M. "The Challenge to Business" in George A. Steiner (ed.), *Selected Major Issues in Business Role in Modern Society*, 7-8.

9. Cf. *TIME*, October 1978, p. 56.

10. "Using a Task Force to Improve Employee Communication—Bank of America Approach," *Management Review* (August 1975), 25-30.

15

Strategy to Communicate with the Underprivileged

BHUPINDER SINGH

The problem before us today are two: national reconstruction and national development. National reconstruction can also be equated with nation-building. Mass media, particularly radio and television should become instruments of both national reconstruction and national development. In contradistinction to the entertainment-commercial advertisement aspect, they should have a missionary, purposive and educative role.

Role in National Reconstruction

In the sphere of national reconstruction, the pride of place should be occupied by forces cementing national integration. One has only to recall the observation of Jawaharlal Nehru at the time of Independence: If India dies, who lives? Both radio and television should contribute to the forces of unity and cohesion. The media should undermarke a campaign for inter-communal, inter-ethnic, inter-regional, inter-linguistic amity. The harmony should be based on understanding and tolerance among the various segments of the society. In the context of the underprivileged people, this has a special significance as, notwithstanding the fact that the Constitution guarantees equality of status and citizenship rights, by and large, the forward sections exhibit an air of superiority towards the weaker sections. This attitude not only hinders the progress and development of sections like the scheduled caste and scheduled tribe people but also creates a sense of alienation. In a country of continental proportions with contentious multitudes, the basic need is to disseminate the message of oneness, good-will and harmony based on constructive understanding of the urges and the aspirations of the constituent groups. For example, in the context of the tribal situation topay, it has to be understood that:

(a) A tremendous intellectual-moral ferment is going on among the tribals: On account of lack of understanding, it might be looked upon as anti-national or potentially anti-national Sociologists and anthropolo. gists feel that the ferment represents a process of transformation from a local to a universalistic stance of tribal culture, through the use of their own cultural symbols and idioms. Imaginative media policy is necessary in interpretation.

(b) A process of identity, consolidation and expansion is currently taking place among tribals. The media can help in crystallisation and consolidation of tribal identities on the one hand and their fitment into the national socio-cultural matrix, on the other.

(c) The tribal communities have evolved over generations their own technological systems through adaptation to their physical and social environment. These cannot be replaced and substituted wholesale by modern technology without disruption of their own socio-cultural ethos. But the transformation of the existing technology can be stimulated. For the purpose the ethno-science, ethno-ecology, ethno-philosophy of th tribal communities being studied today, should receive attention of the nation through radio and television.

Role in National Development

The part to be played by radio and television in the field of national development can be as significant, if not more. Just as in the case of nation-building, with the greater mass of the people unlettered, the print medium has small relevance while audiovisual media can be of infinite advantage.

Since 80 per cent of the Indian population live in rural areas, it is imperative that the media should focus their attention on rural programmes. Three types of beneficiaries of development programmes in rural areas can be identified: the scheduled tribes living on the periphery of the society's physical and cultural habitat, the scheduled castes physically intermixed but socially ostracised and the non-SC and and non-ST rural mass. The seventh Five-Year Plan lays great stress on distributive justice. As such, the three seclions of the population are the target gronps of development programmes during the next five years.

Software

If the radio and TV have to emerge as potent allies of national development, they must adapt themselves to the changing needs. Rural development, and scheduled caste and scheduled tribe development have become complex. Taking the simple examples of agriculture and allied (*e.g.*, horticulture, animal husbandry) sectors. production techniques, loan subsidy components, banking methodologies, cooperative rules, marketing arrangements and many more aspects have to be understood by the peasant, scheduled caste farmer and tribal farmer to avail of the benefits provided by the Government. These intricacies need to be explained and the general message of development has to reach them simply and effectively. There is no better method than through participatory process. The approach document of the Planning Commission for the Seventh Five-

Year Plan emphasises representation of beneficiary-participants in both formulation and implementation of plans giving due representation to the weakest groups and urges that wide publicity should be given in local languages so that the people become aware of policies and programmes meant for them. Sharing of experience and though about a common subject by the persons on the T.V. screen and viewers can have electrifying effect. This implies that the participants on the screen should be drawn from among the viewers. In fact, in the process of conscientisation and awakening of critical awareness of the masses, regional or rural TV centres can play a critical role.

This is indeed the crux of the matter. Creation of software is as important, if not more, as developing hardware. Tremendous progress has been made in expansion of the TV and sceond broad, casting programme, particularly in the recent months. About 47 high power transmitters (HPT) and 133 low power transmitters (LPT) *i.e.*, 180 transmitter stations have been set up in the country reportedly covering 75 per cent of the population, it is a moot point whether more than 2 per cent of the population can afford to watch the programmes. But one really wonders if the programmes have relevance to the target groups.

It might be possible to communicate with the underprivileged, provided healthy programmes for rousing the critical consciousness of the mass are introduced in lieu of what has been dubbed as "degenerative and debilitating consumerism". Secondly, the task of creating adequate knowledge of the schemes, programmes and plans of development should be undertaken by assigning relevant responsibilities to local (district and below), state, regional and national levels. In other words, there has to be a deliberate move towards decentralisation, though the task of beaming integrative national programmes to all the corners, of the country has also to be achieved within the overall time-frame.

A clear distinction should be recognised in the software programmes meant for urban, semi-urban, rural and tribal audiences. They may represent modern-folk-tribal continuum, but the cultural ethos of each of the sections is different. Hence, the cultural idiom through which these audiences can be reached differ. As a result, the programme contents for the concerned audiences should also vary.

The scheduled tribes live in remote areas of the country. The scheduled castes and non-SC non-ST rural poor may not inhabit as inaccessible areas but they are located away from the urban and semi-urban areas, Hence, their cultural idiom is different from those of the urbanites as well as among each other. The programmes should adopt their cultural idiom, instead of bringing to them indiscriminate urban programmes creating psychological distortions. The first principle of Nehru's Panchsheel of tribal development stressed that development should be along the lines of the genius of the tribal community. The media should respect this principle. We have to communicate with the tribals in the cultural idiom they understand. Specific programmes for them have to be prepared. Hence, both the programme content and cultural idiom have to be evolved carefully.

It is sometimes stated that HPTs are more cost-effective. This does not take into account social costs and long-term objectives of development. HPTs likely to be located in urban areas, would imply common programmes for urban and rural areas to the deteriment and disadvantage of the rural people. On the other hand, a large number of LPTs will help reach out to the rural population inclusive of scheduled castes and particularly to scheduled tribes. There should, therefore, be a decentralised net-work of TV LPTs.

A massive effort has been launched recently in extending the TV and radio network; 180 TV transmitting stations have been established. The effort in the Seventh Plan period may be even larger. It appears that commensurate attention has not been given to the reception side. In other words, it has not been seen whether viewers and listeners have adequate number of sets. The vast majority of the rural, SC and ST population cannot afford to buy reception sets. Community sets, therefore, is the answer. This requires attention and financial provisions.

Some Operational Issues

With the objectives coming in view, some operational issues arise.

Firstly, the contents of the programmes, whether relative to nation-building or national development, must be evolved by men and women who are fully conversant and possess professional expertise. Half-baked. ill-conceived programmes lacking perspective and maturity will do more damage than good. The contents have then to bs projected in a convincing presentation; here the media experts should work in close harmony with sociologists, anfiropologists, economists, administrators, etc.

Secondly, the question of language of transmission. The radio has done a good job in the use of local and tribal languages. This policy needs expansion.

Thirdly, the question of reception. With the best software the rich hardware, the result can be naught, if at the receiving end the people cannot afford receiving sets. Arrangements for such sets should be made.

Fourthly, there cannot be too much stress on decentralisation of hardware and software.

16

Communications and How to Make Them More Effective

AIR CMDE. R.K. MEHRA

Introduction

"Our administrative system must become goal-oriented. A new works-ethic, a new work-culture must be evolved in which Government is result-bound and not procedure-bound. Reward and punishment must be related to performance. A strong concern for efficiency must premeate all institutions."

The history of communication is as old as the history of mankind. Even when he lived in caves, man learnt to convey his feelings, desires and intentions to other human beings by grunts, squeaks and clicks. But in olden days, life was simple and performance of tasks required little specialized knowledge. The working units were small and people knew each other well. Communication between people was therefore easy.

With advance in civilization, the organizations have become large and impersonal. Tasks have become complex and demand combined effort by a number of people with different specializations. While the means for communication have increased tremendously, the understanding between people has not improved accordingly. Creating common ground and mutual understanding between people and thus paving the way to meaningful action is the basic purpose of good communication.

In this paper, the process of communication would be studied in context of organisations and ways and means would be suggested to make these more satisfying and result oriented.

Communication Channels

The flow of communication in a typical organization is shown in Fig. 16. 1 The Chief Executive passes down decisions and instructions for execution a lower levels. He also passes down limited information on policies, plans and programmes so that

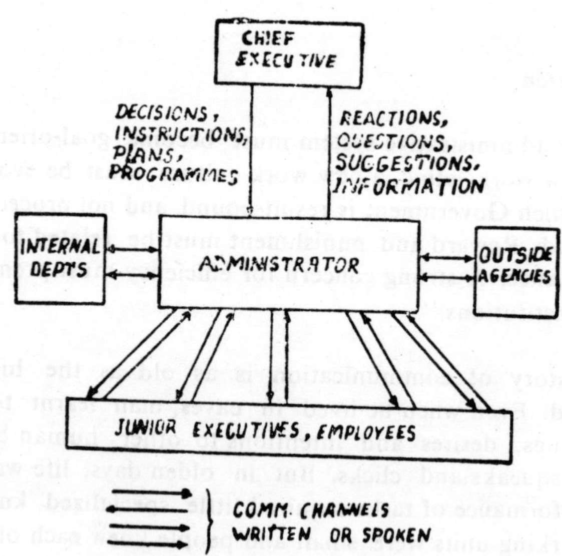

Fig. 16. 1 Communication Channels in a Typical Organization

all levels are aware of the latest thinking and future perceptions. This is important as lack of downward flow of information gives rise to rumours, anxieties and a 'grapevine' which eventually destroys the usefulness of the normal communication channels.

It would be seen from the diagram that the middle level manager or the administrator plays a vital role. From the point of view of employees, he is the "face" of the management while the chief executive depends upon him to interpret the needs of the employees. The ability of the person at this level to communicate upwards, downwards and sideways becomes a vital issue in the smooth running of the venture, be it a Government office or a private business house.

Before an administrator can hope to become an effective communicator, he needs to have a clear understanding of his key role in administration and to develop a healthy self-image about his ability to meet the challenge.

Process of Communication

Whether the communication takes place up, down or sideways, essentially it involves a Sender, the Message and the Receiver. This is shown in Fig. 16. 2.

The process starts with the sender having a desire for achieving a certain result. This he transforms into an idea and evolves a plan of action to achieve it. The point to note is that the thought process at this stage is generally in the form of an outline. Much more work has to be put in before a sound plan can be evolved. The sender now chooses the medium through which he would like to send his message. As an example, he may decide to speak, either directly or through a telephone; or he may prefer to write a letter or send a telegram.

This is then followed by the transmission of the message through the medium chosen.

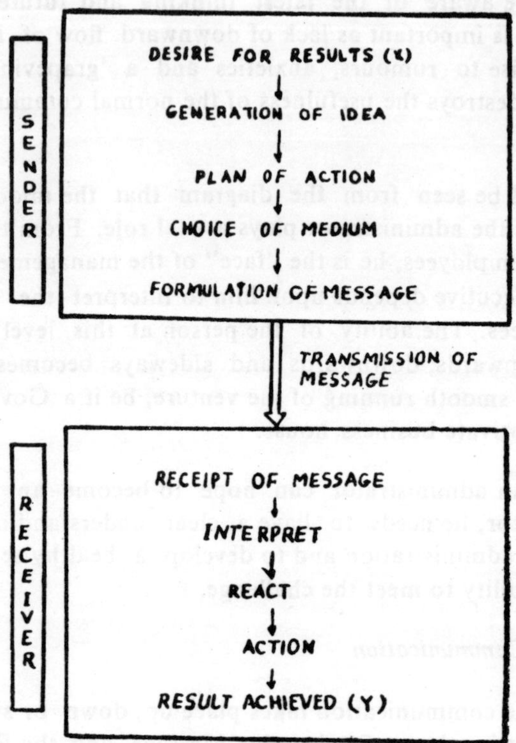

Fig. 16. 2 Process of Communication

On the receiving end, the process involves the receipt of the message and its interpretation by the receiver. He then reacts to it in accordance with his own views and previous knowledge of the subject. Thereafter. he decides upon the course of action to be taken and allots a degree of priority to the task, depending upon his own assessment. Finally, the action is taken and some result is achived.

In the final analysis, the true test of effective communication is the proximity between the result achieved and that desired. The objective of the communicator should be to achieve or excel the desired result along with maximum economy in effort and expenditure.

Common Barriers to Communication

It is a common experience in management and administration that somewhere down the channel, the effectiveness of the communication is lost and the result achieved fall far short of the expectations. Sometimes, quite to the surprise of the sender, the end result may even be contrary to his expectations. This can broadly be termed as a failure in communication. Such failures occur because of the existence of barriers in communication. It is essential to recognize these barriers before one can hope to eradicate them.

The common barriers which come in the way of communication are shown in Fig. 16.3 and are self explanatory. The

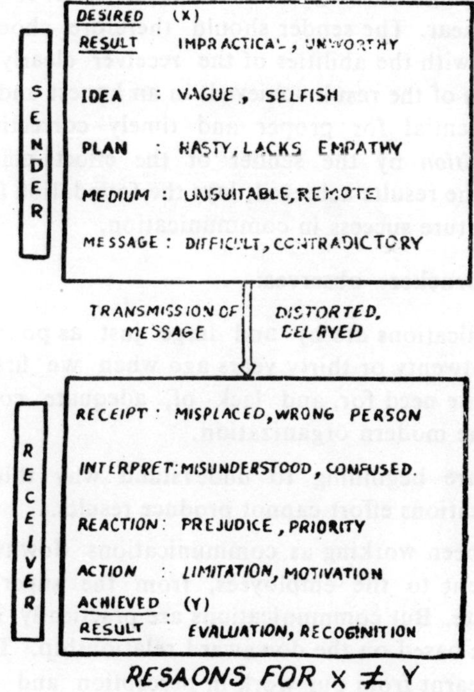

Fig. 16.3 Common Barriers to Communication

reader will no doubt be able to recognize the presence of several of these in his own work environment and may even be able to identify some more from his own experience. He would greatly benefit if he lists out the barriers which are relevant to his particular situation.

Perhaps a few comments on some of these barriers would be in order. At the sender's end, an *unworthy cause* or a *selfish motive* eventually stands revealed and may cause irreparable damage in the long run. *Empathy* is the ability of the sender to place himself in the shoes of the receiver. The so-called "uncanny knack" and the receiver. As a general rule, the more direct the communication, the more effective it would be.

At the receiver's end, one of the common reasons for misunderstanding a message is that people tend to hear what they want to hear. The sender should therefore choose a style of expression with the abilities of the receiver clearly in mind. The *evaluation* of the result achieved, in an honest and impartial manner, is essential for proper and timely corrective action. Proper *recognition* by the sender of the efforts made by the receiver and the results achieved, lays the foundation for mutual respect and future success in communication.

Peter F. Drucker—observes:

"Communications are by and large just as poor today as they were twenty or thirty years ago when we first became aware of the need for, and lack of, adequate communications in the modern organization.

But we are beginning to understand why this massive communications effort cannot produce results.

We have been working as communications downward from management to the employees, from the superior to the subordinate. But communications are practically impossible if they are based on the downward relationship. This much we have learnt from our work in perception and communications theory. The harder the superior tries to say something to his subordinate, the more likely is it that the subordinate will mishear. He will hear what he expects to hear rather than what is being said."

Strategy for Effective Communications

A practical strategy for increasing the effectiveness of communications is shown in Fig. 16 4. The basis of good communication is the consultative approach.

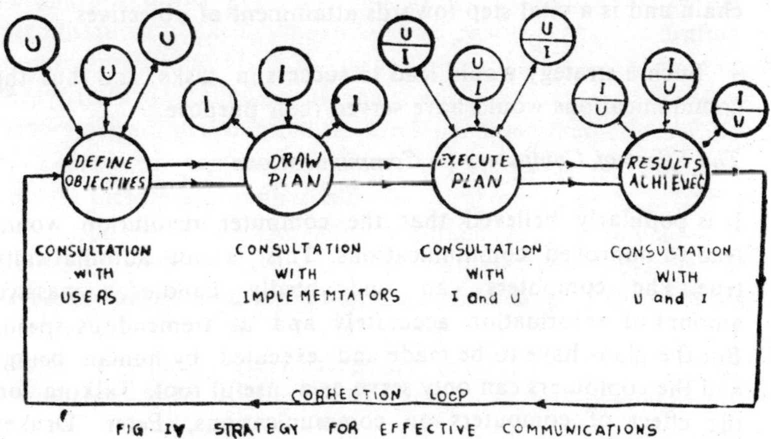

FIG IV STRATEGY FOR EFFECTIVE COMMUNICATIONS

The process starts with proper definition of the objectives to be attained. Active consulation with the "USERS" is essential here to ensure that the attainment of the objectives would bring satisfaction to the users.

The next stage is the drawing up of a plan of action. Here the active involvement of the "IMPLEMENTORS" ensure that the plan evolved is practical and achievable. It also helps to commit the implementors to the next stage of execution of the plan.

Once the executive of the plan starts, the administrator maintaing his primary links with the implementors but encourages them to establish direct contact with the users thus enhancing the level of satisfaction attained.

A critical evaluation of the results achieved is the next task of the administrator for which he must shifit his main focus to the user, for it is his satisfaction that will decide the degree of success.

Lastly, the administrator must sit back and compare the attainments against the objectives. He should consult with his superior and may even need to modify the objectives or the plan. This is the "Correction Loop" in the communication chain and is a vital step towards attainment of objectives.

Such a strategy would lead to success in tasks and thus the communications would have served their purpose.

The Effect of Computers on Communications

It is popularly believed that the computer revolution would lead to improved communications. This is not automatically true. The computers can undoubtedly handle a massive amount of information accurately and at tremendous speed. But the plans have to be made and executed by human beings and the computers can only serve as a useful tool. Talking on the effect of computers on communications, Peter Druker says:

> "But now we have the problem of establishing the necessary minimum of communications so that we understand each other, and can know each other's needs, goals, perceptions, and ways of doing things. Information does not supply this. Only direct contact, whether by voice or by written word, can communicate.
>
> The more we automate information-handing, the more we will have to create opportunities for effective communication."

Measurement of Communication Effectiveness in on Organisation

Rensis Likert has devised a scale on which the effectiveness of communications in organisation can be judged. This is given in Table 16.1 Organisations which have poor communications belong to System 1 while those which have the most effective communications belong to System 4. It is claimed by Likert that the most efficient working group tends to have System 3 or 4 type of communications.

Attributes of an Effective Communicator

Based upon the foreging discussion, it is possible to list the attributes of an administrator who hopes to become an effective communicator. These attributes are presented in Table 16.2. While the list looks rather formidable at first scrutiny, a thoughtful study would indicate that it reflects a particular, consistent type of personality, in which a tendency towards consultative approach and a drive for result oriented action with enthusiasm appear as balanced elements. The communicator may like to remember that face-to-face discussion, carried out in an atmosphere of understanding and cordiality, with focus on results, is still the best known method of communication.

To achieve such personality traits, an administrator needs to look inwards and assess his own personal sense of values. For as J. Feiffer says:

> "If you are not able to communicate successfully between yourself and yourself, how are you supposed to make it with the strangers outside?"

Conclusions

Effective communication is the key to the success of tasks undertaken by organization and the best of the plans would flounder without it. In a developing country, with problems of limited resources, this may spell the difference between progress and failure. Research has brought out the successful communications are rooted in the consultative approach backed by

TABLE 16.1

Communication Characteristics of Different Management Systems

S. No.	Characteristic	System 1	System 2	System 3	System 4
1.	Amount of interaction and communication aimed at achieving organisation's objectives	Very little	Little	Quite a bit	Much with both individuals, and groups
2.	Dircetion of information flow	Downward	Mostly downward	Down and up	Down, up, and with peers
3.	Extent to which downward communications are accepted by subordinates	Viewed with great suspicion	May or may not viewed with suspicion	Often accepted but at times viewed with suspicion; may or may not be openly questioned	Generally accepted, but if not, openly and candidly questioned
4.	Accuracy of upward communication via line	Tends to be inaccurate	Information that boss wants to hear flows; other information is restricted and filtered.	Information that boss wants to hear flows, other information may be limited or cautiously given	Accurate

5. Psychological closeness of superiors to subordinates (*i.e.*, how well does the superior know and understand problems faced by subordinates?)	Has no knowledge or understanding of problems of subordinates	Has some knowledge and understanding of problems of subordinates	Knows and under stands problems of suborninates quite well	Knows and understands problems of subordinates very well

enthusiastic, result-oriented action. The administrator can acquire these traits by introspection and self-development. The fruits of such effort would not only bring about prosperity to the organization but inner peace and enhanced prestige to the communicator as well.

ATTRIBUTES OF AN EFFECTIVE COMMUNICATOR

A. Towards Employees

Attitude of genuine concern and helpfulness.
Direct and open approach.
Strict impartiality and integrity.
Consultations: up-down-sideways.
Flexible approach to rules and regulations.
Empathy.
Ability to listen and observe.
Appreciation and awards.
Decisive action against offenders.

B. Towards Task

Action orientation.
Enthusiasm.
Adequate supervision, not under or over supervision.
Pride in work and achievements.
Accent on performance and results.
Honest evaluation of results.
Corrective mechanism.

BIBLIOGRAPHY

1. Laurance J. Peter, *The Peter Prescription*, Bantam Books, 1973.

2. Petre F. Drucker, *The Effective Executive*, Pan Books, 1967.
3. Rensis Likert, *The Human Organization, Its Management and Value*, McGraw-Hill, 1967.
4. C.L. Littlefield *et al.*, *Office and Administrative Management*, Prentice-Hall, 1974.

17

Costing for Management Decisions

K. L. HANDA

Cost is a measurement, in monetary terms, of the amount of resources used for a purpose. The various elements which constitute the cost of making something or of rendering a service may include physical quantittes of material, hours of labour, and quantities of other services. The use of these resources is first reckoned in physical terms and measured according to their respective yardsticks. Then, using the medium of relevant price, rate, salary or wage, the resources consumed are converted into monetary expression.

Money provides a common denominator to combine and determine the total amount of various resources used. For instance, the use of a particular quantity of material would first be measured according to its weight, volume, or length. And, the use of labour would be measured in terms of manhours or mandays. Then, employing the relevant rate, price, wage, etc., the use of the various resources is translated into money terms so that these monetary expressions could be added to determine the total amount of all the resources consumed. When the use of these resources is related to a specific purpose, their monetary expression is called cost, such as, cost of running a hospital or cost of manning a police post.

Cost accounting aims at systematic recording of expenditures related to a specific function, activity, and operation. It involes analysis of expenditure to ascertain the cost of each product, service, process, job, operation, etc. Under a system of cost accounting, transactions are analysed as related to their purpose. It is different from financial accounting in which classification of expenditure is done by its nature, like salary, wage, conveyance, etc.

The Purpose of Costing

The techniques and processes of costing serve a variety of purpose. Costing enables the management to ascertain the cost of a product, process, job, or service. This facilitates exercise of the necessary control to keep costs pegged to an efficient and economical operation. Control over cost can be effective only if it is known before hand, how much should be spent. Standard costing can be of great help for this purpose.

Costing provides guidelines for management policy and is a useful and in taking management decisions, such as, fixing of product prices, whether to make or buy, selection of product mix to maximise profits, taking investment decisions, etc. Cost accounting makes it possible to carry out break-even analysis to ascertain the quantum of production or sales where total revenue will equal total cost. Determination of break-even point is of great help in taking management decisions regarding quantity to be produced, profit earning possible, product pricing, etc.

Classification of Costs

There are a number of ways in which costs can be classified, such as:

(i) by type of expenditure,

(ii) according to functions,

(iii) by allocation,

(iv) according to behaviour,

(v) in terms of products,

(vi) in terms of jobs,

(vii) in terms of processes,

(viii) controllable cost and non-controllable cost,

(ix) opportunity cost,

(x) social cost,

(xi) apparent cost and hidden cost,

(xii) sunk cost,

(xiii) cost unit,

(viv) in terms of cost centres, etc.

The classification of costs by type of expenditure implies the distinction whether it is materials cost, labour cost, or overhead cost. This is the primary method of classifying costs by break ing them into elements of cost, *i.e.*, material, labour an- overhead.

The classification of costs according to functions refers to categorisation of costs in terms of functions like sales, production, administration, etc. The basis for this classification is, why the cost has been incurred. For instance, a foreman's salary is paid to carry out production function and is, therefore part of production cost. A salesman's salary is paid as part of the sales effort and therefore pertains to cost of sales function.

The categorisation of costs by allocation covers direct and indirect costs. Total costs are distinguished as direct and indirect according as these are traced in relation to a purpose. Direct costs are those which can be straightaway traced to a particular product, service, or job, as for instance, cost of cloth used to make a shirt. Direct costs comprise direct material, direct labour and other direct expenses and that sum total of these is called Prime Cost. Direct materials are those materials which become part of the specified finished product, like leather used for manufacturing a pair of shoes. Direct labour cost of a product is that which can be specifically traced to or identified with the product, like time spent in making a shirt. Indirect cost is that which cannot be straightaway traced to a particular product, service or job, and therefore has to be allocated on some acceptable basis. For example, expen diture incurred on the common use of all workers will be indirect cost, such as money spent on materials like lubricants, hand tools, etc., expenses incurred on salaries of supervisors, purchase officers, storekeepers etc.

Fixed and Variable Costs

The treatment of costs according to behaviour is made in terms of fixed and variable costs. Broadly, costs which vary with a change in quantum of output or level of activity are variable costs, and those which change with the passage of time are called fixed costs. Generally, material and labour costs would vary as the volume of production changes, but administrative salaries, factory rent and rates would vary with the passage of time. A fixed cost may also be fixed only in relation to a given range of production or existing installed capacity or a given level of activity.

The behaviour of variable cost is represented in figure 17.1.

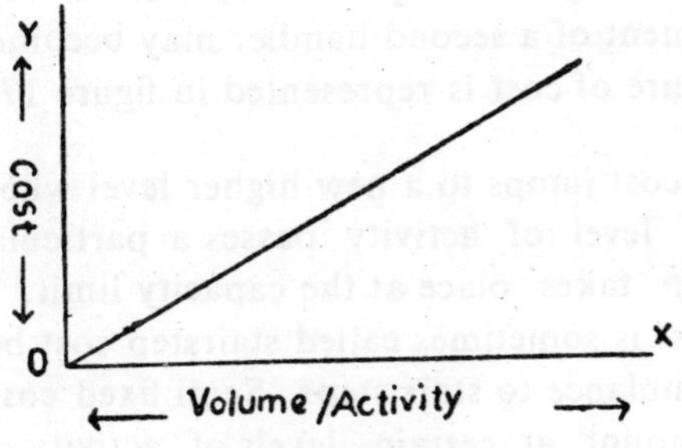

Fig. 17.1

Fixed cost does not vary with the volume, of production or level of activity and is, therefore, represented by the following graph:

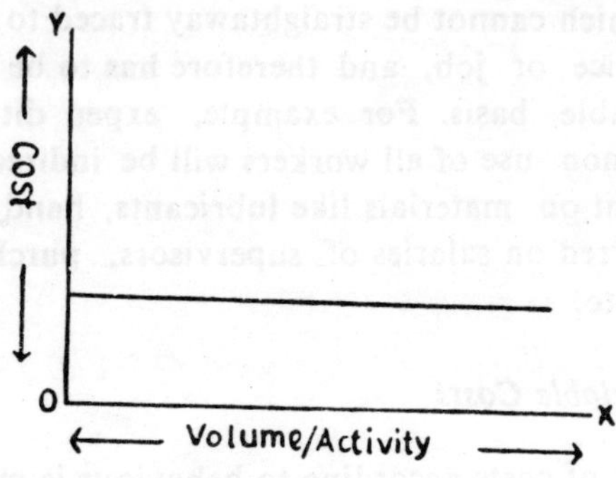

Fig, 17.2

Fixed cost is, however, fixed over a certain range of production or level of activity. If production were to increase manyfold beyond the level over which fixed cost does not change, new premises, machines, staff, etc., would have to be added thereby increasing fixed cost to a new level. In such cases, fixed cost may be thought of as varying with volume at specific levels. Such a behaviour of cost is called semi-fixed cost. Indirect labour would generally fall in this category, because one material handler may be adequate for a certain volume, above which employment of a second handler may become necessary. Semi-fixed nature of cost is represented in figure 17.3.

Semi-fixed cost jumps to a new higher level when volume of production or level of activity passes a particular range. A quantum jump takes place at the capacity limit. That is why semi-mixed cost is sometimes called stairstep cost because of its graphical resemblance to stair steps. Semi fixed cost changes in lump sum amount at certain levels of activity or volume of production instead of changing continuously over all levels of activity. Many types of personnel costs are in the nature of

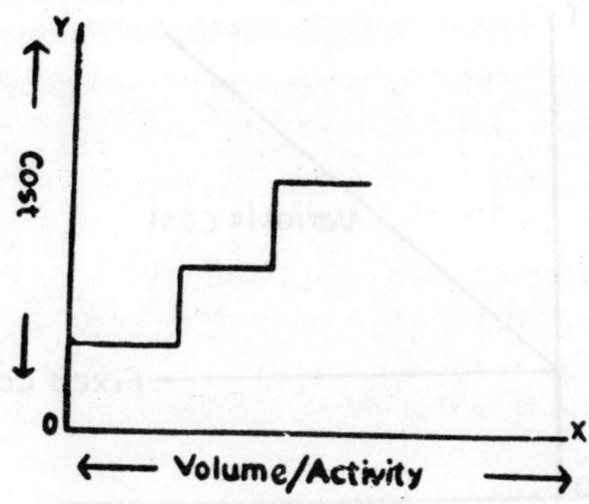

Fig. 17.3

semi-fixed costs. For instance, supervisory cost frequently fits in with this behaviour pattern because each supervisor is able to supervise a limited number of employees, beyond which another supervisor needs to be employed if production passes a particular level necessitating employment of more workers.

Another classification of costs is in terms of semi-variable cost which consists of both fixed cost and variable cost. There is a base amount that remains fixed irrespective of changes in the level of activity. To this, another cost it added that varies directly with changes in the level of activity. Payment to a salesman who is given a fixed monthly salary plus a commission on the sales he transacts would be a case of semi-variable cost. The graphical representation of semi-variable cost is in figure 17.4.

It may be stated that both semi-fixed and semi-variable costs can be bifurcated into 'fixed' and 'variable' components for taking a variety of management decisions for the purpose of cost control, profit planning, etc. The classification of costs by behaviour in terms of fixed cost and variable cost is a useful accounting technique for taking decisions to optimise expenditure. For instance, total cost divided by a number of units produced would determine unit cost or average cost per unit.

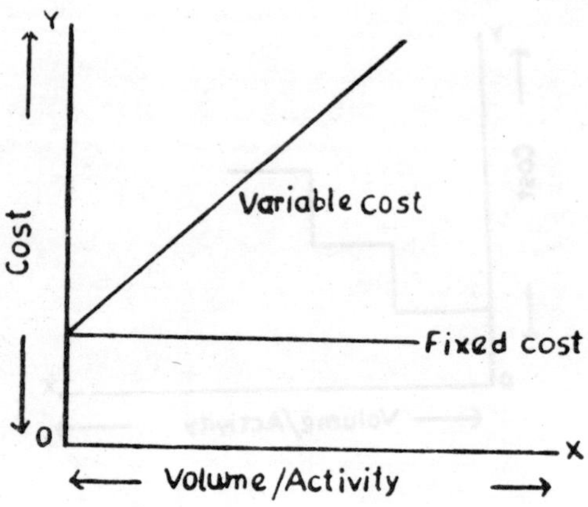

Fig. 17.4

And, the total cost comprises both fiexd cost and variable cost. Therefore, to optimise unit cost, is is necessary that decision to incur fixed cost should be taken with utmost care and after detailed examination of the extent of use to be made of the proposed fixed cost. Normally, fixed cost should be incurred only upto the level that it can be fully made use of. Variable cost should be permitted to be incurred so as to use the fixed cost at its capacity level. This would reduce average cost per unit thereby resulting in optimisation of expenditure.

The traditional approach in government while scrutinising expenditure proposals has been to exercise financial control by restricting expenditure. This has been so whether the proposals pertained to fixed cost or variable cost. But, once an asset gets created by incurring fixed cost, may be the decisions had been taken either because of repeated considerations or otherwise, the same earlier approach in restricting expenditure continues to be applied to variable cost becoming necessary for using such an asset. For instance, if a vehicle has been sanctioned and purchased its use would not be made to its optimum capacity because the running expenditure required or the variable cost needed for operating it optimally may not be sanctioned in order to save on expenditure. This would result in sub-optimal utilisation of the asset and a considerably higher per unit cost. It is, therefore, imperative that when expenditure proposals are examined, both the components of fixed cost and variable cost should be kept in view to base the decision on considerations of achieving the lowest possible per unit or average cost.

Marginal or Differential Costing

It is, however, not always relevant that decision-making should be based on average cost. Sometimes, it is important to consider the net effect on costs of each alternative being considered. It is only the net incremental costs which need to be considered in such circumstances.

Marginal or differential costing refers to ascertainment of costs by differentiating between fixed costs and variable costs. Under marginal costing, fixed cost is not treated as product cost. Fixed cost is recovered from 'Contribution' or 'Gross Profit' which is the difference between sales revenue and variable cost. The following example illustrates the point further:

Product	*X*	*Y*	*Z*	*Total*
Sales Revenue (Rs.)	15,000	25,000	25,000	65,000
Variable Cost (Rs.)	9,000	16,000	12,000	37,000
Contribution or Gross Profit (Rs.)	6,000	9,000	13,000	28,000
Fixed Cost (Rs.)	4,000	11,000	10,000	25,000
Profit (Rs.)	2,000	(—)2,000	3,000	3,000

A firm manufacturing products X, Y and Z as shows in the above example, finding that product Y is giving a loss of Rs. 2,000 would still decide to continue the production and sale of Y because it generates a contribution of Rs. 9,000 against which the fixed cost of Rs. 11,000 is set off to reduce the loss to Rs. 2,000, which would otherwise be Rs. 11,000. In this case, marginal or variable cost has been evaluated against incremental revenue. As long as there is a positive contribution generated, the decision of the management would be to continue production and sale of the product even thought it produces a net loss. Marginal costing helps to ascertain the net effect on profit of changes in quantum of output. Such a system of costing becomes a valuable aid to management in taking a variety of decisions, like product pricing under competitive conditions, whether to make or buy a product, selection of product mix, etc.

Make-or-Buy Decision

A product may be composed of 1, 10, 100, 1000 or more parts that go into making it. A big automobile is made up of hundreds of parts. It is quite often a question faced by management as to which of the parts it should make and which others it should buy from outside. There are also a number of cases where manufacturing firms assemble a product for sale. Some of its component parts are manufactured within the firm and others are incorporated into the product by purchasing them from other manufacturers. For instance, no firm would like to manufacture items like paper, clips, pencils, and erasers required for its use unless it is itself in that business, because specialisation would make their manufacture uneconomical to all firms except those in that particular business.

In such a situation where a firm should manufacture some of the component parts of a product and buy some others from outside, what criteria are valid for taking these decisions? It is logical that a manufacturer should choose an alternative which would be least expensive for him while meeting his need of getting the desired quality and delivery of required components. Such a make-or-buy decision would obviously be based on the criterion of cost. The manufacturer should buy a part from outside if it could be bought cheaper. Otherwise, he should manufacture the part in his firm if that alternative results in cost saving as compared to buying the same part from outside market. Therefore. in evaluating the consequences of a make-or-buy situation, the decision-maker has to compare the cost of manufacturing a product with the cost of buying the same. The following example will illustrate the point further:

A manufacturing concern needs 100,000 values for incorporation in a product. The same quality of valves are available in the outside market for Rs. 2.70 per valve. Also, the firm has the capacity to manufacture the valves itself. If it so does, the various components of costs to be incurred by the firm in manufacturing the valves will be as under:

Material used (per valve)	Rs. 0.60
Cost of machine operation including supplies, oil, electricity, etc. (per valve)	Rs. 2.00
Machine operators' salary (per year)	Rs. 25,000.00
Fixed cost (relevant to the period of one year)	Rs. 70,000.00

The cost analysis relevant to make-or-buy decision is as follows:

	Make	*Buy*
Material @ Rs. 0.60 per 100,000 Valves (Rs.)	60,000	
Machine operation @ Rs. 2.00 for 100,000 Valves Rs.	200,000	
Machine operator's salary (Rs.)	25,000	

Purchase of valves from outside market @Rs. 2.70 (Rs.)		270,000
Fixed cost (Rs. 70,000— not relevant in such decision-making situation)		
Total (Rs.)	285,000	270,000

In such a situation, it is cheaper to buy from outside, which would result in a saving of Rs. 15,000 for the firm. This is so if machine operators' salary of Rs. 25,000 is treated as variable cost implying that if the valves are not manufactured by the firm, the machine operators could be removed and the amount of salary paid to them saved. If the situation present differently, that it is not possible for the firm to retrench the machine operators in the event of its stopping manufacturing of valves, then the salary of the machine operators cant not be considered as variable cost, and has to be treated as fixed cost. In the changed circumitances, the fixed cost of Rs. 25,000 towards salary of machine operators would no more remain relevant for a make-or-buy decision, and therefore, the cost analysis would be presented as:

Make	Rs. 260,000
Buy	Rs. 270,000

In this case, the decision most suitable to the management, on financial considerations, would be in favour of manufacturing the valves within its own firm.

There may, however, be other considerations inherent in a situation because of which an approach different from the one discussed earlier may need to be adopted. For instance, if buying from outside is costlier on marginal costing considerations, the firm may still decide to buy the product if the extra cost it has to incur thereby is more than compensated by manufacturing another product with the production capacity freed and taking advantage of the fresh opportunity emerging for its sale.

In addition, certain decisions may be taken on non-economic and intangible factors. The firm may decide to manufacture a product for certain technical considerations and control of trade secrets. It may also decide to do so for retaining reliability of supply. The firm may in other situations decide to buy the product from outside even though it is costlier to do so as compared to manufacturing it within the firm. Such a decision of the firm may be dictated by considerations of retaining alternative sources of supply or to retain goodwill of an important supplier.

Break-even Analysis

Break-even point refers to that volume of production or level of activity or sale at which total revenue equals total cost. Total cost is made up of fixed cost and variable cost. At break-even point, the firm neither earns a profit nor incurs any loss. A graphical representation of break-even point is given in figure 17.5.

Break-even point (B.E.P.) is determined at the intersection of the total revenue and total cost curves. Vertical distance between the total cost line and the total revenue line to the left of B.E.P. measures loss because total cost exceeds total revenue at that volume of production, while vertical distance between the total revenue line and the total cost line to the right of B.E.P. represents profit.

Break-even analysis or cost-volume-profit analysis in an analytical technique for studying the relationship between costs and revenues at different volumes of production or levels of activity to determine its impact on profit. A firm operating at a volume lower than the break-even point would first like to reach it and then devise strategies for crossing this point if it is to earn profit.

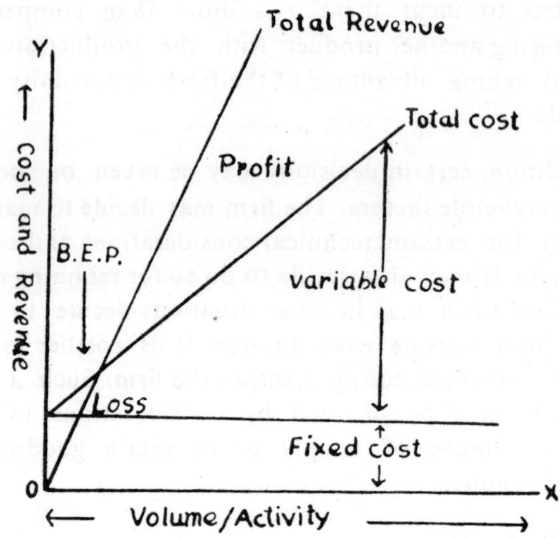

Fig. 17.5

The following assumptions are usually made in break-even analysis:

(i) that total variable costs vary linearly with the volume of production or level of activity. In other words, unit variable cost remains constant;

(ii) that total revenues vary linearly with the volume of sales or, unit selling price is constant;

(iii) that the quantity sold is the same as the quantity produced and there is no inventory change.

From the graphical presentation of the break-even point, the following algebraic analysis can be carried out. At the break-even point:

TR=TC (where TR is total revenue, and TC is total cost)

$P \times Q = F + V \times Q$ (where P is the price per unit, Q is the quantity produced and sold, F is fixed cost, V is variable cost per unit)

Therefore, $Q (P-V)=F$

Or, $Q=\dfrac{F}{P-V}$

The above equation can be used for taking a variety of decisions.

(i) Supposing somebody wants to set up a tea stall and is interested in knowing the break-even point for the number of cups of tea to be sold in a month. The break-up of the total cost he has to incur is as follows:

Fixed cost per month including rent, electricity, etc.
=Rs. 360 or Paise 36,000

Variable cost per cup of tea:

tea leaves	:	8 paise
sugar	:	12 paise
milk	:	4 paise
fuel, etc.	:	6 paise
Total		30 paise

Therefore, break-even quantity $= \dfrac{F}{P-V}$

$= \dfrac{36000}{50-30}$ (where 50 paise is the price per cup of tea that he can charge)

=1,800 cups of tea

Having determined the break-even quantity at 1800 cups to be sold in a month, the vendor can carry out a market study or demand analysis to assess whether it would be possible for him to sell more than 1,800 cups in a month if he is to earn profit.

(ii) If it is intended to earn a profit of Rs. 600 per month, the quantity required to be sold for the purpose can also be determined from the same equation by adding profit desired to the fixed cost. In this case,

$$\text{Quantity} = \frac{36000+60000}{50-30} = 4{,}800 \text{ cups of tea}$$

Therefore, in order to earn a profit of Rs. 600 per month, the vendor has to sell 4,800 cups of tea.

(iii) Supposing the demand for cups of tea which can be sold in a month is fixed at 2,400. But the vendor is in a monopoly position and has discretion in fixing price for a cup of tea to be sold. Then using the same equation, he can determine the price he should charge if he wants to earn a profit of Rs. 600 per month. In that case,

$$2400 = \frac{36000+60000}{P-30}$$

$$\text{Therefore, } P-30 = \frac{96000}{2400} = 40$$

And, $P=40+30=70$ paise.

So, he has determined the price as 70 paise to be charged for a cup of tea if he is to earn a profit of Rs. 600 per month by selling a fixed quantity of 2,400 cups of tea.

(iv) Supposing the vendor finds that he can sell only 4,000 cups of tea in a month at the market price of 50 paise per cup, and he wants to determine the profit he would earn under such a situation. Using the same equation:

$$Q = \frac{F+PR}{V-P} \text{ (where PR is profit to be determined)}$$

$$\text{Or,} \quad 4000 = \frac{36000+PR}{50-30}$$

Therefore, PR=80000—44000 paise or Rs. 440. So, the vendor has determined the profit he would earn under these circumstances as Rs. 440.

A variety of management decisions can thus be taken with the help of the technique of break-even analysis.

Conclusion

Traditionally, the approach in government in exercising financial control has not been appreciably based on cost-consciousness. It has mostly been focussed on restricting expenditure. Modern management requires that the expenditure decision taken should optimise the use of resources by relating the costs incurred to the resulting benefits. It should be aimed to achieve the highest possible productivity by minimising per unit or average cost of activities and operations. Costing techniques can prove of great help in achieving efficiency and economy of expenditure. In government and public sector, cost-consciousness in taking expenditure decisions can immensely rationalise and improve the exercise of financial control to optimise the use of resources.

18

Materials Management and Make/Buy Decision Analysis

A.K. DATTA

Make/Buy Choices

When needs arise in a manufacturing organisation for a material, part or a product, these have to be satisfied either by purchase from an outside source or the firm may seek the alternative course of satisfying the need by undertaking production within the firm's own plant for reasons of cost, convenience and control which outside supply sources do not always provide. For non-manufacturing organisations, such as hospitals, research and educational institutions, government agencies and commercial establishments, it is service rather than the product that matters. Even in manufacturing organisations, the possibility of becoming one's own supplier receives scant attention, yet it is a vital strategy for efficient Materials Management. Probably because most concerns do not have a clear-cut policy on 'make or buy', they prefer to decide each case on cost, volume, service and other considerations. There are, however, some component which tend towards self-sufficiency of the material, part and/or component is vital to their manufacturing operation. On the other hand, there are companies which believe in specialising in a limited production line, even if an opportunity exists for the manufacture of the part or component.

Theoretically at least, any manufacturing concern has three basic alternatives in sourcing a part or a product that it needs:

1. Buy the part/product completely from an outside source;
2. Buy some components/parts or materials and manufacture and assemble others; and
3. Manufacture the part or product completely.

An organisation cannot manage its operations on the basis of the third alternative alone, even though it may have a large base of an integrated operation starting from extraction of basic raw materials down to final production of marketable finished goods. And some companies perfer to stick to the first alternative because they are either a merchandising firm or engineering organisatian and the part or product is not suited to their manufacturing facilities, or may be due to the patent or specialisation of the vendor or the supplier. As a general rule, therefore, a manufacturing company will make some of its parts or components and buy others from outside sources, either in semi-finished or finished state. Even when procurement of an item by purchasing looks plausible, the question 'make or buy' must be settled first in the form of economic analysis if no definite company policy exists. Such decisions have obviously to be made before making the purchase requisition and supply order. Often it is outside the scope and responsibility of the purchasing department to find the answer. Cost considerations and conditions in the supply market may suggest a change even when the part or product was formerly purchased. On the other hand, it may work in quite opposite directions, although the significance and justification of the proposition 'make or buy' largely depends on the volume and cost involved. For this reason, cost-comparison is one of the first considerations that confronts the decision maker, but it may not always be the most important consideration. The estimated total cost of production must be compared against the cost of purchase to know the pay-off. It is apparent, therefore, that when a 'make or buy' decision has to be made, what matters is not the purchasing policy or source of supply but the consultation and cooperation of Production, Cost, Quality and other technical departments. Even marketing executives may have to be consulted. A simple 'make or buy' decision may have such economic implication as that may affect the total organisation interest on a much wider scale which can even threaten the product stability in a highly competitive market.

Formally, 'make or buy' decisions of such vital importance are made by top management and here the Materials Management Department plays the key role in collecting, collating, analysing and interpreting data. It also acts as co-ordinator between other departments so as to assist top management in decision-making. A decision based on minimum cost-point has to be located for an optimum decision and if two or more alternatives possess the same characteristics, the minimum cost-point for each must be determined for a final choice.

Decision Model for Optimum Purchase Quantity

When a decision has to be made to procure an item, it is necessary to determine the optimum purchase quantity which will result in minimum cost. After the demand for the item has been settled, it may be met by procurement at the beginning of the year, or by purchasing day-to-day supply. Since neither of these two extremes it economical from the viewpoint of costs associated with purchasing and holding the item, inventory models are used to arrive at a decision for the most economical purchase quantity. Let

TC = total annual cost of the item

D = annual demand of the item

N = number of purchases during the year

t = time between purchases

Q = purchase quantity

C_i = item cost per unit (purchase cost)

C_p = purchase cost per order

C_h = holding cost per unit per year (cost of storage, rent, term, insurance, interest and handling, etc.)

Assuming that the demand for the item is contant throughout its year, the purchase lead-time is zero and no stock-out is allowed the total cost will be sum total of the annual item cost, purchase cost and the holding cost for the year, that is,

$$TC = IC + PC + HC$$

The yearly item cost will be the time cost per unit times the yearly demand in units, or

$$IC = C_t(D)$$

The purchase cost will be the cost per purchase times the number of purchases during the year, or

$$PC = C_p(N)$$

But N is the annual demand divided by purchase quantity, hence

$$PC = \frac{C_p(D)}{Q}$$

Since the time interval begins with Q and ends in zero, the average inventory during the cycle-time will be Q/2 and, therefore, the holding cost for the year will be the holding cost per unit times the average number of units held in stock during the year, or

$$HC = \frac{C_h(Q)}{2}$$

So that the total annual cost of providing the item by purchase will be the sum total of the item cost, purchase cost and holding cost, or

$$TC = C_i(D) + \frac{C_p(D)}{Q} + \frac{C_h(Q)}{2}$$

For example when the annual demand for an item is 1,000 units cost per unit delivered is Rs. 16.00, purchase cost per order is Rs. 10.00 and the cost of holding one unit in inventory per annum is Rs. 1.32, the total cost may be expressed as a function of Q by substituting the costs and various valves of Q into the total cost equation, as tabulated below:

Purchase Quantity	*Total Cost*
50	Rs. 16,233
100	Rs. 16,166
125	Rs. 16,162
150	Rs. 16,165
200	Rs. 16,182
300	Rs. 16,231
400	Rs. 16,289
500	Rs. 16,350
600	Rs. 16,412

Reading from the table, it may be seen that under conditions specified, the total cost for Q=125 is the minimum, that is to say, it is optimum.

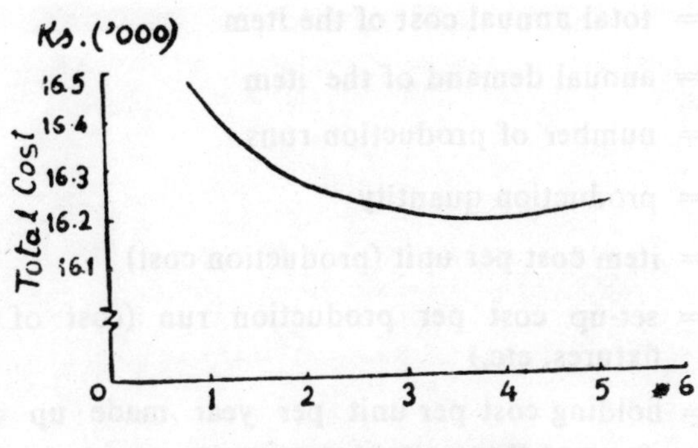

Fig. 18.1 Graph for total cost as a function of purchase quantity

A solution may also be found by applying mathematical optimisation formula, which is very close to the tabulated value, thus

$$Q = \sqrt{\frac{2C_p(D)}{C_h}}$$

Where $A = C_h/2$, $B = C_p(D)$ and $C = C_i(D)$. By substitution, we get

$$Q = \sqrt{\frac{2(\text{Rs. } 10{\cdot}00)\ (1{,}000)}{\text{Rs. } 1{\cdot}32}}$$

$$= 123 \text{ units or say, } 125 \text{ units}$$

Total cost=Rs. 16,160 (apprx.) which will not substantially alter the situation.

Decision Model for Optimum Production Quantity

Similarly, when a decision has to be made to manufacture an item, it is necessary to determine the production quantity that will result in minimum cost. This may also be done in the manner described before, only difference being that when a purchase quantity is received, it is received in lots, but production lot accumulates as the item is produced and this has to be taken into account. Let

TC = total annual cost of the item

D = annual demand of the item

N = number of production runs

Q = production quantity

C_i = item cost per unit (production cost)

C_s = set-up cost per production run (cost of tooling, fixtures, etc.)

C_h = holding cost per unit per year made up of such items as storage rent, taxes, etc.

R = production rate.

Assuming that the demand for the item is constant, production rate is constant during the production run, the production lead-time is zero and no shortage is allowed, the resulting inventory system will operate in the similar fashion as in the purchase quantity. The total yearly cost will be the sum total of the annual item cost, set-up cost and the holding cost for the year, that is,

$$TC = IC + SC + HC$$

The yearly item cost will be the item cost per unit times the yearly demand in units, or

$$IC = C_i(D)$$

The set-up cost for the year will be the cost per set-up times the number of set-ups per year, or

$$SC = C_s(N)$$

But since N is the yearly demand divided by the production quantity,

$$SC = \frac{C_s(D)}{Q}$$

When items are added to inventory at a rate of R units per year and are taken from inventory at a rate of D units per year, where R>D, the net rate of accumulation is (R−D) units per year and the time required to produce D units at the rate of R units per year is D/R years. If D units are made in a single lot, the maximum accumulation will be (R—D) D/R. Since there will be nothing in stock at the end of the year, the average inventory will be

$$\frac{(R-D)/R+O}{2} = (R-D)\frac{D}{2R}$$

If N lots are produced per year, the average number in stock will be

$$(R-D)\frac{D}{2RN}$$

But, since N=D/Q, the average number may be expressed as

$$(R-D)\frac{Q}{2R}$$

The holding cost for the year will be the holding cost per unit times the average number for the year, or

$$HC = C_h(R-D)\frac{Q}{2R}$$

Since the total yearly cost of making the item is the sum total of the item cost, set-up cost and the holding cost, or

$$TC = C_i(D) + \frac{C_s(D)}{Q} + C_h(R-D)\frac{Q}{2R}$$

Again, assuming that the annual demand for an item is 1,000 units. cost of production is Rs. 15.90 per unit (including elements of cost for direct labour, direct material and factory overhead) and the set-up cost per lot is Rs. 50.00 and the item can be manufactured at a rate of 6,000 units per year, the holding cost of one unit in inventory per annum is Rs. 1.30, the total cost may be expressed as a function of Q by substituting costs and various values of Q into the total equation. The result is tabulated below, from which it may be seen that for conditions specified, the total cost for Q=300 is minimum. In other words, this is the optimum production quantity.

Production Quantity	*Total Cost*
100	Rs. 16,454
150	Rs. 16,314
200	Rs. 16,258
300	Rs. 16,229
400	Rs. 16,241
500	Rs. 16,270
600	Rs. 16,307

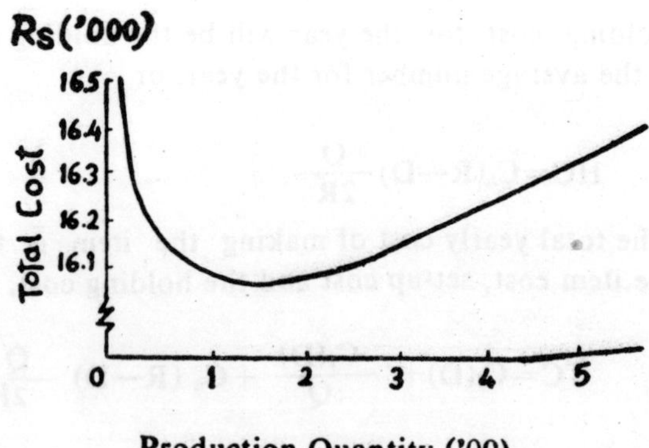

Fig. 18.2 Graph for total cost as a function of production quantity

As before, the economic production quantity may be found by the use of mathematical optimisation formula, which is also close to the calculated figure, thus

$$Q = \sqrt{\frac{2C_s(D)}{C_h(1-D/R)}}$$

where $A=C_h(R-D)/2R$, $B=C_sD$ and $C=C_t(D)$. By substitution we get

$$Q = \sqrt{\frac{2\ (\text{Rs. } 50.00)\ (1{,}000)}{\text{Rs. } 1.30\ (1-1{,}000/6{,}000)}}$$

= 302 units or say, 300 units

Total cost=Rs. 16,230 (apprx.) which will not substantially alter the situation.

Make or Buy Decision

Now, whether to purchase an item or to manufacture it may be resolved by the application of minimum cost-analysis for multiple alternatives. The alternative of manufacturing may be compared with that of purchasing to find out the respective total cost values, and the choice that identifies the minimum cost is better of the two alternatives.

Suppose that an item will have an annual demand of 1,000 units and the costs associated with purchasing and production are as assumed.

	Purchase	*Produce*
Item cost	Rs. 16.00	Rs. 15.90
Purchase cost	Rs. 10.00	—
Set-up cost	—	Rs. 50.00
Holding cost	Rs 1.32	Rs. 1.30

Respecting the assumptions, on the basis of tabulated values total costs as a function of purchase quantity and production quantity two separate graphs were drawn (Figs. 18.1 and 18.2). When superimposed, the resultant new graph will look like the following:

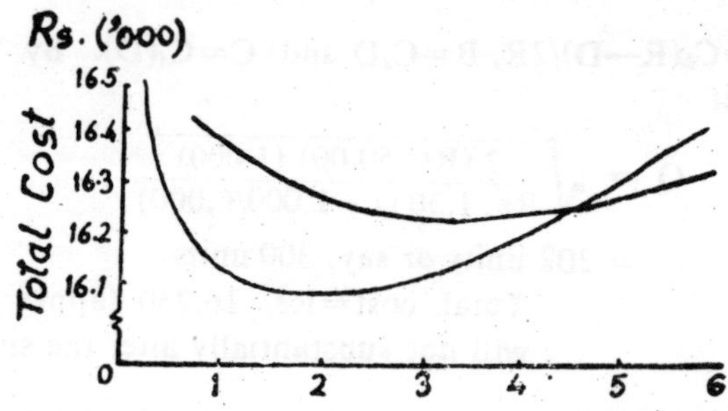

Purchasing and Prodnction Quantity ('00)

Fig. 18.3 Combined graph for total cost as a function of purchase and production quantity

Adecision whether to 'make or buy' may be made by examining and comparing the minimum cost for each alternative. In this particular case, a decision to purchase will be the least cost alternative resulting in a saving of Rs. 70.00 per year (Rs. 6,230—Rs. 6,160). If a decision has to be made on the basis of cost consideration alone, the needed item would be supplied by purchasing. It must be noted, however, that accurate cost information is hard to obtain.

In any case, in order to make sure that no significant factor is over-looked in making a final decision, apart from cost comparison, the following factors should also be properly weighed:

1. *Quality factor*: Adherence to specifications and quality requirements and rejection of defective parts/components and their timely replacement by suitable ones must be considered

2. *Capacity factor*: Is there any spare capacity and possibility of some overhead to be absorbed and how much additional capital is needed to manufacture?

3. *Labour factor*: Whether labour, skilled and semi-skilled, are available or further training is necessary for undertaking the manufacture of the new item.

4. *Skill factor*: Are the technical expertise available within the organisation and is it most profitable to use the experts' time on the new item?

5. *Scheduling factor*: If there is possibility of adjusting capacity to peaks and slow-downs and would it be possible to ensure timely supply?

For a scientific evaluation of the problem of 'make or buy', their are internal factors which must be considered before a switchover is made from buying to manufacturing. It must be pointed on here that apart from internal factors, there are also some long-time external factors which should receive serious attention of top-management for decision-making.

Suppose, as in the example cited, if there are other pressing needs for the manufacture of the item, only a saving of Rs. 70.00 per year will not warrant a decision for purchase.

REFERENCES AND ACKNOWLEDGEMENTS

Ammer, D.S., *Materials Management*, Richard D. Irwin, Inc.' Homewood, III., 1962.

Datta, A.K., *Integrated Materials Management: A Functional Approach*, S. Chand and Co., New Delhi, 1978.

———, *Materials Management: A Total Systems Approach*, Kalyani Publishers, New Delhi, 1982.

———, *Materials Management: Procedures, Text and Cases*, Prentice-Hall of India Pvt. Ltd., New Delhi, 1983.

England, W.B. and Leenders, M.R., *Purchasing and Materials Management*, Richard D. Irwin Inc., Homewood, Ill., 1975 (Indian Reprint edn. D.B. Taraporevala Sons and Co. Pvt. Ltd. Bombay, 1978).

Fabrycky, W.J. and Thuesen, G.J., *Economic Decision Analysis*, Prentice-Hall, Inc., Englewood Cliffs., N.J., 1974.

Heinritz, S.F., *Purchasing: Principles and Applications*, Prentice-Hall. Inc., Englewood Cliffs, N.J. 1961.

19

Productivity and Efficiency in Human Service Organizations as Related to Structure Size, and Age,

CHARLES A. GLISSON &
PATRICIA YANCEY MARTIN

Given widespread interest in and pressures for "accountability" in the public arena (Glisson, 1975), surprisingly little attention has been given to the development and testing of models that explain variation in the performance of human service organizations. In organizations that lack straight-forward output indicators (such as sales volume or annual profits), it is difficult to identify criteria that are either useful or applicable in the assessment of performance (Human and Freeman, 1977). This, perhaps, has stymied the investigation of predictors of success or effectiveness. Nevertheless, the demands of decision makers for relevant and comparable data across organizations underscore the need for establishing performance criteria and, more importantly, for understanding the determinants of successful performance (Whetten, 1978).

The present study presents organizational structure, size and age as determinants of an organization's performance and empirically investigates their effects on the output criteria of productivity and efficiency in a variety of types of human service organizations. Structure is conceptualized in the hypothesized model as directly affecting productivity and efficiency. Size and age are shown as indirectly affecting the performance criteria through their effect on structure. Productivity is defined as the quantity of service provided and efficiency as the per unit cost of providing service. Although these criteria are, in fact, responsive to certain accountability demands, no claim is made that any one is an indicator of the effectiveness of services provided. However, there is general consensus on the meaning or intent of productivity and efficiency, whereas the concept of effectiveness currently is beset by definitional ambiguity in both the human service (Hasenfeld and English, 1974) and organizational literature (Goodman and Pennings, 1977). The prescriptive implications of the model suggest that administrative influence can be wielded over performance through the manipulation of structural dimensions within the constrains imposed by the size and age of the organization.

THEORETICAL MODEL

Structure as a Determinant of Productivity and Efficiency

Figure 19 1 shows the hypothesized theoretical model of the present study. In this model, productivity (number of clients served per week per line worker) and efficiency (number of clients served per week per $ 10,000 annual budget) are determined by the degree to which the organization's internal structure is centralized and formalized. It suggests that the structural dimensions of centralization and formalization have a direct and positive impact on the outcome criteria of productivity and efficiency. Centralization refers to the degree to which the authority and decision making power in the organization is concentrated versus dispersed (Price, 1972 . Formalization refers to the degree to which divisions of labour and procedures are explicit (*e.g.*, written or espoused in the form of guidelines) rather than implicit (Price, 1972). The model in Figure 19.1 proposes that human service organization that are more highly centralized and formalized are also more productive and efficient in terms of number of clients served and the cost of serving them.

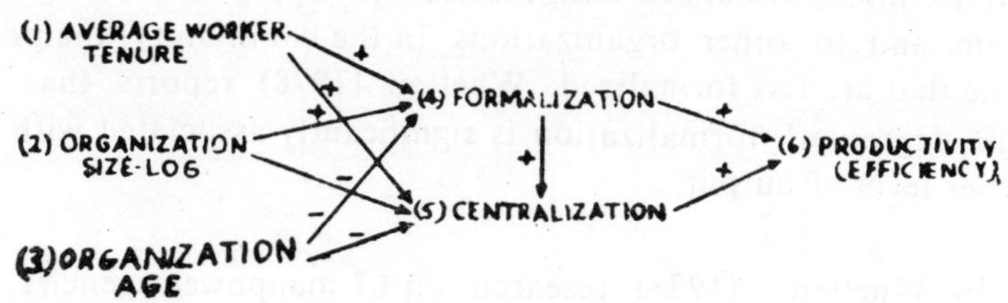

Fig. 19.1 Hypothesized Model of the Influence of Organizational Size, Age, and Structure on Productivity and Efficiency.

When it is difficult to assess relevant differences in the quality of a product or service, Scott (1977) suggests that quantity of services performed may serve as an effectiveness criterion. He notes that for a large number of organizations, quantity indicators are the only "effectiveness" measures that are routinely or systematically collected. Whetten (1978) documents that central administrators of manpower programs view number of clients served (specifically, number of placements or referrals made) as the major "effectiveness" criterion on which funding decisions are based. Finally, Hannan and Freeman (1977) suggest that effectiveness and efficiency are probably closely related for organizations that face resource constraints.

Justification for the positive effects of increased centralization and formalization on productivity and efficiency rasts on research by Hage (1965), Price (1968), Mott (1972), Molnar and Rogers (1976), and Whetten (1978). Mott (1972), in particular, reports positive associations between clarity of rules, policies, and guidelines and the amount of productivity in the organizations he studied. Hage (1965), in his axiomatic theory of organizations, argues that greater formalization is associated with greater productivity and efficiency due to the fact that it minimizes decisional uncertainty. Molnar and Rogers (1976) report (for a sample of 110 public agencies in Iowa) that those that are more formalized both receive and supply more resources (from and to other organizations in the community) than do those that are less formalized. Whetten (1978) reports that a high degree of formalization is significantly associated with a higher level of output.

In Whetten's (1978) research on 67 manpower agencies, a centralized decision making structure is observed to be even more strongly associated with level of output (here, propuctivity) than is formalization ($r=.41$ vs. .31). Whetten concludes that "if an administrator centralizes the decision making process, output will increase. . . ." Reasons for this, similar to those for formalization, rest on the reduction of decisional leeway at the service delivery level. Similar conclusions are reported by Price (1968) and, to some extent, by Mott (1972).

In a highly centralized organization, workers at the service delivery level are allowed minimal say-so in the decision making process of the organization: for example, in regard to the setting of policies and hiring of new employees. On the one hand, this frees the workers from concern with larger organizational issues and increases the time available for direct service delivery. Direct service workers in a centralized organization therefore have more time to deal directly with clients. Logically, productivity, or the number of clients served, should be enhanced. On the other hand, these same workers are likely to resent their lack of opportunity for decisional participation (Holland, 1973; Pondy, 1977). Whetten (1978) reports that although centralization facilitates productivity, it also produces a dissatisfied staff. To the extent that a "satisfied" staff is a necessary component of *effective* service delivery, it may be the case that the goals of productivity/efficiency are in conflict with those of service effectiveness. This, in fact, is a very real possibility and, for this reason, will be discussed later.

As shown in Figure 19.1 formalization is proposed to have a positive effect on the extent to which the authority and discretion of the line workers are centralized. The explicit specification of divisions of labour and operating procedures among line workers reduces the discretion and authority exercised in carrying out their job takes. Workers in more formalized settings simply do not have as much decision making power over what they do or how they do it as do workers in less formalized settings. A higher degree of formalization, therefore, facilitates the concentration of power into the hands of those who specify procedures and divisions of labour, *i.e.* the decision makers in the hierarchical structure.

Size and Age as Determinants of Structure

Size—The organizational literature is fairly consistent in reporting a negative association of organizational size with centralization of authority (Pugh, Hickson, Hinings, and Turner 1969; Blau, 1970). 'As shown in Figure 19.1 a negative relationship is hypothesized here as well. Size, typically indicated by number of organizational members (usually employees), is conceptualized by Blau (1970) as inevitably leading to an increase in structural differentiation (Blau and Schoenherr, 1971). As an organization becomes more differentiated (*e.g.*, into more divisions and departments), decision making authority necessarily becomes more dispersed. (For a contrasting viewpoint, see Hall, 1963, and Hall, Johnson, and Haas, 1967.) As additional organizational units are created, authority migrates away from a single administrative chief to at least a number of lower level administrators in charge of the various subunits. The degree to which the authority of the line worker is affected by this process, however, is seldom addressed. Although the organization *as a whole* may exhibit a less centralized authority structure with an increase in number of employees, little is known regarding the effects of this process on the direct service worker's participation in organizational level decision making.

It should be noted that extrapolation from previous results to the present study may be invalidated by the generally small size of the organizations in the present sample. As shown in Table 19.1 one of the organizations has as few as 14 employees. Fully two-thirds of them have 1,000 or fewer. Thus, previously reported results based on organizations of 25,000 or so employees such as those obtained by Pugh *et. al.* (1969) may be inapplicable here. Pugh *et. al.* (1969) report, in addition, that public organizations have considerably more centralized authority structures than do private ones, regardless of size. In the present sample, therefore, a rather weak association might be expected—of whichever direction—between size and centralization of authority. Finally, it is noted that the observed effects

TABLE 19.1

Characteristics of the Sample

Variable	*Mean*	*Standard Deviation*	*Minimum*	*Maximum*
Organization age (years)	**45.76**	**37.34**	**2**	**134**
Organization size (total workers)	**303.17**	**653.12**	**14**	**3292**
Average worker tenure	**4.48**	**2.79**	**1**	**12**
Centralization	**47.72**	**10.04**	**28**	**69**
Formalization	**41.70**	**6.70**	**28**	**56**
Productivity (clients/ week/worker)	**27.60**	**17.46**	**5**	**82**
Efficiency (clients/ week/$ 10,000)	**35.65**	**45.85**	**7**	**228**

of organizational size on organizational structure typically are reported to be curvilinear in from (Child, 1973; Mileti, Gillespie, and Haas, 1977). Given the restricted range of sizes represented by the 30 human service organizations in the present sample, it may be the case that an increase in size leads *initially* to an increase in centralization up to some point at which it turns downward and leads to a decrease. In light of this possibility, the initial analysis here includes size in both its log-transformed and raw form modes.

The relationship between size and formalization is reported consistently in the literature to be positive (Hall *et. al.*, 1967; Pugh *et. al* , 1969; Kimberly, 1976). A positive association is hypothesized here as well (see Figure 19.). Greater size leads to greater development and utilization of formalized rules, procedures, and guidlines. The reasons for this reflect the increased need for clarity, predictability, and planning prompted by the presence of large numbers of emplyees (Tracy and Azumi, 1976).

It is important to note that formalization is the aspect of organizational structure generally associated in the public mind with "bureaucratic red tape." Popularly damned as a nuisance and a hindrance, it represents an aspect of bureaucratic organization that assures a minimum of fairness and consistency in the treatment of employees and clients alike. In this light, it is important to note recent findings by Anderson (1977). He reports a moderate degree of formalization to be associated with *higher* job satisfaction and *fewer* feeling of alienation among 200 direct service workers in 19 service organizations.

The specification of rules and procedures may be viewed, therefore, as reducing ceertain kinds of work-relevant uncertainty and, in doing so, facilitating the conduct of a worker's job. To the extent that very small organizations lack such specificantions and very large ones have too many of them, it can be expected that they will be both less productive and less efficient than will medium size organizations with a moderate degree of formalization.

Age—Organizational age or "time" is a relatively neglected topic in the literature on human service organizations (Moos, 1974; Kimberly, 1976). Stinchcombe (1965) suggests that this is to be expected because age is largely an irrelevant cancept for understanding organizations (also, Hall, 1963). Others, however, have found age to be moderately associated with aspects of structure (Pugh *et. ul.*, 1969), admissions policies (Martin, 1978), and programmatic emphasis on rehabilitation versus custody (Kimberly, 1975). Heydebrand (1973) reports that among hospitals both higher quality and greater stability are associated with increased organizational age. Age of the organization is examined here as one aspect of organizational time that influences the organization's structure.

In a broader sense, Pfeffer (1977) suggests that the age and tenure distributions of organizational *members* be examined to determine the "time horizons" of an organization. Following his suggestion, staff tenure (or the average length of employment of direct-service staff) is analyzed as a second dimension of organizational time. Although "official" organizational records are likely to antedate the tenure of any given employee, the actual reference to "precedents" or previous actions or events depends to some extent on employees who have memories or habits or their own. In organizations with a more highly tenured staff, one can expect greater reliance on tradition or precedent than would be the case if all the staff were relatively new. To the extent, then, that greater "age" in general means greater knowledge, greater experience, and more extensive behavioral and cognitive repertoires, organizational age may be said to be reflected by the tenure of the employees.

As shown in Figure 19.1 the two dimensions of organizational time are hypothesized to influence formalization and centralization in opposite directions. Actual age of the organization, taken as evidence of the organization's previous success at adaptation, is expected to influence a *decrease* in both formalization and centralization (Pugh *et. al.*, 1969). With increased evidence of survival ability, older organizations may be expected to relax a bit. Confidence in the ability of the system to produce desired results is hypothesized, with the passage of time, to lead to a decentralization of the decision making process and to somewhat lesser emphasis on formalized rules and procedures.

A higher average staff tenure, on the other hand, is expected to have the opposite effect. In the present case, where tenure data are taken from direct service workers, long term employment in a low-level organizational position is expected to encourage greater reliance on formalized rules and procedures and a more centralized authority structure. This process may be conceptualized as the institutionalization of "maintenance structures" in order to preserve a study state (Katz and Kahn, 1966). Thompson (1967) states that "organizations abhor uncertainty," suggesting that people abhor uncertainty in organizational situations. Workers may contribute, therefore, to the institutionalization of maintenance structures over time by following the "well-worn paths" described by March and Simon (1958) in solving organizational problems. Formalization and centralization reflect stability, lack of uncertainty, and lack of contingencies. As workers fall into their slots over the years, they feel comfortable with a steady state situation and thereby contribute to it, maintain it, and support it.

A related consideration is suggested by Kanter (1977). Direct service staff who remain in a front-line position for an extended period of time may be persons who lack attributes necessary for promotion or who have been repeatedly passed over for advancement or promotion (as a result, for example, of institutionalized sexism or racism that limits opportunity and discourages ambition). Kanter (1977) reports that workers who remained locked in to low level organizational positions tend, over time, to become rigid, to encourage turf development, and to oppose innovation and change. Such workers, therefore, are likely to contribute through their behaviour to the creation and maintenance of a more formalized and centralized organizational structure. (It is possible that the causal ordering here is either the reverse of what is proposed here (*i.e.*, with centralization and formalization influencing length of tenure] or else reciprocal in nature. In short, a highly centralized and formalized structure may result in a lack of organizational fluidity and thus chances for advancement by direct service workers. Weick [1977] and Pondy [1977] caution against "too much stability" as a liability to the long term adaptability of the organization.) Whether or not this is an otherwise desirable occurrence, the model in Figure 19.1 suggests that it will contribute indirectly to a higher degree of organizational productivity and efficiency.

At any rate, results of the present analysis will allow an assessment of the relative effects of the age of the organization *per se versus* the average tenure of the staff as predictors of structure (and ultimately productivity and efficiency) in human service organizations. (Because "older" organizations have greater *potential* for staff with longer tenure, it may be the case that consequences sometimes attributed to years of operation are, instead, consequences of staff seniority or tenure, or *vice versa*. While the two variables no doubt are highly collinear in some organizations, they are conceptually distinctive aspects of organizational time.)

METHOD

Each of the 30 organizations in a large, mid-western city selected from the 34 that agreed to participate in the study had at least one administrative level above the line workers who had direct contact with the clients. The selected organizations provided the following: corrections (2), services to the aged (1), children's services (7), drug abuse treatment (2), family counseling (6), welfare services (5), mental health services (3), services to the mentally retarded (1), and services to the physically handicapped (3). Each of the organizations attempted to improve the affective, cognitive or behavioral functioning of their clients and used a variety of intensive technologies (Thompson, 1967) to produce those changes. The 408 workers participating in the study were well educated (89 per cent college graduates and 52 per cent with a master's degree or above), with the majarity of the degress held in the social sciences or "helping" professions (88 percent). The most frequently occurring degree was a master of social work (35 per cent).

All of the workers in each organization whose primary job responsibility involved direct interaction with clients for the purpose of facilitating changes in these clients responded to the questionnaire, except that in two correctional institutions, a medical-psychiatric hospital, a state mental hospital, and a large community service organization, the questionnaires were administered only to workers in the social services departments. The questionnaires were completed anonymously during staff meetings and returned unsigned during the meeting. Organizational scores for formalization and centralization were derived by arithmetically averaging the worker responses within each organization.

Centralization was measured with the participation in decision making scale developed by Hage and Aiken (1967) and the hierarchy of authority scale developed by Hall (1961). Formalization was measured with the division of labour and procedural specifications scales developed by Hall (1961). For both dimensions of structure, items were combined within each pair of scales and scored so that possible values for centralization and formalization ranged from 0 to 100. Split-half reliabilities calculated for each scale were .88 for participation in decision making, .89 for hierarchy of authority, .75 for division of labour, and .79 for procedural specifications. The total number of worker responses for establishing scale reliabilities was 408.

Average worker tenure was calculated by arithmetically averaging the number of years all present workers had been with the organization. Organizational age was simply the number of years the organization had been in existence. These are two measures of "time" in an organization, with the former measure hypothesized to have greater significance for internal organizational characteristics, such as structure, and the latter having greater significance perhaps for certain relationships with the environment important to funding, legitimation, or marketing.

Organization size was measured both as the total number of workers in the orgnnization and as a natural log transformation of the number of workers in the organization. The log transformation was conducted because of the expected curvilinear relationship between size and structure as reported by prior investigators (Child, 1973; Mileti *et al.* 1977).

The measure of productivity consisted of the average number of different clients served by each line worker per week. A measure of efficiency was calculated as the number of clients served per week per $10,000 annual budget (Goodman & Pennings, 1977; Price, 1968). Although it is emphasized that these variables certainly are not indicators of the quality of service being delivered, the "accountability controversy" (Glisson, 1975) dictates a need for such data if only for purposes of description and discussion. The absence of productivity and efficiency data serves to increase unfounded speculation and misdirect inquiry into accountability.

RESULTS

Table 19.1 presents the means, standard deviations, and ranges of the variables measured. The productivity and efficiency data are of particular note because of the present dearth of such information in the literature. The frequency distributions of the average number of clients served per week per worker and of number of clients served per week per $10,000 budget indicate considerable differences among organizations. The effects of type of service organization (residential vs. non-residential, physiological vs. psychological etc.) on productivity and efficiency were controlled for by standardizing the measures in week-units. Simply because of the different rates of turnover, an organization providing residential care could service significantly fever clients on a yearly basis than if it provided only outpatient care. On a weekly basis, however, the differences according to type of organization have an insignificant impact on productivity and efficiency. For example, one correctional institution had the highest productivity score (82 clients/week/worker), but the other correctional institution scored below the mean (26 clients/week/worker). Also, one organization delivering welfare services had the third highest efficiency score (110 clients/week/$10,000), and another tied for the lowest (7 clients/week/$10,000). An exception to the observation that type of organization had no effect on productivity is that the two least productive organizations (5 and 8 clients/week/worker) both treated drug abuse problems. However, the organizations also were similar in structure (with stores of 36 and 31 on centralization; 39 and 31 on formalization), which was significantly correlated with productivity across the total sample. Also there was a greater discrepancy in the two organizations' efficiency scores (20 and 11 clients/week/$10,000), with ordinal rankings of 16 and 24 in the sample of 30.

The discrepancies in any organization's productivity and efficiency rankings depend on the size of its budget per staff, which is determined, to some extent, by salaries. For example, a child guidance clinic was more productive than nine other organizations (21 clients/week/worker) but, because a number of psychiatrists were employed as line workers, it along with one other organization proved to be the least efficient of all the organizations (7 clients/week/$10,000). The richness of these productivity and efficiency data, in short, provide convincing evidence that this is an area long overdue for close examination.

As shown by the Pearson correlations in Table 19.2, neither organizational size, age, nor average worker tenure is significantly related to either productivity or efficiency, although the two structural dimensions are positively correlated with both. Also, organization size-log and average worker tenure are positively correlated with both structural dimensions, but organization size and organization age are not correlated with

TABLE 19.2

Pearson Correlation Matrix (N=30)

	(1)	(2)	(2a)	(3)	(4)	(5)	(6)
(1) Average worker tenure							
(2) Organization size·log	.28						
(2a) Organization size	.05	.79*					
(3) Organization age	.33*	.19*	.15				
(4) Formalization	.34*	.33*	.01	−.03			
(5) Centralization	.49*	.42*	.11	−.05	.79*		
(6) Productivity	.15	.19	−.08	.07	.32*	.50*	
(7) Efficiency	.01	.21	−.10	−.07	.30*	.40*	.70*

*$p < .05$

either structural dimension. The very high correlation (.79) between formalization and centralization supports the hypothesized relationship between the formalization of divisions of labour and procedures and the centralization of authority and discretion at the line worker level.

Figure 19.2 presents the results of a path analysis of the hypothesized model which decomposes the zero-order correlations into direct and indirect effects. Centralization has a very large, positive, direct effect on productivity as predicted; formalization has an unpredicted smaller, negative, direct effect. Because of the high correlation between centralization, formalization, formalization is suppressing a portion of the variance in centralization uncorrelated with productivity. In removing the

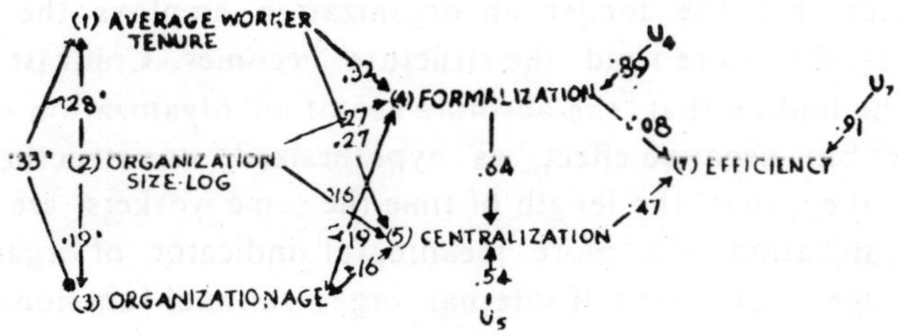

Fig. 19.2 Path Analysis of Hypothesized Model with Productivity as an Outcome Variable
*Zero-order correlations.

variance in centralization associated with formalization, centralization's impact on productivity is increased. Formalization, as a result, negatively affects productivity after the variation explained by centralization has been accounted for. This indicates that limiting the authority and participation in decision making of line workers increases the number of clients they serve, if formalization is held constant, but that increasing formal divisions of labour and procedural specifications slightly decreases the number of clients served by each worker if centalization is held constant. However, formalization has the proposed positive, direct effect on centralization and, therefore, a positive, indirect effect on productivity of .44. The total effect of formaliz tion on productivity, then, is also positive as suggested vy the zero-order correlation. As divisions of labour and procedural specifications are formalized within an organization, the power and discretion of the line workers are decreased. They apparently become less involved in administrative or management problem solving and are freed to devote their time to clients. Although this increases productivity, it is not an indicator of effectiveness. Formalization, in fact, may have a negative impact on effectiveness as suggested in an earlier analysis (Glisson, 1978).

Of the three predictors of structure included in the model, average worker tenure had the greatest impact on both formalization and centralization. This predicted, positive effect indicates that the longer an organization employs the same workers, the more rigid the structure becomes. Contrast this with the finding that the absolute age of an organization had a smaller but negative effect, as hypothesized, on structure. It seems, then, that the length of time the same workers are with an organization is a more meaningful indicator of organizational age, particularly if internal organizational functioning is the focus.

When log transformed, organizational size shows the proposed positive effect on formalization and, also, an unexpected positive, although small, effect on centralization. The log transformation was necessary because the relationships between size and both formalization and centralization were found to be curvilinear, with the impact of size leveling off at around 200 workers and a slight downward trend beginning at around 400 workers for both variables. The fact that the majority of the sample had less than 400 employees could therefore explain the discrepancy between the present findings and other studies reporting a negative relationship between size and centralization. This curvilinear relationship may explained by the tendency of departments, divisions, or offices to become the units of reference for workers as organizations become larger. That is, the structural variables measured here cease to be a function of total size as departments, divisions, or offices begin to assume a degree of autonomy within larger organizations and become the units of reference for policy and planning.

It should also be emphasized that, although size-log and centralization enjoyed a significant zero-order correlation, the direct effect of size-log on centralization proved negligible after the variation in centralization explained by formalization was accounted for. The high correlation between size-log and centralization, therefore, could be interpreted as an artifact of their shared high correlalions with formalization.

The adequacy of the path model was tested by predicting correlations that were not constrained to be reproduced automatically by the path model, using the basic theorem of path analysis, $r_{ij}=\Sigma p_{iq} r_{jq}$, where r equals the correlation coefficient, p equals the path coefficient, the subscripts i and j denote two variables in the model, and q ranges over all variables from which paths directly effect x_i (Land, 1969). The initial subscript of the path coefficient indicates the dependent variable, and the second subscript indicates the independent variable in that particular direct causal relationship. The path model should enable the investigator to reproduce, closely, correlations that were not used in the derivation of the path coefficients. The crucial correlations to be reproduced are between those variables that have no predicted direct effect on each other, excluding correlations. between two exogenous variables, which are assumed to be known. Table 18.3 shows the observed and predicted correlations for the hypothesized path model. The crucial correlations are r_{16}, r_{26}, and r_{36}, and the predicted correlations deviate from the observed by .10, .03, and .10, respectively. The model reproduces the correlation matrix fairly well, but there is no test of the degree of fit to determine if the model is the "right" model. The adequacy of the model in explanining variance was supported using the test reportee by Kim and Kohout (1975), where L=−1.4974 with 3 degrees of freedom, indicating that the variance explained by the restricted model did not differ significantly from that explained by the general model. The theoretical rationale underlying the model, however, is the true test of the model. That rationale combined with the ability to repoduce accurately the observed correlations and to explain variance provides support for the specified model.

TABLE 19.3

Observed and Predicted Correlations for Hypothesized Model in Figure 19.1

Observed r_{ij}[a]	*Predicted* r_{ij}	*Difference* $\vert r_j - r_{ij} \vert$
$r_{16}=.15$	$r_{16}=.15$	.10
$r_{26}=.19$	$r_{26}=.21$	.03
$r_{36}=.07$	$r_{36}=.03$	.10

[a]Correlations constrained to be automatically reproduced by the model are not included. Those listed are the crucial correlations which determine the predictive ability of the model.

The model in Fig. 19.3 shows efficiency, rather than productivity, as the outcome variable. It differs from the previous model

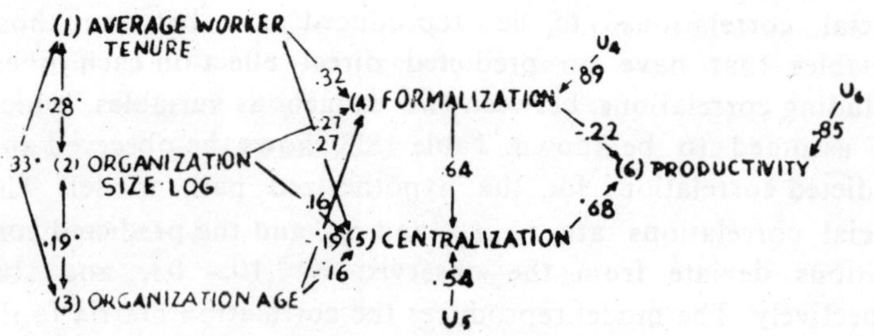

*Zero-order correlations.

Figure 3: Path Analysis of Hypothesized Model with Efficiency as an Outcome Variable

only in the path coefficients from formalization and centralization to efficiency. These were —.08 for the path from formalization and .47 for the path from centralization. This is the same pattern observed for productivity; centralization exhibits a larger, positive effect, and formalization exhibits a smaller, negative effect efficiency. The sizes of the effects of both structural dimensions on efficiency, however, are substantially smaller than on productivity, with formalization having almost no impact whatsoever. The differences between the predicted correlations based on the efficiency model and the observed correlations are the same as for the productivity model except that the predicted correlation for r_{16} based on the efficiency model deviates from the observed by only .05, rather than by -10.

SUMMARY AND DISCUSSION

As suggested by Whetten (1978), present results confirm the importance of centralization of authority in accounting for quantity of organizational output. A highly centralized human service organization is likely to be highly productive and, to a lesser degree, efficient as well. A heightened reliance on formalized rules and procedures apparently facilitates concentration of decision making power in the hands of a few. (Rather than being alternative modes of organizational "control as suggested by Pugh *et al.* [1969], formalization and centralization are apparently supportive of each other). Further, it is this concentration of power that facilitates productivity and efficiency. It is emphasized, however, that the *direct* effects of formalization on productivity and efficiency are negative in direction, indicating that gaeater emphasis on formal rules and procedures has the direct consequence of reducing each. As previously stated, this negative direct effect results from the "net" suppression of the variance in centralization (Cohen and Coeen, 1975). To the extent that formalization enhances centralization, however, its overall impact on both output criteria is positive.

The findings suggest the conclusion that average staff tenure is somewhat more important than organizational age for understanding the origins of internal organizational structure. As hypothesized, older organizations are somewhat less formalized and centralized, whereas those with a more senior staff are somewhat more so. Because the two variables are positively associated with each other at the zero-order level (r=.33), their directional divergence in relation to struture suggests that they may be indicative of different theoretical concepts. Perhaps age of the organization is a reflection of its relationship with the environment (*i.e.*, in terms of previous adaptive success), whereas average staff tenure provides clues as to promotional or advancement opportunities for first-line staff inside the organization.

As anticipated, the effects of size on structure proved to be curvilinear and, in relation to formalization, positive as well. Although the positive association of size and centralization was unanticipated, it may be accounted for by the limited range of variation on size of the organizations in the sample. As previously stated, the strong positive relationphip between size and centralization among organizations of less than 200 was not observed in large organizations and, in fact, changed to a slightly negative trend in organizations of more than 400. If this is the case, two substantive conclusions are suggested. First, to the extent that most human service agencies fall within the size-range exemplified by the present sample (from 14 to 3,300 with two-thirds under 1,000 employee), larger size in human service organizations results in an increase (rather than decrease) of centralized decision making procedures. Second, to he extent that other types of organizations (*e.g.*, factories and businesses) typically are larger than the organizations in the present sample, results based on one type of sample may not be generalizable to other types. Present results underscore Kimberly's (1976) recent call for more careful studies of the consequences of size within intratypical versus intertypical samples of organizations.

The rather high association of the productivity and efficiency variables (r=.70) in the present sample is noteworthy. It suggests that, in large part, those organizations that are high producers are also cost efficient in their production activities. Or, viewed in light of the "economies of scale" concept (Price, 1972), it may indicate simply that increased volume of output reduces the per-unit cost of processing any given client or case.

Whetten (1978) criticizes the "resource theory" of organizational effectiveness (Yuchtman and Seashore, 1967) for failing to acknowledge that organizations typically must demonstrate efficiency in the use of previously received resources in order to secure additional ones. This illustrates the point that funding sources external to the human service organization are likely to pressure it to produce and to produce efficiently. In a production and quantitatively-oriented society, organizations that can claim high productivity and cost-efficiency enjoy greater legitimacy in the public arena. As argued by Meyer and Rowan 1977), articulation of and compliance with the values expressed by the larger society assure an organization of goodwill, support, resources, and relative protection from external regulation (including evaluation) as well.

To the extent that high productivity and efficiency require high centralization of authority, however, an important dilemma prevails. As noted by many researchers, a high degree of centralization leads to staff dissatisfaction (Whetten, 1978), a lower quality of client service (Holland, 1973; Hage, 1974), and a diminished level of individual worker and organization level development (Pondy, 1977). Weick (1977) notes that high adaptation in the short run—as indicated, say, by high productivity and/or efficiency—may actually prevent high adaptability in the long run. Certainly to the extent that a centralized power structure stifles worker experimentation, innovation, and openness to change, the chances for discovery of new and better methods appear minimal. The exclusion of professional staff from the decision making process, a characteristic of highly centralized organizations, is known to result in staff members' adoption of an apathetic orientation toward clients (Holland, 1973; Martin and Segal, 1977). One is hard-pressed, therefore, to make the case that a centralized authority structure contributes ro a higher quality of services for clients.

Conflicts between the goals of quantity and quality of services have been noted by Seashore (1965), Freidlander and Pickle (1968), Mohr (1973), and Whetten (1978). Whetten (1978) reports that staff members' evaluation of their own organization's effectiveness (in providing services to clints) is significantly and negatively associated with the organization's productivity (or output) rate (r=—.42). Further, Whetten finds educational level of the staff (indicative of the "degree of professionalism") to be negatively associated with output (r=—.25). This result is replicated by present findings (r=—.25 for education of staff and productivity and—.30 for education and efficiency). Such correlations may merely reflect the oft-reported conflict between "professionalism" and "bureaucracy" in human service settings (Anderson, 1977). Professional staff may be oriented toward long term, in-depth "treatment," whereas funding agencies and administrators favor a short term, quick turnaround approach. Even if this is the case, it appears to constitute a genuine dilemma for the human service administrator.

Present results underscore the bind in which human service administrators find themselves. In regard to organizational well-being (*e.g.*, survival, resource procurement, expansion, and growth), they are advised to emphasize productivity and efficiency. In regard to staff and client satisfaction, they are pressured to stress quality and effectiveness. Conflicting demands from their organizations' multiple constituencies force human service administrators into the political arena in the mere execution of their jobs (Walmsley and Zald, 1976). To the extent that resources continue to come from outside the organization, furthermore, administrators of service programmes can be expected to be more responsive to pressures for productivity and efficiency than to those for quality and effectiveness (Rogers and Molnar, 1976). Conclusions such as this emphasize the need for more refined research on the correlates of effectiveness as well as efficiency. The identification of practice principles that facilitate high quality services in addition to organizational well-being are long overdue.

REFERENCES

1. Anderson, W.A. *Conflict and congruity between bureaucracy and professionalism: Alienation outcomes among social service workers.* Unpublished Ph.D. dissertation, Florida State University. 1977.
2. Blau, P.A. formal theory of differentiation in organizations. *American Sociological Review*, 1970, 35, 201-218.
3. Blau. P.M., and Schoenherr. R. *The structure of organizations* New York: Basic Books, 1971.
4. Child, J. Predicting and understanding organizational structure, *Administrative Science Quarterly*, 1973, 18, 168-185.
5. Cohen, J, and Cohen, P. *Applied multiple regression/correlation analysis for the behavioural sciences*, Hillsdale, N J.: Lawrence Erlbaum Associates, 1975.
6. Freidlander F., and Pickle, H. Components of effectiveness in small organizations. *Administrative Science Quarterly*, 1968, 13, 289-304.
7. Glisson, C.A. The accountability controversy. *Social Work*, 1975, 20. 417-419.
8. Glisson, C. A. Dependence of technological routinization on structural variables in human service organizations. *Administrative Science Quarterly*, 1978, 23, 383-395.
9. Goodman, P.S., and Pennings, J.M. (Eds.). *New perspectives on organizational effectiveness*, San Francisco: Jossey-Bass, 1977.
10. Hage, J. An axiomatic theory of organizations. *Administrative Science Quarterly*, 1965, 10, 289-320 .
11. Hage, J. *Communication and organizational control: Cybernetics in health and welfare settings*, New York: Wiley, 1974.
12. Hage, J., and A ken, M. Relationship of centralization to other structural properties. *Administrative Science Quarterly*, 1967, 12, 73-92.
13. Hall, H. R. *An empirical study of bureaucratic dimensions and their relation to other organizational characteristics*, Doctoral dissertation, Ohio State University, 1961.
14. Hall, R.H. The concept of bureaucracy: An empirical assessment. *American Journal of Sociology*, 1963, 69, 32-40.

15. Hall, R.H., Johnson, N.J., and Hass, J.E. Organizational size, complexity, and formalization. *American Sociological Review*, 1967, 32, 903-912.

16. Hannan, M.T , and Freeman, J. Obstacles to comparative studies. In P.S. Goodman and J.M. Pennings (Eds.), *New perspectives on organizational effectiveness*, San Francisco: Jossey-Bass, 1977, 106-131.

17. Hasenfeld, Y., and English, R. *Human service organizations*, Ann Arbor. The University of Michigan Press, 1974.

18. Heydebrand, W. *Hospital bureaucracy: A comparative study of organizations*, New York: Dunellen, 1973.

19. Holland, T.P. Organizational struture and institutional care. *Journal of Health and Social Behaviour*, 1973, 14, 241-251.

20. Kanter, R.M. *Men and Women of the corporation*, New York: Basic Books, 1977.

21. Katz, D., and Kahn, R.L. *The social psychology of organizations*, New York: Wiley, 1966.

22. Kim, Jae-On, and Kohout, F.J. Special topics in general linear models. In N.H. Nie, C.H. Hull, J.G. Jenkins, K. Steinbrenner, and D.H. Bent, *Statistical package for the Social sciences*, New York: McGraw-Hill, 1975, 368-394.

23. Kimberly, J. R. Environmental constraints and organizational structure: A comparative analysis of rehabilitation organization, *Administrative Science Quarterly*, 1975, 20, 1-9.

24. Kimberly, J.R. Organizational size and the structuralist perspective: A review, critique, and proposal, *Administrative Science Qnarterly*, 1976, 21, 571-597.

25. Land, K.C. Principles of path analysis. In E.G. Borgatta (Fd.) *Sociological methodology*, San Francisco: Jossey-Bass, 1969, 3-37.

26. March, J.G., and Simon, H.A *Organizations*. New York: John Wiley, 1958.

27. Martin, P.Y. Organizational 'time' in halfway houses for alcoholics Assessment and implications. Unpublished manuscript, 1978.

28. Martin, P.Y., and Segal, B. Bureaucracy, size and staff expectation for client independence in halfway houses. *Journal of Health and Social Behaviour*, 1977, 18, 376-390.

29. Meyer, J.W., and Rowan, B. Institutionalized organitions. Formal structure as myth and ceremony. *American Jonrnal of Sociology*, 1977, 83, 340-363.

30. Mileti, D.S., Gillespie, D.F., aud Haas, J.E. size and structure in complex organizations. *Social Force*, 1977, 56, 208-217.

31. Mohr, L. The concept of organizational goal. *American Political Science Review*, 1973, 67, 470-481.

32. Molnar. J.J., and Rogers, D.L. Organizational effectiveness: An empirical comparison of the goal and system resource approaches. *The Sociological Quarterly*, 1976, 17 401-413.

33. Moos, R.H. *Evaluating treatment environments: A social ecological approach*, New York: Wiley-Interscience, 1974.

34. Moti, P.E., *The characteristics of effective organizations*, New York: Harper and Row, 1972.

35. Pfeffer, J. Usefulness of the concept. In S.P. Goodman and J M. Pennings (Eds.), *New perspectives on organizational effectiveness*, San Francisco: Jossey-Bass, 1977, 132-145.

36. Pondy, L.R. Effectiveness: A thick description. In P.S. Goodman and' J.M. Pennings (Eds.), *New perspectives on organizational effectiveness* San Francisco: Jossey-Bass, 1977, 226-234.

37. Price, J.L. *Organizaiional Effectiveness: An inventory of propositions*, Homewood, Ill.: Richard D. Irwin, 1968.

38. Price, J.L. *Handbook of organizational measurement*, Lexington, Mass.: D.C. Heath, 1972.

39. Pugh, D.S , Hickson, D.J., Hinings, C.R., and Turner, C. The context of organization structures, *Administrative Science Quarterly*, 1969, 14, 91-1 4.

40. Rogers, D.L., and Molnar, J. Organizational antecedents of roie conflict and role ambiguity in top-level administrators. *Administrative Science Quarterly*, 1976, 21, 598-610.

41. Scott, W.R. Effectiveness of organizational effectiveness studies. In P.S. Goodman and J.M. Pennings (Eds.), *New perspectives on organizational effectiveness*, San Francisco: Jossey-Bass, 1977, 63-95.

42. Seashore, S. Criteria of organizational effectiveness. *Michigan Business Review*, 1965, 17, 26-30.

43. Stinchcombe, A.L. Social structure and organizations. In James G. March (Ed.), *Handbook of organizations*, Chicago: Rand McNally, 1965, 142-193.

44. Thompson, J.D. *Organization in action*, New York: McGraw-Hill, 1967.

45. Tracy, P., and Azumi, K. Determinants of administrative control: A test of a theory with Japanese factories. *Americal Sociological Review*, 1976, 41, 80-94.

46. Walmsley, G.L., and Zald, M.N. *The political economy of public organizations: A critique and approach to the study of public administration*, Bloomington: Indian University Press, 1976.

47. Weick, K.E. Re-punctuating the problem. In P.S. Goodman and J.M. Pennings (Eds.), *New perspectives on organizational effectiveness* San Francisco; Jossey-Bass, 1977, 193-225.

48. Whetten, D.A. Coping with incompatible expectations: An integrated view of role conflict. *Administrative Science Quarterly*, 1978, 33, 254-271.

49. Yuchtman, E., and Seashore, S.E. A system resource approach to organizational effectiveness. *American Sociological Review*, 1967, 32, 891-903.